STUDY GUIDE

Christopher T. Kilmartin
Mary Washington College

PSYCHOLOGY IN PERSPECTIVE
Third Edition

Carol Tavris
Carole Wade

PRENTICE HALL, UPPER SADDLE RIVER, NEW JERSEY 07458

©2001 by PRENTICE-HALL, INC.
PEARSON EDUCATION
Upper Saddle River, New Jersey 07458

ISBN 0-13-028328-2

Printed in the United States of America

TABLE OF CONTENTS

Introduction.. iv

Chapter One.. 1

Chapter Two.. 16

Chapter Three... 35

Chapter Four.. 53

Chapter Five 76

Chapter Six 95

Chapter Seven 113

Chapter Eight... 132

Chapter Nine.. 152

Chapter Ten.. 169

Chapter Eleven... 187

Chapter Twelve... 206

Answer Keys 230

INTRODUCTION

One of the biggest advantages to learning about psychology is that it can help you in all of your coursework. As you understand the psychological principles involved in processes like learning, memory, and reasoning, you can apply these principles and thereby develop personal methods for academic success.

This introduction will present several ideas about learning, studying, note taking, time management, test taking, motivating yourself, and handling test anxiety. (If you want a more detailed explanation of any of these skills, consult one of the excellent books listed under Suggested Readings at the end of this section.) Many of these methods are relatively easy to apply, and you will discover that taking a little bit of time to learn them will make you a more organized and efficient student in all of your classes, not just in psychology class. Your goal is not necessarily to study harder, but to study *smarter*.

The Organization of This Student Resource Manual

Each chapter in this manual corresponds to a chapter in your textbook. After reading and studying the material in the text and your class notes, you are ready to structure further studying and to check your understanding of the material by going through the relevant chapter in this manual.

You will note that there is a good deal of repetition in this manual; for each chapter, the Chapter Outline and the Chapter Summary follow the text material, and the sample test questions go over the same material again. This is fully intentional; repetition improves learning and retention of the material. By the time you read the chapter, attend class, review your notes, and complete the activities in this manual, you will have reviewed the same information five times or more, and you should know it very well.

Each chapter in this manual contains:

Learning Objectives: You should begin by reading each of these carefully. Together, they describe the skills and the body of knowledge that are the outcome of your studying. After you finish studying, turn back to the learning objectives and evaluate yourself on each one.

Chapter Outline: This is a structured summary of the chapter material. It is written in full sentences so that it will make sense by itself. Read it carefully. If there is something in the outline that you do not remember or understand, go back and review the relevant sections of your textbook.

Chapter Summary: This is a more detailed synopsis of the chapter with numbered blanks for you to fill in. The answers can be found in a separate section in the back of the manual. If you answer items incorrectly, review the relevant sections of your textbook. Occasionally, you might give an equivalent term to the one found in the answer key. For instance, you could answer with a term like "reward" and find the term "positive reinforcement" in the answer key. These terms are roughly synonymous, so your answer is different but correct in this case. If you think your term is equivalent, it is still a good idea to check by going back to the textbook.

Multiple Choice Self-test: These sample test items will help you further evaluate your retention of the textbook material. Many of these items require you to *apply* concepts to novel situations. Therefore, you will be able to assess not only your learning of the concepts, but your understanding as well. Read and answer each item carefully. The answers can be found in the back of the manual. If you do not understand why you got an item wrong (or right, for that matter), review your textbook or see your instructor or teaching assistant.

True-false Self-test: These sample test items will allow you to review the material and test your understanding in a different testing format. Follow the same procedure as with the other testing sections. The answers to these tests can also be found in the back of the manual.

Key Terms: These are the same terms and definitions found in footnoted sections of your textbook. Read them carefully and make sure that you understand each term. You can use this section as a reference while you are working on other sections.

Suggested Research Projects: If you want to go beyond textbook learning into the application of psychological principles in the real world, you will find some suggestions here. See your instructor or teaching assistant for help in designing your research projects. If they involve human or animal participants, you will need the approval of your college or university to carry these projects forward.

Suggested Readings: These books provide a more in-depth investigation of topics of interest.

Biological Diagrams: Many students have difficulty with learning the locations of various parts of neurons, the brain, nervous system, and other biological structures. In the back of your textbook, there is a "coloring book" section that will help you become familiar with these biological structures.

How to Study

Following are many suggestions for success in this course. Feel free to tailor techniques to fit your own talents, style, and situation. If you want more detail, consult the books listed under Suggested Readings at the end of this section.

Reading the Textbook

1. *Read each chapter twice, but in different ways.* First, read the chapter the way you read any book. The authors of your text discuss very interesting topics in each chapter, and they write very well. Enjoy the reading and allow your curiosity to get you involved in the subject matter. When you are ready to read the chapter a second time, use the SQ3R method described below.

The SQ3R method. This is a well-documented, effective technique for learning reading material by making the reader more active. SQ3R is shorthand for the five steps of the method, which are followed in sequence:

Survey: Skim the chapter, paying particular attention to headings, pictures, captions, tables, and terms in boldface or italics. Get a general idea of what you will be studying, how the chapter is organized, and how the topics are related to one another. Some people find it helpful to do this again for each new section they study.

Question: Before you read each section, ask yourself some questions about what will be covered and what you should learn. For example, when you get to the section on "psychobabble" in the first chapter, you might ask, "How can someone distinguish between a "psychobabble" self-help book and one that contains more reliable information?" Questioning helps you to become active and involved in learning the material.

Read: Think actively about the material as you read. Note the answers to your questions and the connections between topics. Check the definitions of key terms at the bottom of the page. You might also want to refer to the learning objectives at the beginning of each chapter in this manual.

Recite: When you finish each section, recite its major points in your own words. You can structure this step by referring to relevant learning objectives. You can also write down the main points. This will help you to practice for essay examinations.

Review: Go back over all of the material when you reach the end of the chapter. Try to see the "big picture" of the chapter by again focusing on its overall organization. If you can grasp the chapter's larger framework, the details will be easier to retain because they will fit into a specific place in this framework.

2. *Apply sections in your textbook to the actual process of reading and studying.* Your authors describe memory and learning in Chapters 5, 6, and 8. If you read some of these sections first, you will have a structure for improving your skills as you go along.

3. *Think critically.* Chapter 1 of your text describes the process of critical thinking. If you adopt this as your mindset when you read, you will engage with the material actively.

4. *Reward yourself when you have finished.* It is a well-known fact that behaviors followed by pleasant consequences are more likely to recur; your authors discuss this principle in Chapter 5. After studying, reward yourself. Do some pleasure reading, have a conversation, watch some television, play a video game, or do something you enjoy. This will strengthen the habit of reading and studying.

In Class

1. *Go to class.* This seems like such a simple suggestion that it should go without saying, but it is amazing how often students fail to follow it. If you miss class, you will have to spend several hours learning the material you could have learned in one class hour, and you will have to guess at what the instructor is emphasizing. Students also tend to do something enjoyable, like sleeping or relaxing, when they skip class. The same principle described above in item 4 applies here: behaviors followed by pleasant consequences tend to recur. If you do something pleasant when you skip class, you strengthen the habit of skipping class.

2. *Listen actively.* Try to distinguish major from minor points. Ask yourself questions about the material as you go along. Try to make connections between lecture material, reading, previous lectures, and other things you have learned. Sitting near the front of the room may be helpful.

3. *Be a note taker, not a stenographer.* If you try to write down everything your instructor says, you will be so focused on writing that active listening will be impossible. Your notes will also fail to reflect any emphases, and you will probably have a lot of seemingly unconnected material to study. Good note taking involves actively thinking about what the instructor says, and then summarizing the major points concisely.

4. *Be prepared for class.* Of course, you should be on time, bring a notebook and pen, etc. Most instructors want you to do the reading about a topic before the lecture. Most students wait until exam time to do the reading. If you have read the material before class, you will be better able to become actively engaged in the lecture, and you will reinforce what you have read.

Studying

1. *Review your class notes on a regular basis.* Most forgetting occurs within the first 24 hours after the material is learned. The best strategy for retaining information is to go over your class notes as soon as possible after class. Most students wait until just before a test to review their notes; this is very inefficient. Reviewing your notes does not take a long time, and it can pay off in time saved when the test comes up. It is also a good idea to do a second review of the week's class notes at the end of the week.

2. *Set learning goals.* Chapter 6 details the research on setting learning goals as opposed to setting performance goals. If you focus on learning, then you will study on a regular basis in order to learn what you want to know. If you focus on performance,

you are more likely to study once a month in order to pass a test. You have more control over learning than you do over performance. If you concentrate on learning, you will perform better, and you will enjoy the class more.

3.   *Spaced practice is better than massed practice.* Studying for an hour a day for 5 days is more beneficial than studying for 5 hours in one day. Spaced practice makes it easier to combat the effects of fatigue and inattention. Of course, you should study more on the days immediately preceding the test, but don't let "cramming" be your only technique.

4.   *Take frequent breaks from studying.* A 10-minute rest period can be very rejuvenating and can help you to refocus your attention.

5.   *Study in groups.* There are many benefits to organizing a study group with your classmates. For example:

You can explain things to each other. This allows you to pool your resources.

Your studying time can be structured. If your study group meets at 7:00 on Tuesday evenings, you will study psychology every week at that time.

You have to learn something well in order to teach it. The process of explaining concepts to your fellow group members will improve your understanding.

You can split up the work. Assign each group member a certain section to teach the group.

There are social benefits. You will get to know the members of your group, and being part of a group makes studying less painful.

If you decide to study in a group, *set goals for each session* in order to provide a structure, and *make assignments for the next session* so that group members can be prepared. Most importantly, *resist the temptation to socialize until the session is over*. Make socializing the reward for studying.

6.   *Put yourself in an environment that is conducive to studying.* Most students set up their dormitory rooms for enjoyment. You have a bed there, and perhaps also a phone, a stereo, or other distractions. Friends may stop by to converse. All of these aspects of the dormitory environment will compete with your studying. For studying, find a quiet environment without distractions.

7.   *Use strategies for prolonging retention.* Chapter 8 details the relative benefits of maintenance and elaborative rehearsal. Maintenance rehearsal involves the rote repetition of material and is not very effective or efficient. Elaborative rehearsal involves imposing meaning on the material by relating it to information that is already stored in long-term memory. For example, you might study classical conditioning (Chapter 5) by comparing its various components to behavior you have observed in

your cat, who salivates at the sound of the electric can opener. Anything you can do to make the information more familiar will help. For another method to help you retain information, read the section in Chapter 8 on mnemonic devices. For example, a way to remember that dreaming occurs in REM sleep is to see the word as dREaMing. You can also use visualization to help you retain material. It is easy to remember that the brain structure called the hippocampus (Chapter 4) is involved in memory when you picture a hippopotamus going to college (get it?). Often the most ridiculous images are the easiest to remember. Because humans tend to be visually dominant, including visual images usually makes material more memorable than limiting your thinking to words and sounds. Using many senses and abilities (writing, reading, hearing, speaking, drawing, etc.) helps you to organize, retain, and recall information. The more you make material *meaningful* to you by creating associations to things you already know, the less likely you will be to forget the material.

8.   *Reward yourself for studying.* Behaviors followed by pleasant consequences are more likely to recur. Rewarding yourself for studying will lead you to study more often and to *want* to study more often.

Taking Tests

1.   *Learn how to handle your anxiety.* The long, slow, deep breath is an excellent stress manager. You can also talk to yourself reassuringly as you go through tasks. Look at an exam as an opportunity to demonstrate what you know, not to have what you don't know exposed. If you need help in this area, consult a reputable self-help book on test anxiety or visit your campus counseling center.

2.   *Underline key words.* Regardless of whether you are taking a multiple choice, true-false, or essay exam, underlining serves to help you focus on the most important aspects of the question. Look for qualifiers such as "always" and "never." Ask yourself if there are any exceptions to the statement being made. If so, these answer choices are incorrect.

3.   *On essay exams, underline what the question asks you to do, and be sure to do it.* There are two basic approaches to answering an essay exam. One is to answer the question. The other is to write everything you know about the subject and hope that the answer is in there somewhere. The first method is obviously preferable. If the question asks you to compare and contrast, underline those words, briefly outline your answer, and go back to the question when you are finished writing to make sure that you have addressed it fully.

4.   *On multiple choice exams, formulate your own answer first.* Read the question and decide what you think the answer is. Then look at the choices, carefully considering each one. If a question is especially difficult, put a mark next to it on your answer sheet and come back to it after you have finished answering the other questions.

5.   *Prepare specifically for the format of the test*. Ask your instructor what the format of the test (e.g., multiple choice, essay, short answer) will be, and practice answering questions in that format.

Motivation and Time Management

1.   *Think about studying in positive terms*. When you tell yourself "I *have* to study," you may feel resentful and deprived. The truth is, you don't have to study. You *want* to study because it will benefit you. This doesn't mean that you have to like it, but it does mean that you are in control of your own behavior. Chapter 6 explains how interpretations of events have important implications for emotion and behavior.

2.   *Let curiosity, not fear, be your motivation*. Approach the class as an opportunity to learn something interesting, not as a rite of passage in which you can fail if you don't suffer through the work.

3.   *Prioritize your time*. Make lists of things to do and put them in order of importance. Get the most important things done first.

4.   *Set small goals*. Break large tasks down into smaller ones. This will make them more manageable. Large tasks provoke anxiety; it is easier to think in terms of learning a section than learning a chapter.

5.   *Use the 5-minute plan*. A good way to get yourself started is to decide to study or read for 5 minutes. At the end of 5 minutes, ask yourself if you can do 5 more, and continue until you are unwilling to do another 5 minutes. This gets you past the difficulty of beginning the task.

6.   *Schedule some flexibility*. If at all possible, overestimate the time needed to do any task. If it takes you less time than expected, you can relax or work on a low-priority task.

7.   *Schedule time for relaxation and fun*. We all need to take it easy and play once in a while. This is no waste of time - it will refresh you and prepare you for other tasks. Use enjoyable activities as rewards for your hard work.

Suggested Readings

Ellis, A.E., & Knaus, W.J. (1977). *Overcoming procrastination*. New York: Signet. A description of thinking styles and behaviors that perpetuate procrastination, along with strategies for dealing with the problem.

Flemming, L.E., & Leet, J. (1994). *Becoming a successful student*. New York: HarperCollins. A collection of strategies for maximizing your potential as a student.

Greenberg, J.S. (1994). *Comprehensive stress management* (3rd ed.). Dubuque, IA: Brown and Benchmark. A textbook on the effects of stress and a large variety of strategies for dealing with stress.

Lakein, A. (1973). *How to get control of your time and your life.* New York: Signet. A time management self-help guide.

Mealy, M. (1995). *Studying for psychology.* New York: HarperCollins. A description of study skills for specific application to psychology.

Schmitt, D.E. (1992). *The winning edge: Maximizing success in college.* New York: HarperCollins. A guide for making the most of your academic potential.

Wade, C., & Tavris, C. (1993). *Critical and creative thinking: The case of love and war.* New York: HarperCollins. A detailed approach to critical thinking, written by the authors of your textbook.

CHAPTER 1

Explaining Human Behavior

Learning Objectives

After reading and studying this chapter, you should be able to:

1.   Explain the difference between scientific psychology and pseudoscience.

2.   Define critical thinking.

3.   Demonstrate critical thinking in approaching some problem or question.

4.   Describe the origins of psychology as a formal science.

5.   List the three disciplines from which psychology emerged.

6.   Describe the three basic types of psychologists and their training.

7.   Distinguish between psychologists, psychiatrists, psychotherapists, and psychoanalysts.

8.   Describe the five leading psychological approaches.

9.   Apply each of the five leading psychological approaches to some problem or question.

10.   Describe humanistic psychology.

11.   Describe feminist psychology.

Chapter Outline

I.   Introduction

    A.   **Psychology** is the scientific study of behavior and mental processes.
        1.   Its aim is to examine and explain how humans and animals think, feel, and behave.
        2.   Behavior and mental processes are affected by an organism's physical state, mental state, and external environment.
        3.   Psychology is based on **empirical** evidence, gathered by careful observation, experimentation, and measurement.
    B.   Pseudoscience and Psychobabble
        1.   Methods and approaches distinguish psychology from nonscience and pseudoscience. Psychology relies on research evidence.
        2.   The distinction between pseudoscience and psychology is

important because major decisions are often based on psychological information.

    3.   Psychobabble confirms existing beliefs and prejudices; psychology often challenges them.

II.   Thinking Critically and Creatively about Psychology

    A.   **Critical thinking** is the ability and willingness to assess claims and make judgments on the basis of well-supported reasons and evidence, rather than emotion and anecdote.

        1.   Critical thinkers look for flaws in arguments and resist poorly supported claims.

        2.   Critical thinkers have the ability to come up with various possible explanations for events.

        3.   Being open-minded does not mean accepting all opinions as equally valid.

    C.   Critical thinking is fundamental to all science.

    B.   There are eight essential guidelines for critical thinking:

        1.   Ask questions; be willing to wonder.

        2.   Define your terms

        3.   Examine the evidence.

        4.   Analyze assumptions and biases.

        5.   Avoid emotional reasoning.

        6.   Don't oversimplify or argue by anecdote.

        7.   Consider other interpretations.

        8.   Tolerate uncertainty.

III.   Psychology Past and Present

    A.   The goals of psychology are to *describe*, *predict*, *understand*, and *modify* behavior in order to add to human knowledge and increase human happiness.

    B.   Forerunners of modern psychology were philosophy, natural science, and medicine. Early investigators did not always rely on empirical evidence.

IV.   The Birth of Modern Psychology

    A.   Psychology as a formal science began in 1879 with **Wilhelm Wundt**.

        1.   Wundt's method of *trained introspection* -- observation and analysis of one's own mental experience -- was rejected as unscientific.

        2.   **Functionalism** emphasized the purpose of behavior -- how behavior helped adaptation. **William James** was an early leader. Functionalism was inspired in part by **Charles Darwin's** theory of evolution.

    B.   Psychology as a method of psychotherapy began around 1900 with **Sigmund Freud**.

        1.   Freud argued that a major portion of human functioning occurs in the unconscious mind.

2. **Psychoanalysis** is a theory of personality and a method of psychotherapy originally formulated by Freud, which emphasizes unconscious motives and conflicts.

V. Psychology Today

A. Psychology is now a complex field encompassing many specialties, perspectives, methods, and training programs.

B. Despite the stereotype of the psychologist as psychotherapist, psychology is a highly diverse field. Most professional activity falls into one of three categories:

1. *Psychological research*, including:

a. **Basic psychology**, the study of psychological issues in order to seek knowledge for its own sake rather than for its practical application, and

b. **Applied psychology**, the study of psychological issues that have direct practical significance and the application of psychological findings.

2. *Psychological practice*, attempts to understand and improve physical and mental health. Practitioners of psychology include *counseling*, *clinical*, and *school psychologists*. People often confuse the term *clinical psychologist* with:

a. *Psychotherapist* -- anyone who does any kind of psychological therapy (only some of whom are clinical psychologists).

b. *Psychoanalyst* -- persons who practice one specialized form of therapy (psychoanalysis). Some, but not all, are psychologists.

c. *Psychiatrists* -- medical specialists concerned with mental disorders. Psychiatrists are not psychologists.

C. *Psychology in the Community* -- people who apply psychological research in various settings.

VI. The Major Psychological Perspectives

A. There are five leading approaches to studying and explaining mental processes and behavior. Each has its own questions, assumptions, and emphases.

1. **Biological perspective** -- the approach that emphasizes bodily events and changes associated with actions, feelings, and thoughts.

a. Biological psychologists are interested in areas such as hormones, the nervous system, and the relative effects of nature and nurture on the development of abilities and personality.

b. *Evolutionary psychology* is a popular new specialty in which researchers study how a species' evolutionary past may help to explain present behaviors and characteristics.

  c. *Psychoneuroimmunology* is the study of the effects of psychological processes on the functioning of the immune system.

 2. **Learning perspective** -- a psychological approach that emphasizes how the environment and experience affect a person's or an animal's actions. It includes:

  a. *Behaviorism* -- an approach to psychology that emphasizes the study of objectively observable behavior and the role of the environment as a determinant of behavior.

  b. *Social-cognitive learning theory* -- the theory that behavior is learned and maintained through observation and imitation of others, positive consequences, and cognitive processes such as plans and perceptions.

 3. **Cognitive perspective** -- a psychological approach that emphasizes mental processes in perception, memory, language, problem solving, and other areas of behavior.

 4. **Sociocultural perspective** -- a psychological approach that emphasizes social and cultural influences on behavior.

  a. *Social psychologists* study social rules and roles, the influences of groups, why people obey authorities, and how a person is affected by others around him or her.

  b. *Cultural psychologists* study the cultural rules and values that affect human development, behaviors, and feelings.

 5. **Psychodynamic perspective** -- a psychological approach that emphasizes unconscious dynamics within the individual, such as inner forces, conflicts, or the movement of instinctual energy.

VII. Two Influential Movements in Psychology

 A. Throughout the history of Psychology, movements and intellectual trends have emerged which do not fit neatly into the perspectives already described. Two of the most important are:

  1. **Humanistic psychology** -- a psychological approach that emphasizes personal growth and achievement of human potential, rather than the scientific understanding and assessment of behavior.

  2. **Feminist psychology** -- a psychological approach that analyzes the influence of social inequities on gender relations and on the behaviors of the two sexes.

VIII. About This Book

 A. The five perspectives represent qualitatively different approaches to the study of psychology.

 B. No single perspective operates in isolation from the others.

 C. In order to understand the complexity of behavior, we must look at it from many angles, explore its strengths and weaknesses, and understand its social and political implications.

D. **Reductionism** is the process of reducing a phenomenon to a single type of explanation or to a limited set of elements of a particular type (for example, biological or cognitive). The dangers of reductionism are demonstrated throughout the book.

Chapter Summary

Scientific psychology differs from the popular conception of psychology as a special body of knowledge that allows a person to magically transform his or her life. The aim of modern scientific psychology is to examine and explain how people and animals learn, remember, solve problems, perceive, feel, and interact with one another.

Modern psychology is the scientific study of 1._____ and 2._____, and how they are affected by biology, mental states, and environments. Psychology is based on 3._____ evidence, gathered by careful observation, experimentation, and measurement.

The popular marketplace contains a great deal of pseudoscience and quackery that is often labeled 4._____. Its common elements are the promise of quick fixes for emotional problems and a reliance on vaguely psychological and scientific language. Examples of psychology's nonscientific competitors include fortune tellers, astrologers, and graphologists. Pseudoscience tends to confirm existing beliefs and evidence, whereas serious psychology often 5._____ them.

6._____ is the ability and willingness to assess claims and make judgments on the basis of well-supported reasons. It involves looking for flaws in arguments and resisting poorly supported claims on the basis of inadequate evidence. The critical thinker is a creative and constructive person who can generate a range of possible explanations for a single event, as well as understand the implications of research findings. Being 7._____ does not mean accepting all opinions as equally valid. Critical thinking is fundamental to all science.

Critical thinking involves several elements: being willing to ask questions, defining problems in 8._____ terms, examining the 9._____ that supports an argument or the 10._____ behind an argument, avoiding reasoning that is based solely on 11._____, not oversimplifying or arguing by anecdote, considering alternative explanations for phenomena, and being willing to tolerate 12._____.

The goals of psychology are to describe, 13._____, understand, and modify behaviors. Psychology's history as a formal science only dates back to the 14._____ century, although great thinkers in history have long been interested in behavior and mental processes. Philosophers have speculated about these processes, but without psychology's reliance on 15._____. Later research has often disconfirmed their theories, although they were sometimes correct.

The first psychological laboratory was established in 1879 by 16._____. His favorite research method was 17._____, a method of analyzing one's own mental experiences. This method was abandoned because it was not 18._____.

The early school of 19._____ emphasized the purpose of behavior, how it furthered 20._____ to the environment. It was strongly influenced by the theories of 21._____. One of its leaders was 22._____.

Around 1900, psychology as a method of 23._____ was born. Its founder, 24._____, theorized that mental disorders were caused by conflicts, memories, and traumas that occurred in early childhood. These ideas evolved into a broad theory of personality and a specific method, called 25._____, for treating people with emotional problems.

Psychology has grown into a complex field consisting of differing perspectives, methods, and training. Most people think of psychologists as therapists, but many psychologists do not fit this stereotype. Two types of psychological research are 26._____, the attempt to gain knowledge for its own sake, and 27._____, the attempt to relate research to practical problems. In general, the professional activities of psychologists fall into three broad categories: college or university 28._____ and 29._____, providing 30._____ services, and conducting 31._____ in nonacademic settings.

32._____ psychologists diagnose, treat, and study mental or emotional problems. People often confuse this term with 33._____, anyone who does any kind of psychological therapy, psychoanalysts, who practice a specialized form of therapy, and 34._____, physicians with a specialty concerned with mental disorders. The application of psychological knowledge to various settings is called 36._____ psychology.

The five leading psychological approaches to studying and explaining mental processes and behavior each have their own explanations, assumptions, and emphases.

The 37._____ perspective assumes that all psychological processes involve physiological events. Its focus is the study of the complex interactions between mind and body. For instance, the specialty called 38._____ is the study of the ways in which psychological processes affect the body's immune system.

The 39._____ perspective emphasizes the acquisition of behavior through interactions with the environment. One of its founders, 40._____, advocated the abandonment of introspection in favor of observable and measurable behavior. Russian physiologist 41._____ studied the acquisition of involuntary behaviors. Later, 42._____ extended the behavioral approach to voluntary behaviors. Still later, an outgrowth of behaviorism known as 43._____ theory combined research on behaviorism with research on thinking and consciousness in an effort to better understand self-regulated behavior.

In the 1950s and 1960s, new computer-based models of the mind gave rise to the 44._____ perspective, the study of people's thoughts, memories, beliefs, perceptions, explanations, and other mental processes. One of its most important contributions has been to demonstrate how a person's explanations and perceptions influence his or her behavior. This approach has inspired a great deal of current psychological research.

The 45._____ perspective attempts to move beyond the study of the individual into the study of the effects of cultural values and political systems on everyday experience. Researchers from this perspective point out that a great deal of behavior is powerfully influenced by the social context in which it occurs. 46._____ psychologists study social rules and roles, the influence of groups, and how people affect each other. Cultural psychologists study the effects of cultural rules and values on human behavior.

An emphasis on unconscious forces within the individual is provided by the 47._____ perspective. Freud's view was that an understanding of consciousness only provides surface explanations of human functioning. His followers believe that the important regions of the mind lie outside of conscious awareness.

Other schools of psychology depart from these five major perspectives. For example, 47._____ psychology emphasizes the spiritual and free will aspects of the person. 48._____ psychology focuses on the influence of gender on behavior and thought. It has also pointed out the inherent subjectivity of psychology and other sciences.

Each of these perspectives has its strengths, weaknesses, and limits. We can combine and integrate many of these perspectives with the goal of achieving a fuller understanding of human functioning in all of its complexity rather than falling prey to 50._____, the use of a single explanation to describe a phenomenon.

Multiple Choice Self-Test

1. Nadine is interested in studying the process by which people come to believe in astrology. Nadine is most likely a:
   a. pseudoscientist.
   b. psychologist.
   c. psychotherapist.
   d. psychoanalyst.

2. Psychology differs most from other attempts to understand behavior in:
   a. the material it studies.
   b. its reliance on empirical evidence.
   c. its historical development.
   d. its philosophical tradition.

3. A speaker talks about the unconscious as "the area of the mind that holds both the blocks to creativity and the power to unleash creativity." He says that "we now have the technology to bypass the psychological "guard" of the unconscious and thereby improve people's creativity." This speaker is most likely a:
   a. psychologist.
   b. psychoanalyst.
   c. psychiatrist.
   d. quack.

4.   Stephanie says, "the Scholastic Aptitude Test is worthless because my sister got a low score on it and got excellent grades in college." A good critical thinker knows that Stephanie is:
a.   arguing by anecdote.
b.   tolerating uncertainty.
c.   using Occam's razor.
d.   being open-minded.

5.   If a psychological study is empirical, it:
a.   is subjective and counterintuitive.
b.   yields unambiguous results.
c.   relies on careful measurements of behavior.
d.   describes naturally occurring behavior.

6.   Dr. Muldaur, a high school principal, wants to reduce the incidence of violence at her school by changing its social environment. What kind of psychologist should she consult?
a.   a school psychologist.
b.   a community psychologist.
c.   a cognitive psychologist.
d.   a psychoanalyst.

7.   Phrenology was abandoned as a science because:
a.   it was very unpopular.
b.   it failed to be useful in predicting phenomena.
c.   it yielded predictions that were offensive to people.
d.   it threatened to replace organized religion.

8.   A popular book claims that men are naturally more sexually promiscuous than women because this characteristic maximizes the probability of producing many offspring. This explanation is based in the assumptions of:
a.   evolutionary psychology.
b.   structuralism.
c.   clinical sexology.
d.   sexual dimorphism theory.

9.   Chris keeps his "good" shaving razor at home and also keeps a disposable razor in his locker at the gym. He notices that the disposable razor seems to give him a better shave than the "good" razor. If Chris is a critical thinker, he will:
a.   begin to use only disposable razors.
b.   generate some alternative explanations for getting a better shave at the gym.
c.   think about the implications for companies that make razors.
d.   imagine what might be involved in making an even better razor.

10. Jarrod argues that gun control is counterproductive because it would prevent law-abiding citizens from arming themselves against dangerous criminals. In evaluating Jarrod's argument, a good critical thinker would:
a. ask Jarrod for evidence supporting his view.
b. ask Jarrod if he owns a gun himself.
c. watch for signs of anxiety or anger as Jarrod expresses his view.
d. accept the argument only if Jarrod is an expert on gun control.

11. Critical thinking and creative thinking:
a. are interrelated.
b. are mutually exclusive.
c. occur together only coincidentally.
d. are the provinces of scientists and artists, respectively.

12. In a discussion of the merits of welfare, Barry says, "Think about how many millions of lazy people are sitting on their rear ends collecting welfare without contributing to society at all." This statement is best characterized as:
a. empirical evidence in support of abolishing welfare.
b. evidence of critical thinking.
c. an evaluation of available evidence, but without precision.
d. the use of unanalyzed assumption in constructing and argument.

13. Which of the following is TRUE about critical thinking?
a. It is a continuing process, not a finished accomplishment.
b. It should remain uninfluenced by emotions.
c. It is only achieved by a very few people.
d. It is only exhibited by trained professionals.

14. Jeanine says, "I never go to church, but when I have children, I'm going to start, because children need to have some god to believe in while they're growing up." A critical thinker might say to her:
a. "You may find it hard to start going to church later because you've already established a different pattern."
b. "Doesn't your argument assume that children who don't grow up with formal religion will be damaged in some way? Where is the evidence for that?"
c. "If you think that you're okay, and you don't go to church, what makes you think that your children won't be okay if they don't go to church?"
d. "Psychologists all agree that formal religion does little more than make children fearful and constricted."

15. Deeanne, a gun control advocate, says, "According to the U.S. Justice Department, over 50% of gunshot wounds that happen in the home are inflicted by the homeowner's own gun." If this statement is true, it means that:
a. gun control works.
b. there is some evidence that gun control might be a good idea.
c. the U.S. Justice Department supports gun control.
d. there is no evidence that gun control will work; this is simply an emotional appeal.

16. Towanda dreams of her classmate asking her out on a date. The next day, this actually happens. According to the principle of Occam's Razor, the best explanation for these events is:
a. dreams predict the future.
b. Towanda unconsciously communicated her availability to the classmate.
c. a coincidence occurred.
d. Towanda sensed that the classmate was ready to ask her out, and this in turn affected her dream.

17. In studying the formation of language, a functionalist would focus on:
a. how language functions to allow the individual to adapt to the environment.
b. how language serves an emotionally expressive function.
c. how language changes as a function of thought.
d. how language functioning is impaired by brain injury.

18. Psychology had its early beginnings in:
a. law, sociology, and philosophy.
b. chemistry, literature, and social science.
c. philosophy, natural science, and medicine.
d. art, economics, and drama.

19. A clinical psychologist:
a. works in a hospital.
b. is a specialized type of researcher.
c. consults with various organizations on psychological topics.
d. is trained in the treatment of psychological problems.

20. Imagine that you have just tasted a new dessert. It is delicious. A behaviorist would predict that you would eat some more. Why?
a. You have been exposed to many adult role models who engage in similar activities.
b. Eating is a reflexive action like salivation.
c. The consequences of our actions affect future actions.
d. Humans have evolved to prefer sweet-tasting substances.

21. A psychoanalyst:
a. can be a psychiatrist, but can also be a psychologist.
b. is always a psychiatrist.
c. s always a psychologist.
d. is never a psychotherapist.

22. Dr. Washington specializes in devising programs to prevent teen pregnancy. She is most likely to be a:
a. community psychologist.
b. psychotherapist.
c. psychiatrist.
d. psychoanalyst.

23. Behaviorists resist theorizing about things like the unconscious and the mental state because these things:
a. have no explanatory value.
b. have long been demonstrated to not exist.
c. are too difficult to work with.
d. are not directly observable.

24. Antoinette tells her psychology teacher that she became angry when her friend failed to show up for lunch after she said she would. The teacher tells Antoinette that her anger occurred because she told herself that her friend did not care about her. The teacher's perspective is:
a. cognitive.
b. behavioral.
c. sociocultural.
d. pseudoscientific.

25. A humanistic psychologist is most likely to study:
a. paranormal events.
b. the neurological basis of behavior.
c. learning and memory.
d. altruism and creativity.

26. Marie is a highly ambitious person. The sociocultural perspective asserts that:
a. Marie unconsciously competes with her parents.
b. ambition is a strong value in Marie's community.
c. Marie has been punished for failing to achieve.
d. ambition is a displacement for the aggressive drive.

27. Historians of psychology recall that slaves who wanted to escape were said to suffer from a psychological disorder called *drapetomania*. Persons from which of the following perspectives would be most likely to point this out?
a. sociocultural.
b. learning.
c. humanistic.
d. cognitive.

28. Lee is conducting research to investigate perceptions of "femininity" and "masculinity" among college students. His choice of topics reveals the influence of:
a. the psychodynamic perspective.
b. feminist psychology.
c. humanistic psychology.
d. the behaviorist perspective.

29. A psychologist tells the following story: Jake is walking through a dark forest and sees a long, narrow, slender object on the path in front of him. It is too dark to tell for certain what the object is. If Jake believes it to be a stick, he will continue to be relaxed. However, if he believes it to be a snake, he will become frightened (even though it might, in actuality, be a stick). The psychologist tells this story to illustrate which of the following perspectives?
a. psychodynamic
b. social learning
c. cognitive
d. feminist

30. The claims of each of the five major theoretical perspectives:
a. compete with one another.
b. are made about different subjects.
c. are accepted by all psychologists.
d. reflect qualitatively different views of the same phenomenon.

True-False Self-Test

T   F   1.   Self-help books are never written by psychologists with integrity.

T   F   2.   Psychology is the science of behavior and mental processes.

T   F   3.   Scientific language cannot be used without the scientific method.

T   F   4.   Wundt is generally considered the first psychologist.

T   F   5.   Behaviorists avoid explaining behaviors by referring to mental states.

T   F   6.   Feminist psychology emerged in the 1940s.

T   F   7.   Psychologists should not consider the social and political implications of their work.

T   F   8.   A good scientist always tries to think critically.

T   F   9.   A good critical thinker is also a creative person.

T   F   10.   Generating a range of explanations for a single event is an important process for science.

T   F   11.   A social learning theorist would suggest that people learn through observation, imitation, and insight.

T　F　12.　Empirical evidence is used to support scientific theories.

T　F　13.　Emotions have no place in scientific reasoning.

T　F　14.　The explanation that requires the fewest assumptions is usually the most useful.

T　F　15.　Good scientists have always been objective.

T　F　16.　Reductionism is a useful tool in scientific psychology.

T　F　17.　As a formal discipline, psychology dates back to the Renaissance.

T　F　18.　Charles Darwin was a major influence on the process of introspection.

T　F　19.　Functionalists were very interested in the adaptive value of behavior.

T　F　20.　Some fields of psychology grew out of the field of medicine.

T　F　21.　Pure research does not primarily concern itself with the applications of findings.

T　F　22.　Legally, the vast majority of psychologists cannot write prescriptions.

T　F　23.　Compared with most disciplines, psychology is highly diverse.

T　F　24.　Biological theories always compete with cognitive theories.

T　F　25.　Environmental events cannot affect hormone levels in the body.

T　F　26.　Behaviorism attempts to deal only with directly observable material.

T　F　27.　A cognitive psychologist might design a computer program to help her understand how the brain processes information.

T　F　28.　Cultural values have a strong effect on behavior.

T　F　29.　Few modern psychologists hold psychodynamic views.

T　F　30.　Feminist psychologists are all women.

Key Terms

empirical Relying on or derived from observation, experimentation, or measurement.

psychology The discipline concerned with behavior and mental processes and how they are affected by an organism's physical state, mental state, and external environment.

critical thinking The ability and willingness to assess claims and make judgments on the basis of well-supported reasons and evidence, rather than emotion or anecdote.

functionalism An early psychological approach that emphasized the function or purpose of behavior and consciousness.

psychoanalysis A theory of personality and a method of psychotherapy, originally formulated by Sigmund Freud, which emphasizes unconscious motives and conflicts.

basic psychology The study of psychological issues in order to seek knowledge for its own sake rather than for its practical application.

applied psychology The study of psychological issues that have direct practical significance and the application of psychological findings.

biological perspective A psychological approach that emphasizes bodily events associated with actions, feelings, and thoughts.

learning perspective A psychological approach that emphasizes how the environment and experience affect a person's or an animal's actions; it includes *behaviorism* and *social-cognitive learning theories*.

behaviorism An approach to psychology that emphasizes the study of objectively observable behavior and the role of the environment as a determinant of behavior.

social-cognitive learning theory The theory that behavior is learned and maintained through observation and imitation of others, positive consequences, and cognitive processes such as plans and perceptions.

cognitive perspective A psychological approach that emphasizes mental processes in perception, memory, language, problem solving, and other areas of behavior.

sociocultural perspective A psychological approach that emphasizes social and cultural influences on behavior.

psychodynamic perspective A psychological approach that emphasizes unconscious dynamics within the individual, such as inner forces, conflicts, or the movement of instinctual energy.

humanistic psychology A psychological approach that emphasizes personal growth and achievement of human potential, rather than the scientific understanding and assessment of behavior.

feminist psychology A psychological approach that analyzes the influence of social inequities on gender relations and on the behaviors of the two sexes.

reductionism The process of reducing a phenomenon to a single type of explanation or to a limited set of elements of a particular type (for example, biological or cognitive).

Suggested Research Projects

1. Select a few psychology books from your campus library and read the authors' theoretical explanations about behavior. Try to identify which of the perspective(s) the author is arguing from. Try to construct some alternative explanations based on a different perspective.

2. Newspaper editorial sections often contain speculations about the causes of behaviors like violence, risky sexual practices, politically corrupt actions, and the like. Read a few editorials or letters to the editor and try to discern each writer's assumptions, biases, and psychological perspective. Identify the writer's claim. Design a research experiment to gather empirical evidence in support or against the writer's claim.

3. Browse through the popular psychology section of a local bookstore. Judging from the claims each book makes, distinguish between those that seem reputable and those that seem pseudoscientific. What percentage of popular psychology appears to be "psychobabble"?

Suggested Readings

Bem, S. (1998). *An unconventional family*. New Haven, CT: Yale University Press. A leading feminist psychologist explains how she applied her theories to the way in which she raised her children.

Kuhn, T. S. (1962). *The structure of scientific revolutions*. Chicago: University of Chicago Press. A description of the processes of change in scientific explanations.

Segerstrale, U. (2000). *Defenders of the truth: The battle for science in the sociobiology debate and beyond*. Oxford, England: Oxford University Press. A thorough and scholarly examination of the debates over evolutionary psychology.

CHAPTER 2

Studying Human Behavior

Learning Objectives

After reading and studying this chapter, you should be able to:

1.   Describe the attitudes and procedures that make research scientific.

2.   Compare and contrast descriptive and experimental research.

3.   Summarize the advantages and disadvantages of various research methods.

4.   Distinguish between correlation and causation.

5.   Design a simple experiment or other research study.

6.   Describe some sources of bias in experiments and suggest ways to avoid or control for these biases.

7.   Explain the function of statistics.

8.   Distinguish between descriptive and inferential statistics.

9.   Define statistical significance.

10.   Distinguish between cross-sectional and longitudinal research.

11.   Describe meta-analysis.

12.   Discuss the controversy between traditional science and postmodern views.

Chapter Outline

I.   Introduction

      A.   Research methods are important because they:
      1.   Allow scientists to separate truth from unfounded belief.
      2.   Help to sort out conflicting views.
      3.   Help to correct misconceptions.

II.   What Makes Research Scientific?

      A.   Precision
      1.   Scientists start out with a general **theory** -- an organized system of

assumptions and principles that purports to explain a specified set of phenomena and their interrelationships.

        2.   From the theory, the scientist derives a **hypothesis** -- a statement that attempts to predict or to account for a set of phenomena; scientific hypotheses specify relationships among events or variables and are empirically tested.

        3.   An **operational definition** is a precise definition of a term in a hypothesis, which specifies the operations for observing and measuring the process or phenomenon being defined.

        4.   The prediction can then be tested, using systematic methods.

   B.   Skepticism -- accepting conclusions with caution.

   C.   Reliance on empirical evidence.

   C.   Willingness to make "risky" predictions

        1.   The **principle of falsifiability** – the principle that a scientific theory must make predictions that are specific enough to expose the theory to the possibility of disconfirmation; that is, the theory must predict not only what will happen, but also what will not happen.

   E.   Openness to share ideas, methods, and results with other scientists so that they may *replicate*, or repeat, studies to verify findings.

III.   **Descriptive Research. Descriptive methods** are methods that yield descriptions of behavior but not necessarily causal explanations.

   A.   A **case study** is a detailed description of a particular individual being studied or treated. Case studies:

        1.   produce a more detailed picture of an individual than other methods.

        2.   may have vital information missing, making them hard to interpret.

        3.   often depend on people's memories, which may be inaccurate.

        4.   are limited in usefulness because the person may not be representative of the group of interest.

        5.   can be useful when there are no other ways of studying a phenomenon, for example with humans with brain damage.

        6.   are more often sources rather than tests of hypotheses.

   B.   An **observational study** is a study in which the researcher carefully and systematically observes and records behavior without interfering with the behavior. It may involve either naturalistic or laboratory observation.

        1.   The primary purpose of naturalistic observation is to find out how people or animals act in their normal social environments.

             a.   Observational researchers must count, rate, or measure behavior in a systematic way and disguise their intentions to those they are studying.

        2.   In laboratory observation, the experimenter has more control and more access to sophisticated equipment, but subjects may behave differently than they would in their natural surroundings.

C. **Psychological tests** are procedures used to measure and evaluate personality traits, emotional states, aptitudes, interests, abilities, and values.
   1. *Objective tests* ("inventories") measure beliefs, feelings or behaviors of which the individual is aware.
   2. *Projective tests* are designed to tap unconscious feelings and motives.
   3. A good psychological test:
      a. is **standardized** -- has uniform administration and scoring procedures.
      b. uses **norms** -- established standards of performance.
      c. is **reliable** -- produces consistent results. Reliability can be established in two ways:
         i. *test-retest reliability* is measured by giving the test twice to the same group and comparing the two sets of scores statistically.
         ii. *alternate forms reliability* is measured by giving different versions of a test to the same group on separate occasions.
      d. is **valid** -- measures what the test sets out to measure. There are several different kinds of validity, including:
         i. *content validity* -- the extent to which test items represent the trait in question.
         ii. *criterion validity* -- the ability to predict independent measures, or criteria, of the trait in question.
D. **Surveys** are questionnaires or interviews that ask people directly about their experiences, attitudes, or opinions. Good surveys:
   1. involve a **representative sample** -- a group of subjects, selected from a population for study, which matches the population on important characteristics such as age and sex.
   2. avoid **volunteer bias** – a shortcoming of findings derived from a sample volunteers instead of a representative sample; the volunteers may differ from those who did not volunteer.
   3. guarantee anonymity so that subjects are less likely to lie.
   4. avoid biased questions.
E. **Correlational research** involves measuring the strength of relationship between **variables**.
   1. A **positive correlation** is an association between increases in one variable and increases in another.
   2. A **negative correlation** is an association between increases in one variable and decreases in another.
   3. If there is no relationship between variables, then the variables are *uncorrelated*.
   4. The **coefficient of correlation** is measure of correlation that ranges in value from -1.00 to +1.00.
   5. +1.00 is a perfect positive correlation; -1.00 is a perfect negative correlation

6. Correlation does not imply causation.
7. If two variables, A and B, are correlated, it could be that A causes B, B causes A, or a third variable causes both A and B.

IV. Experimental Research

A. An experiment is a controlled test of a hypothesis in which the researcher manipulates one variable to discover its effect on another.
B. Experimental Variables: A basic experimental design involves:
1. An **independent variable** -- a variable that the experimenter manipulates.
2. A **dependent variable** -- a variable that the researcher predicts will be affected by manipulations of the independent variable.
3. Control of all variables except the independent variable.
C. Experimental and Control Conditions:
1. In a **control condition**, subjects are treated exactly like those in the experimental condition except that they are not exposed to the independent variable.
2. **Random assignment** is a procedure for assigning people to experimental and control groups in which each individual has the same probability of being assigned to a given group.
3. Drug research also usually involves **placebo** groups, in which subjects are given inactive substances or fake treatements in order to measure the effects of subjects' expectations about the drug on their behavior.
D. **Experimenter effects** are unintended changes in subjects' behavior due to cures inadvertently given by the experimenter. To avoid these, researchers use:
1. **single-blind study,** in which subjects do not know what group they are in.
2. **double-blind study,** in which neither the subject nor the experimenter has information about group assignment.

V. Advantages and Limitations of Experiments

A. Advantages:
1. Experiments allow conclusions about cause and effect.
2. Experiments permit researchers to distinguish real from placebo effects.
B. Disadvantages:
1. Participants are not always representative of the larger population.
2. Participants may not act in ways they normally would.
C. The more control an experimenter exercises, the more unlike real life the situation becomes.
D. Many psychologists are calling for more **field research** -- descriptive or experimental research conducted in a natural setting outside the laboratory.

VI.   Evaluating the Results

    A.   Statistics help researchers to:
        1.   describe results.
        2.   assess the reliability and meaning of results.
        3.   figure out how to explain results.
    B.   **Descriptive statistics** organize and summarize a body of data. They include:
        1.   the **arithmetic mean**, an average that is calculated by adding up a set of quantities and dividing the sum by the total number of quantities in the set.
        2.   the **standard deviation**, a commonly used measure of variability that indicates the average difference between scores in a distribution and their mean.
    C.   **Inferential statistics** permit the researcher to draw inferences (conclusions based on evidence) about how statistically meaningful a study's results are.
        1.   **Significance tests** show how likely it is that a study's results occurred merely by chance.
        2.   The convention is to consider a result to be *statistically significant* if it would be expected to occur by chance 5 or fewer times out of 100 (the .05 level).

VIII.   Interpreting the Results. Researchers should:

    A.   Choose the best explanation, which often does not emerge until the hypothesis has been tested in several ways, including:
        1.   **Cross-sectional study**, which involves comparing subjects of different ages at a given time.
        2.   **Longitudinal study**, in which subjects are followed and periodically reassessed over time.
    B.   Judge the result's importance.
        1.   Because statistically significant findings may be unimportant or statistically insignificant ones important, researchers are paying more attention to the **effect size**, the amount of variance in the data accounted for by the independent variable.
        2.   **Meta-analysis** is a procedure for combining and analyzing data from many studies; it determines how much of the variance in scores across all studies can be explained by a particular variable.

IX.   Keeping the Enterprise Ethical

    A.   College and university ethics committees must approve studies to be sure that they conform to federal regulations, and the American Psychological Association (APA) has a code of ethics for its members.
    B.   The ethics of studying human beings.

1. Psychologists must respect the dignity and welfare of human subjects.
2. *Informed consent* means that subjects participate voluntarily and know enough about the study to decide whether or not they want to do so.
3. Sometimes, psychologists mislead subjects in order to watch a participant behave naturally. If they use deception, researchers must:
   i. justify it by demonstrating the potential value of the research.
   ii. consider alternative procedures.
   iii. thoroughly debrief participants about the true purpose and methods of the study afterwards.

C. The ethics of studying animals. Animals are used in a small percentage of studies, and researchers are governed by federal regulations and the APA's ethical code in this area. Psychologists study animals:
1. to conduct basic research on a particular species.
2. to discover practical applications.
3. to study issues that cannot be studied experimentally with human beings because of practical or ethical considerations.
4. to clarify theoretical questions.
5. to improve human welfare.

X.   The Meaning of Knowledge

A. Most scientists embrace a vision of their work as objective, detached, and value-free.
B. In contrast, **postmodernism** is a school of thought holding that an observer's values, culture, worldview, and status in society inevitably affect the person's observations and explanations.
C. The postmodern view of *social constructionism* holds that knowledge is constructed more than it is discovered.

Chapter Summary

Psychological research methods allow researchers to separate truth from unfounded belief. In evaluating the findings of a study, one must consider how the information was 1._____.

Several attributes are characteristic of scientists. They begin with a general 2._____, a set of assumptions and principles that purports to explain phenomena. Then, the scientists derives a 3._____, a statement that attempts to specify a relationship among events that can be empirically tested. The construction of 4._____ definitions consists of taking vague terms and specifying how the behavior or situation is to be observed and measured. Scientists do not accept ideas on faith. Rather, they employ a good deal of 5._____, which means that they tend to be very cautious about accepting conclusions. In evaluating claims, scientists search for 6._____ evidence that is based on careful and systematic observation.

The principle of 7._____ is that an idea must be stated in a way that allows it to be refuted by counterevidence. In other words, a scientist must predict not only what will happen, but also what will not happen. Scientists must also be willing to share their methods and results with other scientists who may want to 8._____ their studies and verify their findings.

Psychologists may use several different methods in their research. 9._____ methods yield detailed accounts of behavior but not necessarily causal explanations. These methods include 10._____, which are in-depth descriptions of individuals. These are especially useful in investigating a new topic, or when information cannot be gathered in other ways. However, this method often relies on people's memories, which may be 11._____, and are more often sources, rather than 12._____ of hypotheses.

13._____ studies involve systematically watching and recording behaviors without interfering with those being watched. A common form of this method is called 14._____observation, which is used to describe behavior as it occurs in the environment. When using these methods, it is important to count, rate, or measure behavior in reliable and consistent ways. Sometimes this involves the use of sophisticated equipment, in which case the psychologist must often use the method of 15._____ observation. In this case, however, the presence of the equipment and/or the researchers may cause subjects to behave differently than they would otherwise.

16._____ are procedures used to measure and evaluate personality traits, emotional states, aptitudes, interests, abilities, and values. This process helps to clarify differences among individuals. Good psychological tests have several features. First, they are 17._____, so that the same instructions and procedures are used every time. Second, they are scored according to 18._____, or established standards of performance. Third, test constructors have demonstrated that they are 19._____, producing similar results from one time and place to the next. Last, but not least, they are also demonstrated to be 20._____, that is, they actually measure what they set out to measure.

Reliability is evaluated by giving the test twice to the same group of people and doing a statistical comparison of their scores. This is known as 21._____ reliability. A similar approach is to use two different versions of the same test in evaluating 22._____ reliability.

Validity is determined in several ways. 23._____ validity involves an analysis of test items to evaluate if they are representative of the trait in question. Tests are also judged by their ability to predict an independent measure of the same trait in a process known as 24._____ validity.

Questionnaires and interviews, or 25._____, are direct ways of gathering information from people. In order to be done well, the group of subjects, known as the 26._____, must be 27._____ of the larger population that the researcher wishes to describe. Information from a survey can be distorted by volunteer bias, subjects' lying, or by biased questions. Sometimes surveys actually influence as well as reflect people's attitudes and opinions.

The degree of relationship between two variables is known as a 28._____. This relationship can be 29._____, meaning that increases in one variable are associated with increases in the other, or 30._____, where increases in one variable are associated with decreases in the other. When there is no relationship between variables, they are said to be 31._____. Statistically, the degree of relationship is expressed by a number called a 32._____, which ranges from the perfect positive relationship of 33._____ to the perfect negative relationship of 34._____. A 35._____ correlation means that the variables are unrelated.

While correlations allow researchers to make general predictions about one variable from a second variable, they must be interpreted with caution, for two reasons. First, they cannot make precise predictions about a particular 36._____. Second, one cannot tell from a correlation whether or not one variable is actually the 37._____ of the other.

The descriptive methods provide speculations about explanations of behaviors, but cause can only be established by 38._____ methods that allow the researcher to 39._____ the one variable in order to discover its effect on another. The aspect of an experimental situation that the researcher manipulates or varies is known as the 40._____ variable. The behavior that the researcher attempts to predict is the 41._____ variable.

Experiments usually require an 42._____ condition, in which subjects receive some "treatment," and a 43._____ condition, in which subjects are treated exactly like the other subjects with the exception of the "treatment." In putting subjects in the two groups, researchers often use 44._____, so that each subject has the same probability of being in either group. Drug studies often include a 45._____ group in order to control for the influence of subjects' expectations on their behavior. When subjects are unaware of which group they are in, they are said to be taking part in a 46._____ study.

Researchers' expectations can also affect subjects' behavior, a phenomenon known as 47._____ effects. In order to avoid these, the person who administers the experiment should also not know which group the subjects are in. This is known as a 48._____ study. Because laboratory studies create artificial situations, many psychologists are calling for more 49._____ studies, which are conducted in a natural setting outside of the laboratory.

Psychologists use statistics to describe, assess, and explain data. 50._____ statistics organize and summarize data. The group average, or 51._____, is one commonly used statistic. While it describes the central point of a group's scores, it does not provide any information about the variation in scores. The

52. _____ indicates the average difference between scores and the center of the distribution.

53. _____ statistics permit a researcher to estimate the likelihood that the results of the study were due to 54. _____. When this likelihood is very low, the findings are said to be statistically 55. _____, which usually means that the results would be expected by chance 56. _____ times or fewer out of 100.

The last step in any study is to 57. _____ the results. Sometimes the best explanation does not emerge until a hypothesis is tested in several different ways, as one study can be used to confirm, disconfirm, or extend the results of another. For example, psychologists might compare test scores from two different groups such as young and old people. This approach is called 58. _____ research. Or the same group of people can be followed over longer periods of time in a 59. _____ study. 60. _____ is a recently developed technique in which data from several studies are combined and analyzed.

Researchers must conduct themselves according to ethical standards in order to protect human and animal subjects from physical or psychological harm. Subjects participate voluntarily and with 61. _____ meaning that they know enough about the study to judge whether or not they want to participate. Sometimes, psychologists mislead subjects intentionally in order to study something of interest. If they do so, they must thoroughly 62. _____ subjects afterwards and inform them of the true purpose of the study.

Scientists have traditionally considered themselves to be detached and objective. Recently, however, adherents of the viewpoint known as 63. _____ have argued that the observer's values, judgments, world view, and social status inevitably affect his or her approach to study and explanation. One of these theories, 64. _____, holds that knowledge is not so much discovered as it is invented.

Multiple Choice Self-Test

1.   Bettleheim's theory of the "refrigerator mother" was largely based on:
a.   empirical support.
b.   case studies.
c.   surveys.
d.   observations of mothers' behaviors.

2.   Sven is a member of a college faculty. He believes that guest speakers on the campus have more credibility than the college faculty ("household saints don't make miracles"). Sven's belief constitutes a/an:
a.   hypothesis.
b.   theory.
c.   operational definition.
d.   scientific attitude.

3. Marlene is interested in studying popularity. For the purposes of her study, she describes popularity as "the number of times the person's classmates report him or her to be one of three best friends." This description is:
a. a hypothesis.
b. a theory.
c. an operational definition.
d. a prediction.

4. The coefficient of correlation conveys information about:
a. the strength and direction of correlation.
b. the strength of correlation only.
c. the direction of correlation only.
d. the mean score and variability.

5. LaToya reads a study which says that depressed people tend to have more health problems than nondepressed people. She is skeptical about the findings, so she does a similar study to the one described by the original author. This procedure is known as:
a. falsifying.
b. scientific criticism.
c. reconfiguration.
d. replication.

6. The case study is a/an:
a. descriptive method.
b. unscientific method.
c. inferential method.
d. outmoded method.

7. Darren has a job giving pills to research volunteers. Some of these pills contain a drug, but others contain only sugar. Darren is not told which of these pills the subject is getting in order to avoid:
a. random assignment.
b. placebo effects.
c. experimenter effects.
d. single-blind effects.

8. Phineas Gage was a 19th century railroad foreman in Vermont who suffered a brain injury. His behavior was of interest to psychologists because brain injury in humans can only be studied using:
a. the experimental method.
b. the inferential method.
c. the case study.
d. cross-sectional research.

9. Jane is a psychologist who does research by measuring the interactional style of children on school playgrounds. Her method is:
a. the observational study.
b. the case study.
c. experimental.
d. developmental.

10. In a study designed to measure interpersonal influence, volunteers are asked to work together constructing stories from pictures. Their behavior is videotaped with their permission. This method is an example of:
a. naturalistic observation.
b. laboratory observation.
c. casual observation.
d. cross-checking.

11. The measurement and evaluation of personality traits, emotional states, aptitudes, interests, abilities, and values is known as:
a. the scientific method.
b. observational study.
c. hypothesis testing.
d. psychological testing.

12. After the first response in the Rorschach inkblot test, the tester is instructed to say, "most people see more than one thing." If the tester instead says, "do you see anything else?," he or she has violated the test's:
a. norms.
b. hypothesis.
c. reliability.
d. standardization.

13. When people take an intelligence test, their performance is compared with that of other people of their same age group, not with people who are older or younger. This procedure illustrates the use of:
a. standardization.
b. cross-sectional research.
c. longitudinal research.
d. norms.

14. Dr. Mfume is a psychologist who is developing a test of political conservatism. She gives her test to 1000 volunteers. Three weeks later, she gives the same test to the volunteers again, in order to check for:
a. reliability.
b. standardization.
c. validity.
d. variability.

15. Eight-year-old Juanita takes an intelligence test in order to qualify for a gifted program in her school. She must score 130 in order to be admitted to the program, but she scores only 120. However, a week later, she takes the same test and scores 150. If the second score is NOT a result of practice, we might question whether the test is:
a. standard.
b. normed.
c. reliable.
d. stable.

16. Mr. Andretti is a high school math teacher who teaches a six-week unit on factoring, linear combinations, solving equations, and combining like terms. After his students are tested at the end of the six weeks, they complain that the test had only factoring on it. Although they may not know it, their objection was based on the test's poor:
a. criterion validity.
b. content validity.
c. standardization.
d. reliability.

17. John thinks that "Laughter is the best medicine" and he decides to test this idea. What should he do first?
a. Develop a comedy routine which reliably makes people laugh.
b. Advertise for research subjects.
c. Generate a more precise hypothesis.
d. Ask a large number of doctors to participate as comedians in this research.

18. One way to investigate the value of the Scholastic Aptitude Test (SAT) is to follow a group of people through college and correlate their SAT scores with their senior grade point averages. This study is:
a. a cross-sectional study of content validity.
b. a longitudinal study of content validity.
c. a cross-sectional study of criterion validity.
d. a longitudinal study of criterion validity.

19. A feature in a popular magazine called "Are you a good friend?" contains a series of questions and gives a "friendship score" on the basis of your response to the questions. If this is like most of these types of features, it is probably:
a. pseudoscience.
b. hypothesis testing.
c. a validity study.
d. cross-sectional.

20. If a researcher is interested in college students' conceptions of love, he or she should survey students of all ages in several regions of the world at all different kinds of colleges, so that the sample used in the study will be:
a. valid.
b. reliable.
c. representative.
d. stable.

21. A magazine publishes a survey on dating attitudes. Readers can fill out the survey and send it to the magazine in a postage-paid envelope. However, one should interpret the findings of this survey with extreme caution, as these findings might well be distorted by:
a. unreliability.
b. a negative halo effect.
c. volunteer bias.
d. a lack of content validity.

22. Eunice's study reveals that membership in motorcycle clubs is highly and positively correlated with the number of tattoos on one's body. The correct interpretation of her finding is that:
a. being in a motorcycle club causes one to get tattoos.
b. having tattoos causes one to join motorcycle clubs.
c. tattoos and motorcycle club membership tend to go together.
d. tattoos are a statement of nonconformism.

23. A study reveals that the correlation between the number of classes attended and the final grade point average of students is -0.93.* This means that:
a. students who miss classes tend to get poor grades.
b. students who miss classes tend to get better grades.
c. missing class affects one's grade.
d. attending class causes one to get a poor grade.

* (We made this up. It's not true! Keep going to class.)

24. If A is highly correlated with B, then:
a. A causes B.
b. B causes A.
c. C causes both A and B.
d. A and B occur together often.

25. Tanya designed a paper-and-pencil test of shyness. She administered the test to a large population of subjects and then compared the results to behavioral observations of the same subjects. Tanya has therefore assessed the test's:
a. content validity.
b. criterion validity.
c. test-retest reliability.
d. alternate forms reliability.

26. Dr. Ivanisevich finds that popularity and considerateness are highly related to each other. Popularity and considerateness are:
a. variables.
b. norms.
c. standards.
d. phenomena.

27. Which correlation coefficient indicates the LOWEST degree of relationship?
a. + .22
b. - .16
c. + .09
d. - .37

28. A researcher is trying to find out if same-sex classes allow one to learn more. She takes 100 students and randomly assigns 25 males and 25 females to a same-sex classroom. The remaining 50 students are split randomly into two mixed-sex classrooms, and all students' learning is measured by test scores. The students in the mixed-sex classroom are what aspect of the experiment?
a. independent variable
b. control group
c. placebo group
d. dependent variable

29. A researcher is trying to find out if same-sex classes allow one to learn more. She takes 100 students and randomly assigns 25 males and 25 females to a same-sex classroom. The remaining 50 students are split randomly into two mixed-sex classrooms, and the students' learning is measured by test scores. The test score is the:
a. control.
b. dependent variable.
c. independent variable.
d. hypothesis.

30. Lisa conducted a study to learn if goldfish have color vision. She trained her subjects to swim forward when they saw a red light and to hold still when they saw a blue light. In order to show that the goldfish performed better than could be expected by chance alone, Lisa must use:
a. descriptive statistics.
b. meta-analysis.
c. the coefficient of correlation.
d. inferential statistics.

True-False Self-Test

T   F   1.   Operational definitions add precision to research.

T   F   2.   Scientists must balance skepticism with openness.

T   F   3.   Scientists rely on empirical evidence.

T   F   4.   Psychologists never deceive their subjects.

T   F   5.   The American Psychological Association has a code of ethics for animal research.

T   F   6.   Replication of research studies helps to verify research findings.

T   F   7.   Descriptive methods allow for judgments of cause and effect.

T   F   8.   The case study is an experimental method.

T   F   9.   The case study is sometimes the only ethical way to research certain areas of interest.

T   F   10.   It is not usually important to count, rate, or measure things when one is using naturalistic observation.

T   F   11.   Cross-checking is a technique used in case study research.

T   F   12.   Standardization involves comparing a person's test scores with other scores from persons in the same age group.

T   F   13.   A test is reliable if it measures consistently.

T   F   14.   A test can be reliable but not valid.

T   F   15.   A test can be valid but not reliable.

T   F   16.   Criterion validity studies involve the comparison of test scores to some independent measure.

T   F   17.   A sample should always be representative of the population the researcher wants to describe.

T   F   18.   Volunteers rarely differ from nonvolunteers in any important way.

T   F   19.   In an experiment, the dependent variable is manipulated by the researcher.

T   F   20.   A correlation coefficient provides information about the cause-and-effect relationship between two variables.

T   F   21.   In psychology, the standard for statistical significance is 0.85.

T   F   22.   Negative correlations reflect a low degree of relationship between two variables.

T   F   23.   A social constructionist would argue that humans do not discover knowledge as much as they construct knowledge.

T   F   24.   An experiment allows the researcher to control the situation being studied.

T   F   25.   In the ideal experiment, everything is controlled except for the dependent variable.

T   F   26.   A placebo group is a kind of control group.

T   F   27.   The double-blind method allows one to control both experimenter and placebo effects.

T   F   28.   Statements about probability are a part of descriptive statistics.

T   F   29.   Cross-sectional studies are better than longitudinal studies.

T   F   30.   Meta-analysis always involves several studies.

Key Terms

theory An organized system of assumptions and principles that purports to explain a specified set of phenomena and their interrelationships.

hypothesis A statement that attempts to predict or account for a set of phenomena; scientific hypotheses specify relationships among events or variables and are empirically tested.

operational definition A precise definition of a term in a hypothesis, which specifies the operations for observing and measuring the process or phenomenon being defined.

principle of falsifiability The principle that a scientific theory must make predictions that are specific enough to expose the theory to the possibility of disconfirmation; that is, the theory must predict not only what will happen, but also what will not happen.

descriptive methods Methods that yield descriptions of behavior but not necessarily causal explanations.

case study A detailed description of a particular individual being studied or treated.

observational study A study in which the researcher carefully and systematically observes and records behavior without interfering with the behavior; it may involve either naturalistic or laboratory observation.

psychological tests Procedures used to measure and evaluate personality traits, emotional states, aptitudes, interests, abilities, and values.

standardize In test construction, to develop uniform procedures for giving and scoring a test.

norms In test construction, established standards of performance.

reliability In test construction, the consistency of scores derived from a test, from one time and place to another.

validity The ability of a test to measure what it was designed to measure.

surveys Questionnaires or interviews that ask people directly about their experiences, attitudes, or opinions.

representative sample A group of subjects, selected from a population for study, which matches the population on important characteristics such as age and sex.

volunteer bias A shortcoming of findings derived from a sample of volunteers instead of a representative sample; the volunteers may differ from those who did not volunteer.

correlational study A descriptive study that looks for a consistent relationship between two phenomena.

correlation A measure of how strongly two or more variables are related to each other.

variables Characteristics of behavior or experience that can be measured or described by a numeric scale; variables are manipulated and assessed in scientific studies.

positive correlation An association between increases in one variable and increases in another.

negative correlation An association between increases in one variable and decreases in another.

coefficient of correlation A measure of correlation that ranges in value from -1.00 to +1.00.

experiment A controlled test of a hypothesis in which the researcher manipulates one variable to discover its effect on another.

independent variable A variable that an experimenter manipulates.

dependent variable A variable that an experimenter predicts will be affected by manipulations of the independent variable.

control condition In an experiment, a comparison condition in which subjects are not exposed to the same treatment as in the experimental condition.

random assignment A procedure for assigning people to experimental and control groups in which each individual has the same probability as any other of being assigned to a given group.

placebo An inactive substance or fake treatment used as a control in an experiment or given by a medical practitioner to a patient.

single-blind study An experiment in which subjects do not know whether they are in an experimental or a control group.

experimenter effects Unintended changes in subjects' behavior due to cues inadvertently given by the experimenter.

double-blind study An experiment in which neither the subjects nor the individuals running the study know which subjects are in the control group and which are in the experimental group until after the results are tallied.

field research Descriptive or experimental research conducted in a natural setting outside the laboratory.

descriptive statistics Statistical procedures that organize and summarize a body of data.

arithmetic mean An average that is calculated by adding up a set of quantities and dividing the sum by the total number of quantities in the set.

standard deviation A commonly used measure of variability that indicates the average difference between scores in a distribution and their mean.

inferential statistics Statistical tests that allow researchers to draw inferences about how statistically meaningful a study's results are.

significance tests Statistical tests that show how likely it is that a study's results occurred merely by chance.

cross-sectional study A study in which subjects of different ages are compared at a given time.

longitudinal study A study in which subjects are followed and periodically reassessed over a period of time.

effect size In an experiment, the amount of variance in the data accounted for by the independent variable.

meta-analysis A procedure for combining and analyzing data from many studies; it determines how much of the variance in scores across all studies can be explained by a particular variable.

postmodernism A school of thought holding that an observer's values, culture, worldview, and status in society inevitably affect the person's observations and explanations.

Suggested Research Projects

1. Select a problem of interest to you and design an experiment to study it. Does your design include a descriptive or experimental approach? Does it involve control groups, operational definitions, and other important considerations? Why are these considerations important to your design?

2. Select a problem of interest to you and list several different ways of approaching it. For example, if you were interested in the effects of politeness, you could do a case study, a naturalistic observation, a laboratory observation, and an experiment. Describe your general approach to each of these methods.

Suggested Readings

Hock, R. R. (1999). *Forty studies that changed psychology: Explorations into the history of psychological research* (3rd ed.). Upper Saddle River, NJ: Prentice-Hall. A description of landmark research in the field.

Leavitt, F. (2001). *Evaluating scientific research: Separating fact from fiction*. Upper Saddle River, NJ: Prentice-Hall. A textbook on critical thinking about science.

CHAPTER 3

The Genetics of Behavior

Learning Objectives

After reading and studying this chapter, you should be able to:

1.   Compare and contrast the nativist and empiricist positions.

2.   Explain the concept of the interaction of heredity and environment, using examples from research.

3.   Describe the genetic process by which traits are produced.

4.   Distinguish between sensation and perception.

5.   Explain the concept of critical period.

6.   Summarize the research on the capacity for language.

7.   Describe some universal behavioral tendencies, such as emotional expression, color perception, and language acquisition.

8.   Explain the concept of heritability.

9.   Discuss the research problems involved in separating genetic from environmental influences on behavior.

10.   Describe some research methods for studying heritability and some of the findings of important heritability studies.

11.   Discuss the controversy over racial differences in IQ.

Chapter Outline

I.   Introduction

    A.   In explaining human differences, psychologists tend to split into two camps:
        1.   *Nativists* emphasize genes and inborn characteristics (nature).
        2.   *Empiricists* focus on learning and experience (nurture), the focus of this chapter.
    B.   **Evolutionary psychology** is a field of psychology emphasizing evolutionary mechanisms that may help explain human commonalities in

cognition, development, emotion, social practices, and other areas of behavior.

C. **Behavioral genetics** is an interdisciplinary field of study concerned with the genetic bases of behavior and personality.

D. All scientists understand that heredity and environment interact to produce psychological and even physical traits.

E. A person's body weight is strongly influenced by **set point** -- a genetically-influenced weight range for an individual, thought to be maintained by a biological mechanism that regulates food intake, fat reserves, and metabolism. At the same time, obesity in the United States has increased due to environmental factors.

II. Unlocking the Secrets of Genes

    A. **Genes** are the basic units of heredity. They are located on **chromosomes**, which contain threadlike strands of **DNA**.
        1. Human egg cells and sperm cells each contain 23 chromosomes.
        2. At conception, the fertilized egg contains 46 chromosomes (23 pairs), as do all cells that develop from it (except sperm cells and ova).
        3. The **genome** is the full set of genes in each cell of an organism.
        4. Most traits depend on more than one gene pair.

    B. **Linkage studies** look for patterns of inheritance of genetic markers in large families in which a particular condition is common.

    C. A **genetic marker** is a segment of DNA that varies among individuals, has a known location on a chromosome, and can function as a genetic landmark for a gene involved in a physical or mental condition.

III. The Genetics of Similarity

    A. **Evolution** is a change in gene frequencies within a population over many generations; a mechanism by which genetically influenced characteristics of a population may change when genes *mutate*.

    B. **Natural selection** is the evolutionary process in which individuals with genetically influenced traits that allow adaptation to a particular environment tend to survive and to reproduce in greater numbers than other individuals. As a result, their traits become more common in a population.

    C. Evolutionary psychologists look to the prehistoric past to draw inferences about behavioral tendencies that might have solved survival problems and enhanced reproductive fitness.

    D. Because of evolutionary history, some qualities are universal among human beings, including:
        1. reflexes.
        2. attraction to novelty.
        3. a desire to explore and manipulate objects.

4. an impulse to play and fool around.
5. basic mental skills.

IV. Our Human Heritage

    A. The Origins of Perception
        1. **Sensation** is the detection of physical energy emitted or reflected by physical objects; it occurs when energy in the external environment stimulates receptors in the sense organs.
        2. **Perception** is the process by which the brain organizes and interprets sensory information.
        3. The development of some abilities depends on having certain experiences during critical periods of development.
        4. Complex features of the visual world are processed by special *feature detector cells*.
        5. Depth perception in children is tested using the "visual cliff."
        6. Some perceptual abilities appear to be inborn, including:
            a. being startled by a loud noise.
            b. perceiving sound as localized in space.
            c. distinguishing a person's voice from other kinds of sound.
            d. discriminating among certain odors and tastes.
    B. The Face of Emotion
        1. Some emotional expressions are present from birth.
        2. Universal facial expressions function in communication.
    C. Sociability and Attachment
        1. Synchrony and sociability: Newborns are sociable from birth. They pay attention to human faces and show other responses such as *synchrony*, the adjustment of one person's nonverbal behavior to coordinate with another's.
        2. **Attachment** is the emotional tie that children and their caregivers feel toward each other.
            a. **Contact comfort** is the innate pleasure derived from close physical contact; it is the basis of the infant' first attachment.
            b. Infants who do not develop secure attachments to adults may develop persistent emotional and physical problems.
    D. The Capacity for Language
        1. **Language** is a system for combining meaningless elements into utterances that convey meaning.
            a. Children's vocabulary increases at a rapid rate.
        2. Language development requires learning a large set of rules that make up the grammar of the language including:
            a. *surface structure* -- the way the sentence is actually spoken.
            b. *deep structure* -- the meaning inferred by a sentence.
            c. *syntax* – the rules of grammar.
        3. Children do not simply imitate adults. They are able to perceive deep structure. Chomsky theorized that this is due to a

biologically-based **language acquisition device**, an innate mental module that facilitates the young child's development of language. He cites several arguments in support, including:

    a.   Children of different cultures go through similar stages of linguistic development.

    b.   Children combine words in ways that adults never would.

    c.   Adults do not consistently correct their children's syntax, yet children learn to speak or sign correctly anyway.

    d.   Even children who are profoundly retarded acquire language.

    e.   Infants as young as 7 months can derive simple linguistic rules from a string of sounds.

4.   Imitation also plays a role.

    a.   Parents recast children's ungrammatical sentences.

5.   There may be a critical period for language development.

V.   Evolution, Courtship, and Mating

    A.   The evolutionary viewpoint on mating practices has been strongly influenced by **sociobiology**, an interdisciplinary field that emphasizes evolutionary explanations of social behavior in animals, including human beings.

    B.   The sociobiological view is that nature has selected psychological traits and social customs that aid individuals in propagating their genes.

    C.   Sociobiologists argue that males and females have evolved different mating strategies,

        1.   males to inseminate as many females as possible and females to be more selective, as females must invest much more time and resources in mating than males.

        2.   As a result, males are thought to be more promiscuous and drawn to sexual novelty, while females are more interested in stability and security.

    D.   Sociobiologists tend to argue by analogy to nonhuman animals, but most evolutionary biologists recognize these analogies as simplistic and misleading.

    E.   Critics argue that evolutionary explanations are based on stereotypes of gender, which differs from the actual behavior of humans and other animals.

    F.   Critics also argue that evolutionary theories are nonfalsifiable and that human sexual behavior is varied and changeable.

VI.   The Genetics of Difference

    A.   **Heritability** is a statistical estimate of the proportion of the total variance in some trait that is attributable to genetic differences among individuals within the group.

1. An estimate of heritability applies only to a particular group living in a particular environment.
2. Heritability estimates do not apply to individuals, only to variations within a group.
3. Even highly heritable traits can be modified by the environment.

B. Computing Heritability
1. Research methods are used in an attempt to infer heritability by studying people whose degree of genetic similarity is known.
   a. Adopted children share half their genes, but not their environments, with their birth parents.
   b. **Identical (monozygotic) twins** develop when a fertilized egg divides into two parts that develop into separate embryos. **Fraternal (dizygotic) twins** develop from two separate eggs fertilized by different sperm; they are no more alike genetically than are any other pair of siblings.
   c. Identical twins raised apart from each other are of special interest to researchers because they have identical genes but have been raised in different environments.

VII. Our Human Diversity

A. Heritability and Intelligence
1. **Intelligence quotient (IQ)** is a measure of intelligence originally computed by dividing a person's mental age by his or her chronological age and multiplying the result by 100; it is now derived from norms provided for standardized intelligence tests.
   a. IQ is controversial; many critics argue that intelligence comes in many varieties and cannot be captured by a single score.
   b. The concept of intelligence is culture-bound.

B. Genes and Individual Differences
1. IQ scores are highly heritable, with estimates averaging around .50 in children and .60 to .80 in adults.
2. Scores of identical twins are always more highly correlated than those of fraternal twins.
3. Scores of adopted children are more highly correlated with birth parents than adoptive parents.

C. The Question of Group Differences
1. Race differences in average IQ are controversial.
   a. As a group, Asians score higher than whites, who score higher than African-Americans.
   b. Some theorists have confused the findings that IQ differences within groups are partly genetic with speculation that IQ differences between groups are genetic.
   c. Minority children tend to have access to fewer educational and material resources.
   d. Well designed studies have failed to reveal genetic

differences between blacks and whites.

D.   Genes and Personality
  1.   **Temperaments** are physiological dispositions to respond to the environment in certain ways; they are present in infancy and are assumed to be innate.
  2.   Heredity and Temperament:
    a.   Differences in children's temperaments appear early in childhood.
    b.   Temperaments tend to remain stable throughout childhood.
  3.   Heredity and Traits
    a.   A **trait** is a characteristic of an individual, describing a habitual way of behaving, thinking, and feeling.
    b.   The study of personality traits has been greatly enhanced by applying **factor analysis**, a statistical method for analyzing the intercorrelations among different measures or test scores; clusters of measures or scores that are highly correlated are assumed to measure the same underlying trait or ability (factor).
    c.   Most psychologists agree on the centrality of five robust factors of personality (the *Big Five*):
      i.   *introversion versus extroversion*: the extent to which people are outgoing or shy.
      ii. *neuroticism* or *negative emotionality*, which includes traits like anxiety, poor impulse control and a tendency toward negative emotions.
      iii. *agreeableness*, the extent to which people are good-natured or irritable.
      iv. *conscientiousness*, the degree to which people are responsible or undependable.
      v.   *openness* to experience, the extent to which people are original and imaginative.

VIII.   Behavioral Genetics Research in Perspective

  A.   Some reasons why genes are not everything:
    1.   Not all traits are equally heritable or unaffected by shared environments.
    2.   Some studies may underestimate the impact of the environment.
    3.   Even traits that are highly heritable are not rigidly fixed and can be modified by experience.

IX.   In Praise of Human Variation

  A.   Heredity and environment always interact to produce the unique mixture of qualities in a person.
  B.   The survival of the species depends in part on diversity.

Chapter Summary

Psychologists have long been interested in the nature-nurture question. Historically, two positions tended to emerge: the 1._____, who emphasized inborn characteristics, and the 2._____, who focused on learning and experience. More recently, very few people argue for one or the other, as scientists have come to understand that heredity and environment 3._____ to produce traits. For example, research on weight has revealed that heaviness is not caused by 4._____, but rather that biological factors place certain limits on how much a person will weigh. The two major fields that emphasize biological roots of behavior are 5._____ psychology, which emphasizes our ancestral past, and 6._____, which studies the biologically inherited bases of behavior and personality.

7._____ are the basic units of heredity. They are located on rod-shaped structures called 8._____, which consist of threadlike strands of a substance called 9._____. Because there are thousands of genes that can be combined in thousands of ways, and because genes can spontaneously change, or 10._____, genetic diversity is huge.

Genetic research is difficult because most human traits depend on more than one gene pair. One method that is used to investigate genetics is the 11._____ study, in which scientists look for genetic markers in large families in which a particular condition is common.

12._____ is a change in gene frequency within a population over many generations. The environment determines which genes will survive through the process of 13._____. Because of our evolutionary history, some abilities, traits, and characteristics are universal among human beings, including reflexes, the attraction to novelty, and certain perceptual tendencies.

14._____ is the process by which sense receptors respond to changes in physical energy. The brain interprets and organizes this information in the process called 15._____. This ability can develop abnormally without certain experiences during 16._____ of development.

There is a good deal of evidence that infants can discriminate different sizes and colors as well as contrasts and shadows, at a very early age. Depth perception may also be present, as indicated by studies involving the "visual 17._____." Newborns can also discriminate among certain tastes and sounds. For instance, they can distinguish salty from sweet tastes and tell the difference between a human voice and other kinds of sound. The biological predisposition to respond to certain stimuli evolved in order to help us survive.

Certain emotional expressions are present at birth and universal. Newborns are also sociable from birth, responding to human 18._____, and showing 19._____, the adjustment of nonverbal behavior to others. 20._____ is the emotional tie that children and their caregivers feel toward each other. It is based on physical closeness, or 21._____.

22._____ is a system for combining meaningless elements into communications that convey meaning. In order to learn this system, children must internalize a large set of grammatical rules. A child must not only learn the 23._____ structure of a sentence (the way a sentence is actually spoken), but must also infer an underlying 24._____ structure that contains meaning. Apparently, the capacity to do so is biologically present in humans in the form of a 25._____ device that enables children to readily understand 26._____, the grammatical rules of a language.

Chomsky and others have advanced several arguments to support the proposed existence of this device. First, children everywhere seem to go through similar stages of linguistic development. Second, they combine words in ways that adults do not. Third, adults do not always correct children's linguistic errors. These arguments dispute the once widely-held belief that language is acquired only through 27._____, although it is clear that children's speech is affected by their parents. There appears to be a 28._____ for normal language development, and children who do not acquire language by a certain age are likely to have longstanding problems.

The evolutionary viewpoint on mating practices has been heavily influenced by 29._____, a field that emphasizes evolutionary explanations for social behavior. This view holds that males and females evolved different mating strategies to propagate their genes. Critics argue that these explanations are based on 30._____ of gender rather than actual behavior, and that these theories are not falsifiable.

31._____ is an estimate of the proportion of the total variance in a trait that is attributable to genetic variation within a group. Although the terms "heritable" and "genetic" are sometimes used interchangeably, "heritable" only refers to traits that 32._____ within a population. Estimates of heritability apply only to a particular group living in a particular environment. These estimates may differ for different groups, and they do not apply to 33._____. Even highly heritable traits can be modified by the 34._____. Heritable behavioral traits are usually influenced by many 35.____ working in combination.

Scientists interested in heritability try to study people whose degree of genetic similarity is known. Their studies often include comparisons of adopted children with their birth parents and adopted parents, as well as comparisons of two kinds of twins, 36._____ (identical) and 37._____ (fraternal). Of special interest is the study of identical twins who were raised 38._____.

One major area of heritability study is intelligence. Historically, the measure of intelligence was the IQ, or intelligence 39._____, which is the mental age divided by the 40._____ age times 100. Although modern measures of intelligence are still termed "IQ," these scores now reflect comparisons of a person with others in his or her age group. The concept of intelligence is controversial and culture-bound.

Heritability estimates for IQ scores in children and adolescents average around
41. _____ . 42. _____ twins always have more highly correlated scores than
43. _____ twins, and IQ scores of adopted children correlate higher with their
44. _____ parents than with their 45. _____ parents.

The study of group differences in IQ scores has produced some controversy. Different racial groups have different average scores. However, the fact that differences
46. _____ groups have some genetic basis does not mean that differences
47. _____ groups are genetic. Minority children have less access to important resources, and well-designed studies have failed to reveal genetic differences between blacks and whites.

Personality is another major area for heritability studies. Infants are born with
48. _____, characteristic styles of responding to the environment. This tends to remain stable throughout childhood. Other characteristics, called 49. _____, also have been shown to be both heritable and stable. Several personality factors seem to turn up in adults in many cultures. These include introversion-extroversion, neuroticism, agreeableness, conscientiousness, and openness to experience, the so-called
50. _____ personality factors.

It is clear that not all traits are equally heritable, and some studies are though to
51. _____ the impact of the environment. Even highly heritable traits can be modified by 52. _____ .

Multiple Choice Self-Test

1.   In the nature-nurture debate, those that emphasize learning and experience are known as:
a.   nativists.
b.   empiricists.
c.   nurturists.
d.   cognitivists.

2.   Few modern theorists emphasize nature or nurture, because it has been well established that traits result from:
a.   the interaction of heredity and environment.
b.   the imitation of parents.
c.   the choices of the individual.
d.   prenatal events.

3.   Body weight is MOST affected by:
a.   diet.
b.   overeating.
c.   food preferences.
d.   set point.

4. Your friend Juan says that men are sexually aroused much easier than women because of how things were millions of years ago. His view is closest to that of:
a. sociobiology.
b. behavior genetics.
c. psycholinguistics.
d. insemination theory.

5. A major criticism of sociobiology is that this theory is:
a. unfalsifiable.
b. not based on evolutionary claims.
c. overly complex.
d. genetically based.

6. Most human traits depend on:
a. multiple gene pairs.
b. a single gene.
c. the X chromosome.
d. the Y chromosome.

7. Major depression is found disproportionately among people in some Amish communities. Genetic research on depression in these communities is carried out in a:
a. meta-analytic study.
b. case study.
c. population representation study.
d. linkage study.

8. Penny is a newborn child. What will she need in order to develop a healthy attachment to her caregivers?
a. time with her biological mother.
b. time to overcome her innate shyness.
c. an strict mother.
d. contact comfort.

9. Genetic variation is nearly limitless because of:
a. the number of different chromosome combinations only.
b. the number of different chromosome combinations and mutations.
c. the number of mutations only.
d. natural selection.

10. The attraction to novel stimuli:
a. is learned in certain cultures.
b. is learned in all cultures.
c. is innate to humans and many animals.
d. appears only in humans.

11. A person who is blind from birth but later has his or her sight restored as an adult will likely have problems with visual perception because he or she has missed the:
a. critical period.
b. window of opportunity.
c. transductive interval.
d. optimal stimulus load.

12. Very young infants respond most positively to a:
a. brightly colored object.
b. pleasant face.
c. slightly sour substance.
d. soft toy.

13. Ten students from ten different cultures are watching a pantomimed play when something happens in the play that all of them think is funny. What is the most likely outcome?
a. They will each express their delight in a way that is indigenous to their culture.
b. They will exhibit similar facial responses.
c. Western students will smile; Eastern students will open their eyes wide.
d. The students will communicate with each other.

14. Shadrach and Abednigo are researchers who want to combine and analyze intercorrelations from different personality tests into clusters or measures of scores. They will use a statistical technique called:
a. personality regression.
b. binomial factoring.
c. non-linear combination procedure.
d. factor analysis.

15. Children who have been deprived of contact comfort at an early age show physical and emotional deficits because they:
a. did not have optimum experiences during the critical period.
b. did not attach to their birth parents.
c. did not get fed properly.
d. did not develop a sense of self separate from their mothers.

16. Maria is playing with her newborn baby. She stares joyfully at the baby, who gazes back. After a few seconds, the baby looks away and so does Maria. After another few seconds, the baby looks back at Maria and smiles. Maria smiles back. This exchange between mother and baby is characterized by:
a. contact comfort.
b. infant dominance.
c. synchrony.
d. therapeutic touch.

17. Children seem to learn language because they:
a. have an inborn ability for understanding the deep structure of language.
b. are always rewarded for using new words.
c. imitate their parents, although they are seldom rewarded for doing so.
d. usually do not get their parents' attention without it.

18. Gregory is six months old. His father is his primary caregiver and therefore Gregory has developed a strong attachment to his father. This means that:
a. Gregory will grow up unable to form a healthy relationship with women.
b. Gregory will never learn to exhibit normal facial expressions.
c. Gregory's father will never be able to provide child care equal to that of a woman.
d. Gregory will use his father as a secure base from which to explore his environment.

19. Which of the following supports the existence of the language acquisition device?
a. Children of different cultures pass through different stages of language development.
b. Children can make up sentences of a structure they have never heard adults use.
c. Children's vocabulary increases at a highly rapid rate.
d. Children differ in the pace of their language development.

20. Which of the following is NOT one of the *Big Five* personality factors?
a. neuroticism.
b self-esteem.
c. agreeableness.
d. openness to experience.

21. One apparently <u>unique</u> aspect of human language is that it allows us to:
a. communicate with others of our species.
b. express or comprehend novel utterances.
c. affect the behavior of others of our species.
d. express emotions.

22. If we knew that hypnotizability was highly heritable in Americans of European descent, what would that tell us about the heritability of this trait in Americans of Asian descent?
a. That heritability is high for them also.
b. That heritability is low for them.
c. Nothing.
d. That hypnotizability is not an important cultural concept for Asians.

23. On the average, what percentage of genes in common do dizygotic twins share, compared with monozygotic twins?
a. 100%
b. 50%
c. 200%
d. 18%

24. For her group of subjects, Dr. Craig estimated the heritability of shyness to be about 0.65. Based on this information alone, Dr. Craig should NOT:
a. assume that the heritability of this trait is 0.65 for any single subject.
b. assume that environmental experience affects shyness.
c. assume that genetic inheritance influences shyness.
d. assume that shyness is influenced by multiple factors.

25. Adam, a quiet baby, and Eve, a cranky baby, differ in:
a. prenatal environment.
b. postnatal environment.
c. temperament.
d. attachment level.

26. Shy babies:
a. tend to remain shy throughout childhood.
b. always remain shy throughout childhood.
c. tend to become outgoing adults.
d. are no more likely to be shy throughout childhood than other babies.

27. Personality traits are:
a. unchangeable.
b. highly heritable and highly stable.
c. highly heritable but unstable.
d. highly stable but not highly heritable.

28. Martin and Margo believe that human personality is almost completely shaped by biology. They are:
a. nativists.
b. empiricists.
c. behavior geneticists.
d. natural selectionists.

29. Children can derive simple linguistic rules from a string of sounds when they are as young as:
a. 16 months.
b. 3 years.
c. 7 months.
d. 3 months.

30. Across different cultures, stages of language development are:
a. similar.
b. qualitatively different.
c. quantitatively different.
d. identical.

True-False Self-Test

T   F   1.   Psychology is separate and distinct from biology.

T   F   2.   Most modern researchers are neither nativists nor empiricists.

T   F   3.   Obesity is not caused by overeating.

T   F   4.   French children acquire language similarly to German children.

T   F   5.   Genes contain chromosomes.

T   F   6.   Linkage studies help to separate out the relative influences of genetics and environment.

T   F   7.   Gene mutation adds to genetic diversity.

T   F   8.   Natural selection always adds to genetic diversity.

T   F   9.   All birds and mammals are motivated to explore and manipulate objects.

T   F   10.   Sociobiological theories are nearly universally accepted.

T   F   11.   A baby can tell a human voice from another kind of sound.

T   F   12.   IQ scores are highly heritable.

T   F   13.   Some emotional expressions are universal across cultures.

T   F   14.   Emotional attachment is established through the caregiver's feeding of the child.

T   F   15.   Babies who are not touched and held often grow up with emotional problems.

T   F   16.   There is no identifiable critical period for visual perception.

T	F	17.	Children learn the rules of language mainly through imitation and formal instruction.
T	F	18.	Children in different cultures go through different stages of linguistic development.
T	F	19.	IQ scores of adopted children are more similar to their birth parents than to their adopted parents.
T	F	20.	The heritability scores on IQ for adults are even greater than those of children.
T	F	21.	"Heritable" is synonymous with "genetic."
T	F	22.	Most behavioral traits are influenced by single genes.
T	F	23.	Dizygotic twins have identical genes.
T	F	24.	The definition of intelligence is similar across cultures.
T	F	25.	If the heritability of a trait is 0.50, then for any individual, the trait is half genetically inherited and half environmentally influenced.
T	F	26.	One can see differences in children's temperaments shortly following birth.
T	F	27.	Monozygotic twins share more genetic material than dizygotic twins.
T	F	28.	The IQ scores of 100 pairs of identical twins are always more highly correlated between twins than the scores of 100 pairs of dizygotic twins.
T	F	29.	Temperament is a highly stable trait.
T	F	30.	Highly heritable traits are almost impossible to change.

Key Terms

evolutionary psychology A field of psychology emphasizing evolutionary mechanisms that may help explain human commonalities in cognition, development, emotion, social practices, and other areas of behavior.

behavioral genetics An interdisciplinary field of study concerned with the genetic bases of behavior and personality.

set point A genetically-influenced weight range for an individual, thought to be maintained by a biological mechanism that regulates food intake, fat reserves, and metabolism.

genes The functional units of heredity; they are composed of DNA and specify the structure of proteins.

chromosomes Within every body cell, rod-shaped structures that carry the genes.

DNA (deoxyribonucleic acid) The chromosomal molecule that transfers genetic characteristics by way of coded instructions for the structure of proteins.

genome The full set of genes in each cell of an organism (with the exception of sperm and egg cells).

linkage studies Studies that look for patterns of inheritance of genetic markers in large families in which a particular condition is common.

genetic marker A segment of DNA that varies among individuals, has a known location on a chromosome, and can function as a genetic landmark for a gene involved in a physical or mental condition.

evolution A change in gene frequencies within a population over many generations; a mechanism by which genetically influenced characteristics of a population may change.

natural selection The evolutionary process in which individuals with genetically influenced traits that are adaptive in a particular environment tend to survive and to reproduce in greater numbers than other individuals; as a result, their traits become more common in a population.

sensation The detection of physical energy emitted or reflected by physical objects; it occurs when energy in the external environment stimulates receptors in the sense organs.

perception The process by which the brain organizes and interprets sensory information.

contact comfort The innate pleasure derived from close physical contact; it is the basis of the infant's first attachment.

language A system that combines meaningless elements such as sounds or gestures into structured utterances that convey meaning.

language acquisition device According to many psycholinguists, an innate mental module that facilitates the young child's development of language.

sociobiology An interdisciplinary field that emphasizes evolutionary explanations of social behavior in animals, including human beings.

lateralization Specialization of the two cerebral hemispheres for particular psychological operations.

heritability A statistical estimate of the proportion of the total variance in some trait that is attributable to genetic differences among individuals within the group.

identical (monozygotic) twins Twins that develop when a fertilized egg divides into two parts that develop into separate embryos.

fraternal (dizygotic) twins Twins that develop from two separate eggs fertilized by different sperm; they are no more alike genetically than are any other pair of siblings.

intelligence quotient (IQ) A measure of intelligence originally computed by dividing a person's mental age by his or her chronological age and multiplying the result by 100; it is now derived from norms provided for standardized intelligence tests.

temperaments Physiological dispositions to respond to the environment in certain ways; they are present in infancy and are assumed to be innate.

trait A characteristic of an individual, describing a habitual way of behaving, thinking, and feeling.

factor analysis A statistical method for analyzing the intercorrelations among different measures or test scores; clusters of measures or scores that are highly correlated are assumed to measure the same underlying trait or ability (factor).

Suggested Research Projects

1.   Organize several of your classmates to search for a trait, such as left-handedness, in their families of origin. Draw genograms of family trees with left-handed family members highlighted and try to discern patterns of the trait.

2.   Try to find a place where you can observe the behavior of very young children. See if you can distinguish between temperaments. Perhaps your instructor could help you find a set of behavioral guidelines for observed temperamental styles. If the children are in a setting that allows them to interact, try to systematically observe whether or not children with similar temperamental styles tend to associate with each other. Develop some hypotheses as to why this is or is not so.

Suggested Readings

Gould, S. (1996, revised and expanded ed.). *The mismeasure of man.* New York: Norton. A history of the attempts by majority males to classify people in ways that made males and caucasians appear superior to women and people of color.

Plomin, R. (Ed.), Defries, J. C., McClearn, G. E., & Rutter, M. (1997). *Behavioral genetics: A primer.* San Francisco: Freeman. A basic description of the behavior genetics field.

CHAPTER 4

Neurons, Hormones, and the Brain

Learning Objectives

After reading and studying this chapter, you should be able to:

1.   Describe the function of the nervous system.

2.   Distinguish between the various divisions of the nervous system.

3.   Explain how neurons receive and transmit information.

4.   Explain how hormones affect behavior.

5.   Describe several methods used for studying the brain.

6.   Discuss the locations and functions of various parts of the brain.

7.   Compare and contrast the functions of the left and right hemispheres.

8.   Summarize findings about the physiology of memory and sleep.

9.   Compare and contrast theories of dreaming.

10.   Discuss the benefits and misuses of the biological perspective.

Chapter Outline

I.   The Nervous System: A Basic Blueprint

    A.   The nervous system functions to gather and process information, produce responses to stimuli, and coordinate the workings of different cells. It consists of two parts:

        1.   The **central nervous system (CNS)** receives, processes, interprets, and stores incoming sensory information. It also sends out messages to muscles, glands, and body organs. It has two components:

            a.   the brain.

            b.   the **spinal cord**, a collection of neurons and supportive tissue running from the base of the brain down the center of the back, protected by a column of bones (the spinal column). It:

                i.   acts as a bridge between the brain and the parts of the body below the neck.

ii. handles some reflexes.
2. The **peripheral nervous system (PNS)** contains all portions of the nervous system outside the brain and spinal cord. It handles the central nervous system's input and output and includes:
    a. *sensory nerves*, which carry messages from skin, muscles, and other external sense organs to the spinal cord.
    b. *motor nerves*, which carry messages from the central nervous system to muscles, glands, and internal organs. They enable us to move our bodies and cause glands to secrete *hormones*.
3. Scientists further divide the peripheral nervous system into two parts:
    a. **the somatic nervous system**, sometimes called the *skeletal nervous system* -- nerves connected to sensory receptors and to skeletal muscles.
    b. **the autonomic nervous system** -- regulates the functioning of blood vessels, glands, and internal organs. **Biofeedback**, a method for learning to control bodily functions, including ones usually thought to be involuntary, by attending to feedback from an instrument that monitors the function and that signals changes in it, can be used to help a person learn to control some autonomic responses. The autonomic nervous system is divided into two parts:
        i. **the sympathetic nervous system** -- The subdivision of the autonomic nervous system that mobilizes bodily resources and increases the output of energy during emotion and stress.
        ii. **the parasympathetic nervous system** -- The subdivision of the autonomic nervous system that operates during relaxed states and that conserves energy.

II. Communication in the Nervous System

A. **Neurons**, or *nerve cells*, are the basic units of the nervous system.
1. They are held in place by **glial cells**, nervous-system cells that aid the neurons by providing them with nutrients, insulating them, and removing cellular debris when they die.
2. Neurons transmit signals to, from, and within the central nervous system.
B. The Structure of the Neuron
1. A neuron has three main parts:
    a. **dendrites**, neuron branches that receive information from other neurons and transmit it toward the cell body.
    b. the **cell body**, which is the part of the neuron that keeps the cell alive and determines it will **fire** (transmit a message).

c. the **axon**, a neuron's extending fiber that conducts impulses away from the cell body and transmits them to other neurons. The end of an axon is often divided into branches called *axon terminals*.

d. The **myelin sheath**, a layer of fatty insulating material is found on many axons, especially larger ones. It functions to:

i. prevent signals from adjacent cells from interfering with one another.

ii. speed up the conduction of neural impulses by forcing them to "hop" from one break in the myelin to another rather than moving more slowly down the entire length of the neuron.

2. A **nerve** is a bundle of neural fibers (axons and sometimes dendrites) in the peripheral nervous system.

a. Most nerves enter or leave the spinal cord.

b. The human body has 43 pairs of peripheral nerves, and the 12 *cranial nerves* are connected directly to the brain.

3. Until recently, neuroscientists thought that neurons could not reproduce or regenerate, however there is evidence that *precursor cells* can give birth to new neurons and that these cells exist in the brain.

C. How Neurons Communicate

1. The **synapse** is the site where a nerve impulse is transmitted from one nerve cell to another. It includes:

a. the axon terminal of one axon.

b. the *synaptic cleft* where the axon terminal of one neuron nearly touches a dendrite or cell body of another neuron.

c. the membrane of the receiving dendrite or cell body.

2. Synapses form, are lost, and reform throughout life. New learning results in the establishment of new synaptic connections.

3. The brain's flexibility, called *plasticity*, allows people to recover from strokes and head injuries.

4. The process of neural transmission begins when a neural impulse, or *action potential*, travels down the transmitting axon.

a. In unmyelinated neurons, the action potential at each point on the axon gives rise to a new one at the next point.

b. In myelinated neurons, the action potential "hops" from one node to the next, allowing the impulse to travel faster.

5. When the impulse reaches the the tip of the axon terminal, *synaptic vesicles* (tiny sacs) open and release a **neurotransmitter** (a chemical substance that can alter the activity of receiving neurons).

6. Neurotransmitters bind with *receptor sites*, briefly changing the membrane of the receiving cell in one of two ways:

a. A voltage shift in a positive direction is *excitatory* - making the cell more likely to fire.

      b.   A voltage shift in a negative direction is *inhibitory* - making the cell less likely to fire.

    7.   Neural firing is an *all-or-none* event.

III.   Chemical Messengers in the Nervous System

    A.   Neurotransmitters: Versatile Couriers

        1.   Neurotransmitters exist in the brain, spinal cord, peripheral nerves, and certain glands, affecting specific nerve circuits. Some well-known neurotransmitters are:

            a.   *Serotonin*, which is involved in sleep, appetite, sensory perception, pain suppression, and mood.

            b.   *Dopamine*, which is involved in voluntary movement, learning, memory, and emotion.

            c.   *Acetylcholine*, which is involved in muscle action, cognition, memory, and emotion.

            d.   *Norepinephrine*, which is involved in cognitive and emotional functions and bodily arousal.

            e.   *GABA*, which is the main inhibitory neurotransmitter in the brain.

            f.   Glutamate, an excitatory neurotransmitter involved in long-term memory.

        2.   Harmful effects occur from excesses or deficits of certain neurotransmitters, including:

            a.   sleep, eating, and convulsive disorders (abnormal GABA levels).

            b.   *Alzheimer's disease* (acetylcholine deficits).

            c.   *Parkinson's disease* is caused by degeneration of the brain cells that produce dopamine. Injections of dopamine are ineffective because it cannot cross the *blood-brain barrier*.

                i.   L-dopa can be helpful, but can produce serious adverse effects.

                ii.   Brain tissue transplants are a possible new treatment.

    B.   Endorphins: The Brain's Natural Opiates

        1.   **Endorphins** are chemical substances in the nervous system that are similar in structure and action to opiates. They are involved in pain reduction, pleasure, and memory, and are known technically as *endogenous opioid peptides*.

        2.   They act primarily as *neuromodulators*, which limit or prolong the activity of specific neurotransmitters.

        3.   Endorphins operate when the person or animal is stressed.

        4.   They may also be involved with the pleasure of affection and cuddling in children.

    C.   Hormones: Long-Distance Messengers

        1.   **Hormones** are chemical substances, secreted by organs called glands, that affect the functioning of other organs.

2. **Endocrine glands** are internal organs that produce hormones and release them into the bloodstream.
3. Neurotransmitters and hormones are not always chemically distinct. Some specific hormones include:
   a. **adrenal hormones**, which are produced by the adrenal glands and that are involved in emotion and stress; they include cortisol, epinephrine and norepinephrine.
   b. **melatonin**, a hormone secreted by the pineal gland, that is involved in the regulation of daily **biological rhythms**, periodic, more or less regular fluctuations in a biological system which may or may not have psychological implications.
      i. There are many biological rhythms of varying lengths, including **circadian rhythm** A biological rhythm with a period (from peak to peak or trough to trough) of about 24 hours; from the Latin *circa*, "about," and *dies*, "a day."
      ii. The **suprachiasmatic nucleus (SCN)** is an area of the brain containing a biological clock that governs circadian rhythms.
   c. **sex hormones** regulate the development and functioning of reproductive and sex organs and stimulate the development of sexual characteristics.
      i. *Androgens* (including *testosterone*) are masculinizing hormones produced mainly in the testes but also in the ovaries and adrenal glands. They activate physical changes in males at puberty and influence sexual arousal in both sexes.
      ii. *Estrogens* are feminizing hormones that bring on physical changes in females at puberty and influence the course of the menstrual cycle.
      iii. *Progesterone* contributes to the growth and maintenance of the uterine lining, among other functions.
      iv. Estrogens and progesterone are both produced primarily in the ovaries but also in the testes and adrenal glands.

IV. The Brain

    A. Mapping the Brain
      1. Several methods for studying the brain have been developed, including:
        a. studying patients who have had a part of the brain damaged or removed.
        b. *lesioning* -- damaging or removing sections of the brain in animals.

      c.   probing the brain with *electrodes* that detect the electrical activities of neurons. Electrical activity is translated into visual patterns called "brain waves" by a device called an **electroencephalogram (EEG)**.

      d.   the use of *needle electrodes* to stimulate specific areas of the brain or record its electrical activity. *Microelectrodes* can be inserted into single cells.

      e.   **PET scan (positron-emission-tomography)** - requires injection of a glucoselike radioactive substance which accumulates in highly active brain areas. Computer-processed radioactive signals are translated into colors on a monitor.

      f.   **Magnetic resonance imaging (MRI)** – a method that uses magnetic fields and special radio receivers.

B.   A Tour Through the Brain

    1.   **localization of function** is the specialization of particular brain areas for particular functions. However, major parts of the brain also perform overlapping tasks.

    2.   The **brain stem** is the part of the brain at the top of the spinal cord. It consists of:

      a.   the **medulla**, which controls automatic functions that such as breathing and heart rate.

      b.   the **pons**, which is involved in sleeping, waking, dreaming, and other functions.

    3.   The **reticular activating system (RAS)** is a dense network of neurons found in the core of the brain stem; it arouses the cortex and screens incoming information.

    4.   The **cerebellum** is a brain structure that regulates movement and balance, and that is involved in the learning of certain kinds of simple responses.

    5.   The **thalamus** relays sensory information to the cortex, except for the sense of smell, which is relayed by the *olfactory bulb*.

    6.   The **hypothalamus** is involved in emotions and drives vital to survival, such as fear, hunger, thirst, and reproduction. It also regulates the autonomic nervous system.

    7.   The **pituitary gland** is a small endocrine gland at the base of the brain, which releases many hormones and regulates other endocrine glands.

    8.   The **limbic system** is a group of structures involved in emotional reactions and motivated behavior. It includes:

      a.   the **amygdala**, which is involved in the arousal and regulation of emotion, particularly fear, and the initial emotional response to sensory information.

      b.   the **hippocampus**, which is involved in the storage of new information in memory.

    9.   The Cerebrum and Cerebral Cortex. The **cerebrum** is the largest brain structure, consisting of the upper part of the brain; it is in

charge of most sensory, motor, and cognitive processes. (From the Latin for "brain."). It is divided into two separate halves, or **cerebral hemispheres**, which are connected by a bundle of nerve fibers called the **corpus callosum**.

    a.   Generally, the right hemisphere controls the left side of the body and the left hemisphere controls the right side of the body.

    b.   Each hemisphere is somewhat specialized, a phenomenon known as **lateralization**.

    c.   The **cerebral cortex** is a collection of several thin layers of cells covering the cerebrum. It contains three-fourths of the brain's cells. It is divided into:

        i.   **occipital lobes** at the lower back part of the brain's cerebral cortex. They contain areas that receive visual information.

        ii.   **parietal lobes** at the top of the brain, contain areas that receive information on pressure, pain, touch, and temperature..

        iii.   **temporal lobes** at the sides of the brain's cerebral cortex, just above the ears, contain areas involved in hearing, memory, perception, emotion, and (in the left lobe, typically) speech production.

        iv.   **frontal lobes** at the front of the brain contain areas involved in short-term memory, higher-order thinking, initiative, social judgment, and (in the left lobe, typically) speech production.

        v.   *association cortex* areas are involved in higher mental processes, such as social judgment, rational decision making, goal setting, and carrying out plans.

V.   The Brain's Two Hemispheres

    A.   Split Brains: A House Divided

        1.   Right and left hemisphere functions have been discovered partly through the study of patients, who have had ***split-brain*** surgery, the cutting of the corpus collosum in order to control severe epilepsy.

    B.   A Question of Dominance

        1.   Nearly all right handed people and most left-handed people process language mainly in the left hemisphere.

        2.   The left side of the brain is more active during logical, symbolic, and sequential tasks and is usually referred to as *dominant*.

        3.   The right side of the brain is involved in spatial-visual abilities and facial recognition.

VI.   The Biology of Memory

    A.   Changes in Neurons and Synapses
        1.   Forming a short-term memory involves a temporary alteration in the neuron's ability to release neurotransmitters.
        2.   Long-term memory involves lasting structural changes in the brain, including **long-term potentiation**, a long-lasting increase in the strength of synaptic responsiveness, which seems to involve
            i.   increased release of glutamate from transmitting neurons.
            ii.   increased glutamate receptor sensitivity in receiving neurons.
            iii.   dendrite growth and increase of certain synapses.
            iv.   decrease in the responsiveness of some neurons.
    B.   Locating Memories
        1.   Different information may be stored in different areas of the brain.
            a.   Forming of *declarative memories* involves the hippocampus and adjacent brain areas.
            b.   Forming of *procedural memories* depends in part on the cerebellum.
            c.   The brain circuits involved in the formation of long-term memories are not the same ones involved in the storage of those memories.
    C.   Hormones and Memory
        1.   The hormone epinephrine facilitates storage of information, but only at low or moderate levels.
        2.   Glucose may enhance memory by altering the effects of certain neurotransmitters.

VII.   The Biology of Sleep and Dreams

    A.   Sleep puts an organism at risk, yet it is a necessity.
    B.   Why We Sleep
        1.   A likely function of sleep is to restore the body.
        2.   Sleep is also important for mental functioning. Sleep deprivation causes a number of adverse psychological effects.
    C.   The Realms of Sleep. Sleep occurs in regular cycles of **rapid eye movement REM sleep**, which is characterized by quick eye movements, loss of muscle tone, and dreaming, and *non-REM (NREM)* sleep. Each stage is characterized by certain brain wave patterns.
        1.   First sleep -- high *alpha-wave* (high amplitude, low frequency) activity.
        2.   *Stage 1* -- small, irregular waves; low voltage and mixed frequencies.
        3.   *Stage 2* -- short bursts of rapid, high-peaking waves called *sleep spindles*.
        4.   *Stage 3* -- slow, high-peaked *delta* waves; deeper sleep.

     5.   *Stage 4* -- deep sleep.

     6.   Following this 30-45 minute sequence, stages occur in reverse order.

     7.   REM sleep occurs after stage 1. It is characterized by:

         a.   rapid, irregular waves.

         b.   increases in heart rate, blood pressure, respiration.

         c.   changes in sex organs.

         d.   most dreaming.

     8.   REM periods get longer and closer together as sleep goes on.

D.   The Dreaming Brain

     1.   Psychological theories emphasize unconscious wishes.

     2.   Another theory is that dreams function for memory enhancement.

     3.   The **activation-synthesis** theory holds that dreaming results from the cortical synthesis and interpretation of neural signals triggered by activity in the lower part of the brain.

VIII.   The Oldest Question

A.   The oldest question is: where is the self?

     1.   The brain is an exceedingly complex mechanism with no identifiable center for the exercise of will.

IX.   Essay One: Evaluating the Biological Perspective

A.   In the past few decades, there has been a huge expansion of the understanding of the nervous system and brain chemistry.

B.   Contributions of this perspective

     1.   The biological perspective has contributed:

         a.   A rejection of extreme environmentalism, stressing humans' commonalities with other animals whose behavior is influenced by genes and neurons.

         b.   An appreciation for the role of physical health in psychological functioning.

         c.   A more accurate our understanding of some mental and emotional disorders.

X.   Misuses and Limitations of This Perspective

A.   *Biological Reductionism*, the tendency to explain complex personal and social problems solely in terms of a few physiological mechanisms.

B.   Premature Conclusions, an overstatement of biological findings on the basis of a few studies.

C.   Unwarranted Inferences about Cause and Effect. Biology influences behavior, but experience also alters biology.

D.   Biological Politics. People can use biological research findings to foster racism, and draw attention away from economic and environmental causes of human suffering.

Chapter Summary

The 1._____ system receives and processes information, produces responses to stimuli, and coordinates the workings of different cells in the body.

The 2._____ nervous system receives, processes, interprets, and stores information, and also sends out messages to various body systems. It is made up of two components, the 3._____ and the 4._____, which handles some reflexes and carries messages to and from the brain.

The 5._____ nervous system contains all of the neural tissue outside of the brain and spinal cord. 6._____ nerves carry messages from the receptors of the skin, muscles, and sense organs to the 7._____, which relays the messages to the brain. 8._____ nerves carry messages from the central nervous system to muscles, glands, and internal organs. They enable us to move our bodies and cause glands to secrete 9._____._____

The peripheral nervous system is divided into two parts. The 10._____ nervous system consists of nerves that are connected to sensory receptors and to skeletal muscles, while the 11._____ nervous system regulates the functioning of blood vessels, glands, and internal organs. It is possible to gain some voluntary control over this system through a process called 12._____.

The autonomic nervous system is further divided into the 13._____ nervous system, which is associated with bodily activation, and the 14._____ nervous system, which is associated with conserving energy.

The basic units of the nervous system are nerve cells, or 15._____, which transmit signals to, from, and within the nervous system. They are held in place, nourished, and insulated by 16._____ cells. Within each neuron, 17._____ receive messages and transmit them to the 18._____, which contains the biochemical machinery for keeping the neuron alive and also determines whether the neuron will "fire." The 19._____ transmits messages to other neurons or to muscle or gland cells. These structures typically divide at the end into branches called 20._____.

Many axons are insulated by a layer of fatty material called the 21._____. This structure prevents signals in adjacent cells from interfering with each other and also speeds up the conduction of neural impulses.

Bundles of neural fibers are known as 22._____, most of which enter or leave the spinal cord. Twelve pairs of nerves, called 23._____ nerves, connect directly to the 24._____.

Neurons are separated by a small space called the 25._____, where the
26._____ of one neuron is in close proximity to a dendrite or cell body of another.
The site of neural transmission, which includes all of these structures, is known as the
27._____. New learning results in the establishment of new neural connections.

When a neural impulse, or 28._____, travels down a transmitting neuron, synaptic
29._____, tiny sacs at the end of the axon, open and release a chemical substance
called a 30._____, which binds briefly with 31._____ sites on other neurons. This
produces a change in the electrical charge of the neuron in one of two directions,
32._____ (positive), or 33._____ (negative). Neural firing is an all-or-none event;
neurons fire at the same "strength" every time.

Well-known neurotransmitters include 34._____, which is involved in sleep and
appetite, among other functions, 35._____, a substance involved in voluntary
movement, learning, memory and emotions, 36._____, which regulates muscle action,
cognition, memory, and emotions, 37._____ involved in bodily arousal, and
38._____ and 39._____, major excitatory and inhibitory neurotransmitters,
respectively.

There can be harmful effects from excesses or deficits of neurotransmitters. For
instance, acetylcholine deficits are implicated in 40._____, a common brain disorder
in the elderly. 41._____ is caused by the degeneration of the brain cells that produce
dopamine.

Endogenous opiod peptides, better know as 42._____, are involved in pain reduction
and the experience of pleasure. Their primary action is as 43._____ which limit or
prolong the activity of specific neurotransmitters.

44._____ are chemical substances produced by the body that affect certain bodily
organs. They originate primarily in 45._____ glands. Some specific hormones
include 46._____, which are involved in emotion and responses to stress 47._____,
which appears to regulate certain biological rhythms, such as the sleep-wake cycle,
and 48._____ hormones, which regulate the development and functioning of
reproductive organs.

There are various methods for studying the brain. One approach is to study patients
who have had a part of the brain damaged or removed because of disease or injury. In
laboratories, scientists sometimes use a procedure called the 49._____ method, in
which parts of animal brains are damaged or removed. The brain can also be probed
by using devices called 50._____, which detect the electrical activity of neurons in
particular regions of the brain. This activity is translated into electrical patterns known
as brain 51._____ by a device called an 52._____. Some of the newest
technologies for mapping the brain include the 53._____, which involves radioactively
generated, computer-processed pictures of changes in brain biochemical activity, and
the 54._____, which produces images through the use of radio waves.

An examination of brain anatomy and functioning reveals that reflexive and automatic behaviors are usually controlled by the 55._____ areas of the brain, while more complex behaviors usually involve the 56._____ areas. The most primitive area of the brain is the brain 57._____. Its two main structures are the 58._____, which is involved in functions like breathing and heart rate, and the 59._____, which is involved in sleeping, waking, and dreaming. The 60._____ system is a dense network of neurons that extends upward from the brain stem, and is involved in screening incoming information for the higher centers of the brain.

The 61._____ is a structure at the back part of the brain that regulates movement and balance. The 62._____ is the sensory relay system at the center of the brain. It receives messages from all of the senses except for 63._____, which is processed by the 64._____ bulb. The 65._____ is involved in regulating drives such as hunger and thirst. It sends chemicals to the 66._____, which releases many hormones and regulates other glands.

The 67._____ system is heavily involved in emotional responses. Among the structures of this system are the 68._____, which evaluates sensory information for its emotional importance, and a structure called the 69._____, which is involved in the storage of new information in memory.

Above the limbic system is the 70._____, where the higher forms of thinking take place. This structure is divided into two separate halves called 71._____, which are connected by a large band of fibers called the 72._____. The brain is described as being 73._____, which means that the right side of the brain controls the left side of the body, and vice versa. The left side of the brain is usually involved in the processing of language and in logical and sequential tasks, while the right side processes visual and spatial information.

The cerebrum is covered by several thin layers of cells known collectively as the 74._____, which is divided into four distinct 75._____. Vision is processed in the 76._____. In the 77._____ lobes, information about pain, touch, and temperature is processed. The 78._____ side of this area is typically involved in speech production. The 79._____ lobes are involved in memory, perception, emotion, and language. Finally, the 80._____ lobes are responsible for planning and creative thinking. 81._____ cortex areas are involved in higher mental processes.

The study of patients who have undergone 82._____ has helped scientists understand the functions of the brain's two hemispheres. This procedure involves the cutting of the 83._____. The 84._____ side of the brain is more active during logical and sequential tasks and is usually referred to as the 85._____ side. The other side of the brain is more involved in facial recognition and 86._____ tasks.

The formation of 87._____ memory appears to involve lasting structural changes in the brain, including the growth of dendrites and increase in 88._____ connections, which also become more excitable as a function of learning. Specific memory functions are somewhat localized in the brain. For example, the cerebellum is involved in

89. _____ memory, while the hippocampus and amygdala are involved in processing
90. _____ memories. Hormones also appear to be involved in memory. Optimal
levels of the hormone 91. _____ enhance learning.

Neuroscientists are also interested in the biology of sleep. While it was previously
thought that bodily restoration is the function of sleep, it appears that sleep performs a
more important role in brain function. The ability to study the physiology of people
while they sleep has revealed that there are different stages of sleep, each having its
own characteristic pattern. Periods of 92. _____ sleep alternate with periods of fewer
eye movements.

Early sleep is characterized by 93. _____ waves, which are associated with relaxation.
In stage 1, brain waves become small and irregular. In stage 2, the brain emits short
bursts of rapid, high-peaking waves called sleep 94. _____.

95. _____ waves characterize stage 3, and the deepest sleep occurs in stage 4. The
sleeper goes through all of these stages and then recycles backward to stage 1, then to
REM sleep, where most 96. _____ occurs. REM periods get longer and closer
together as sleep goes on.

Most theories of dreaming have been psychological, but some newer theories have
emphasized physiology. The 97. _____ theory is that dreams are the result of
spontaneously firing neurons whose messages are interpreted by the cerebral cortex
as sensory stimuli.

The biological perspective emphasizes the similarities between humans and other
animals. However, critics of the biological perspective have spoken of the danger of
biological 98. _____, the tendency to explain complex issues in terms of simple
physiological mechanisms. Students need to realize that experience and biology
interact, and that there is a tendency to draw unwarranted conclusions about cause
and effect from biopsychological findings. There is also a fear that research will be
used to foster racism and draw attention away from the economic and environmental
causes of human suffering.

Multiple Choice Self-Test

1.   The central nervous system is made up of:
a.   the brain and spinal cord.
b.   the brain, spinal cord, and sensory nerves.
c.   all neural tissue.
d.   the brain stem, cerebellum, and cerebrum.

2.   The neurons that pick up the sensation that your feet are cold are part of the:
a.   central nervous system.
b.   peripheral nervous system.
c.   motor nervous system.
d.   autonomic nervous system.

3.   Consuelo is trying to learn how to control her anxiety. She is using a simple
       device that attaches to her fingers and emits a tone. The tone lowers in pitch
       when one of the physiological markers of anxiety decreases. Consuelo is using
       a process called:
a.   parasympathetic arousal.
b.   psychotherapy.
c.   physiofeedback.
d.   biofeedback.

4.   Al was alarmed when his friend yelled at him unexpectedly, but he soon relaxed
       again when he realized that the friend was kidding. What system is responsible
       for Al's returning to a relaxed state?
a.   sympathetic nervous system
b.   parasympathetic nervous system
c.   sensory nervous system
d.   somatic nervous system

5.   The structures that nourish, insulate, and "clean up" neurons are known as:
a.   synapses.
b.   vesicles.
c.   glial cells.
d.   axons.

6.   What part of the neuron determines whether or not it will "fire"?
a.   axon
b.   dendrite
c.   cell body
d.   neurotransmitter

7.   In comparing a radio to a neuron, what part of the radio would be the axon?
a.   the part that receives the radio signal from the air
b.   the dial that tunes the radio
c.   the volume control
d.   the speaker

8.   Neuron A conducts action potentials three times faster than neuron B. What is
       the most likely explanation for this difference?
a.   Neuron A is myelinated; neuron B is not.
b.   Neuron B is myelinated; neuron A is not.
c.   Neuron A belongs to an infant; neuron B belongs to an adult.
d.   Neuron A has received more excitatory inputs than neuron B.

9. Messages travel between neurons:
a. electrically.
b. chemically.
c. mechanically.
d. in an unknown way.

10. A neurotransmitter:
a. will affect any neuron.
b. will only affect certain neurons.
c. is only involved in sending messages within a single neuron.
d. is inhibited by myelin.

11. Compared with a newborn infant, a one-year-old should have:
a. longer axons.
b. faster neurons.
c. more neurons.
d. more synaptic connections.

12. As one continues to sleep, REM periods:
a. get shorter.
b. get longer.
c. disappear.
d. become more sporadic.

13. If a person is injured, he or she will experience an increase in:
a. all hormone levels.
b. all neurotransmitter levels.
c. endorphin levels.
d. dopamine levels.

14. Epinephrine and norepinephrine activate the:
a. vesicles.
b. melatonin.
c. sympathetic nervous system.
d. parasympathetic nervous system.

15. One must place electrodes on the head in order to read:
a. brain waves.
b. a PET scan.
c. an MRI.
d. a lesion.

16. One must inject a person with a harmless radioactive element in order to read:
a. a PET scan.
b. a CAT scan.
c. an MRI.
d. an EEG.

17. Bob touches a hot stove and quickly pulls his hand back. What part of the nervous system causes this reaction?
a. the spinal cord
b. the cerebellum
c. the cerebral cortex
d. the brain stem

18. If the medulla is destroyed, the person will:
a. lose control of fine motor behavior.
b. not be able to dream.
c. have language problems.
d. die.

19. As a result of a brain injury, a person loses control of balance and coordination. Which part of the brain was injured?
a. the limbic system
b. the cerebrum
c. the reticular activating system
d. the cerebellum

20. Jackie hears her mother's voice. This information is relayed to her auditory cortex by her:
a. cerebellum.
b. thalamus.
c. hypothalamus.
d. amygdala.

21. The statement "high hormone levels cause sexual behavior to occur" is an example of:
a. a conclusion based on recently acquired biological evidence.
b. a theoretical mistake; hormone levels are unrelated to sexual behavior.
c. a premature conclusion; not enough study has been done to link hormone levels with sexual behavior.
d. biological reductionism; other causes for sexual behavior exist.

22. Choosing which answer to write down in a multiple choice test is a job for the:
a. cerebral cortex.
b. cerebellum.
c. occipital lobes.
d. hippocampus.

23. Lateralization of brain function was discovered mainly through the study of:
a. Parkinson's disease patients.
b. severe epileptics.
c. "normal" brains.
d. developmentally delayed children.

24. Nikki sprains her ankle slightly in a basketball game but is able to finish the game anyway. What neurotransmitter helps her do so?
a. dopamine
b. endorphins
c. glutamate
d. acetylcholine

25. Which of the following skills is most likely to involve the left side of your brain?
a. reading a map
b. recognizing a friend's face
c. adding two numbers
d. catching a ball

26. Learning something new increases the number of:
a. axons.
b. neurons.
c. synaptic connections.
d. brain stem activations.

27. You are most likely to remember what you study if your norepinephrine levels during studying are:
a. high.
b. low.
c. moderate.
d. absent.

28. The primary function of sleep is probably to:
a. rest the muscles.
b. strengthen the immune system.
c. restore glucose levels in the glands.
d. keep the brain functioning.

29. Most dreaming takes place in:
a. REM sleep.
b. NREM sleep.
c. stage 4 sleep.
d. stage 3 sleep.

30. Immediately after stage 4 sleep, a normal sleeper:
a. awakes.
b. returns to stage 3.
c. begins to dream.
d. enters stage 5.

True-False Self-Test

T   F   1.   The nervous system contains billions of neurotransmitters.

T   F   2.   The brain and spinal cord make up the central nervous system.

T   F   3.   The autonomic nervous system regulates the heart.

T   F   4.   Neurons are held in place by glial cells.

T   F   5.   In general, neural messages are received by axons.

T   F   6.   Myelinated neurons conduct messages faster than unmyelinated ones.

T   F   7.   Nerves are mainly bundles of dendrites.

T   F   8.   Neural impulses travel electrically within the neuron.

T   F   9.   Neural impulses travel electrically across synapses.

T   F   10.   Neurotransmitters are stored in vesicles.

T   F   11.   Neurotransmitters always influence other neurons to fire.

T   F   12.   Hormones are produced by endocrine glands.

T   F   13.   Epinephrine slows down the heart rate.

T   F   14.   The thalamus regulates sleeping and waking.

T   F   15.   Testosterone contributes to sexual motivation in both sexes.

T   F   16.   The PET scan measures brain waves.

T   F   17.   MRIs can map brain activity over time.

T   F   18.   Most reflexes are regulated by the spinal cord.

T   F   19.   The destruction of the frontal lobes results in death.

T   F   20.   The limbic system regulates emotional functioning.

T   F   21.   The left side of the brain is involved mainly in visual-spatial tasks.

T	F	22.	Endorphins resemble opiates in their chemical structure.
T	F	23.	New long-term memory results in structural brain changes.
T	F	24.	The amygdala is part of the limbic system.
T	F	25.	The brain stem is the most primitive part of the brain.
T	F	26.	A person learns best when norepinephrine levels are high.
T	F	27.	Most dreaming occurs in REM sleep.
T	F	28.	Most psychologists agree with the activation-synthesis theory of dreaming.
T	F	29.	Dopamine cannot cross the blood-brain barrier.
T	F	30.	Experience sometimes alters biology.

Key Terms

central nervous system (CNS) The portion of the nervous system consisting of the brain and spinal cord.

spinal cord A collection of neurons and supportive tissue running from the base of the brain down the center of the back, protected by a column of bones (the spinal column).

peripheral nervous system (PNS) All portions of the nervous system outside the brain and spinal cord; it includes sensory and motor nerves.

somatic nervous system The subdivision of the peripheral nervous system that connects to sensory receptors and to skeletal muscles; sometimes called the *skeletal nervous system*.

autonomic nervous system The subdivision of the peripheral nervous system that regulates the internal organs and glands.

biofeedback A method for learning to control bodily functions, including ones usually thought to be involuntary, by attending to feedback from an instrument that monitors the function and that signals changes in it.

sympathetic nervous system The subdivision of the autonomic nervous system that mobilizes bodily resources and increases the output of energy during emotion and stress.

parasympathetic nervous system The subdivision of the autonomic nervous system that operates during relaxed states and that conserves energy.

neuron A cell that conducts electrochemical signals; the basic unit of the nervous system; also called a *nerve cell*.

glial cells Nervous-system cells that aid the neurons by providing them with nutrients, insulating them, and removing cellular debris when they die.

dendrites A neuron's branches that receive information from other neurons and transmit it toward the cell body.

cell body The part of the neuron that keeps it alive and determines whether it will fire.

axon A neuron's extending fiber that conducts impulses away from the cell body and transmits them to other neurons.

myelin sheath A fatty insulation that may surround the axon of a neuron.

nerve A bundle of nerve fibers (axons and sometimes dendrites) in the peripheral nervous system.

synapse The site where a nerve impulse is transmitted from one nerve cell to another; it includes the axon terminal, the synaptic cleft, and receptor sites in the membrane of the receiving cell.

neurotransmitter A chemical substance that is released by a transmitting neuron at the synapse and that alters the activity of a receiving neuron.

endorphins [en-DOR-fins] Chemical substances in the nervous system that are similar in structure and action to opiates; they are involved in pain reduction, pleasure, and memory, and are known technically as *endogenous opioid peptides*.

hormones Chemical substances, secreted by organs called *glands*, that affect the functioning of other organs.

endocrine glands Internal organs that produce hormones and release them into the bloodstream.

adrenal hormones Hormones that are produced by the adrenal glands and that are involved in emotion and stress; they include cortisol, epinephrine and norepinephrine.

melatonin A hormone, secreted by the pineal gland, that is involved in the regulation of daily biological rhythms.

biological rhythm A periodic, more or less regular fluctuation in a biological system; may or may not have psychological implications.

circadian [sur-CAY-dee-un] rhythm A biological rhythm with a period (from peak to peak or trough to trough) of about 24 hours; from the Latin *circa*, "about," and *dies*, "a day."

suprachiasmatic [soo-pruh-KIE-az-MAT-ick] nucleus (SCN) An area of the brain containing a biological clock that governs circadian rhythms.

sex hormones Hormones that regulate the development and functioning of reproductive organs and that stimulate the development of male and female sexual characteristics; they include androgens, estrogens, and progesterone.

electroencephalogram (EEG) A recording of neural activity detected by electrodes.

PET scan (positron-emission tomography) A method for analyzing biochemical activity in the brain, using injections of a glucoselike substance containing a radioactive element.

magnetic resonance imaging (MRI) A method for studying body and brain tissue, using magnetic fields and special radio receivers.

localization of function Specialization of particular brain areas for particular functions.

brain stem The part of the brain at the top of the spinal cord, consisting of the medulla and the pons.

medulla [muh-DUL-uh] A structure in the brain stem responsible for certain automatic functions, such as breathing and heart rate.

pons A structure in the brain stem involved in, among other things, sleeping, waking, and dreaming.

reticular activating system (RAS) A dense network of neurons found in the core of the brain stem; it arouses the cortex and screens incoming information.

cerebellum A brain structure that regulates movement and balance, and that is involved in the learning of certain kinds of simple responses.

thalamus The brain structure that relays sensory messages to the cerebral cortex.

hypothalamus A brain structure involved in emotions and drives vital to survival, such as fear, hunger, thirst, and reproduction; it regulates the autonomic nervous system.

pituitary gland A small endocrine gland at the base of the brain, which releases many hormones and regulates other endocrine glands.

limbic system A group of brain areas involved in emotional reactions and motivated behavior.

amygdala [uh-MIG-dul-uh] A brain structure involved in the arousal and regulation of emotion, particularly fear, and the initial emotional response to sensory information.

hippocampus A brain structure thought to be involved in the storage of new information in memory.

cerebrum [suh-REE-brum] The largest brain structure, consisting of the upper part of the brain; it is in charge of most sensory, motor, and cognitive processes. (From the Latin for "brain.")

cerebral hemispheres The two halves of the cerebrum.

corpus callosum [CORE-puhss cah-LOW-suhm] The bundle of nerve fibers connecting the two cerebral hemispheres.

lateralization Specialization of the two cerebral hemispheres for particular operations.

cerebral cortex A collection of several thin layers of cells covering the cerebrum; it is largely responsible for higher mental functions. ("Cortex" is Latin for "bark" or "rind.")

occipital [ahk-SIP-uh-tuhl] lobes Lobes at the lower back part of the brain's cerebral cortex; they contain areas that receive visual information.

parietal [puh-RYE-uh-tuhl] lobes Lobes at the top of the brain's cerebral cortex; they contain areas that receive information on pressure, pain, touch, and temperature.

temporal lobes Lobes at the sides of the brain's cerebral cortex, just above the ears; they contain areas involved in hearing, memory, perception, emotion, and (in the left lobe, typically) speech production.

frontal lobes Lobes at the front of the brain's cerebral cortex; they contain areas involved in short-term memory, higher-order thinking, initiative, social judgment, and (in the left lobe, typically) speech production.

long-term potentiation A long-lasting increase in the strength of synaptic responsiveness, thought to be a biological mechanism of long-term memory.

rapid eye movement (REM) sleep Sleep periods characterized by quick eye movement, loss of muscle tone, and dreaming.

activation-synthesis theory The theory that dreaming results from the cortical synthesis and interpretation of neural signals triggered by activity in the lower part of the brain.

Suggested Research Projects

1. Test the speed of neural impulses by having several people stand in a line and hold hands. Tell them to close their eyes and to squeeze the left hand of the person next to them when they feel their right hand being squeezed. Using a stopwatch, record the time it takes to get from one end of the line to the other. Then ask the participants to squeeze the next person's shoulder instead of his or her hand. Does the time differ? What neural explanation can you give for this difference?

2. A popular game will teach you something about reaction to visual stimuli. Have someone volunteer to try to catch a dollar bill. The person should spread his or her fingers about an inch apart on either side of the center of a dollar that you are holding. Tell the person that he or she can keep the money if they catch it (you should have no problem getting volunteers). The person will only catch the bill if he or she guesses the exact time you are going to release it. What does this demonstration tell you about the relationship between visual information processing and the grasping response?

Suggested Readings

Damasio, A. R. (1994). *Descartes= error: Emotion, reason, and the human brain*. New York: Avon. An examination of the neural interconnections between cognition and emotion.

Hobson, J. A. (2001). *Dreaming as delirium: How the brain goes out of its mind*. Boston: MIT press. The author lays out the leading biological theory of dreams.

Sacks, O. (1985). *The man who mistook his wife for a hat and other clinical tales*. New York: Harper & Row. A collection of case studies of people with neural abnormalities, written in a highly engaging fashion.

CHAPTER 5

Behavioral Learning

Learning Objectives

After reading and studying this chapter, you should be able to:

1.   Explain the basic theoretical stance of behaviorism.

2.   Describe the components of classical conditioning.

3.   Describe the components of operant conditioning.

4.   Compare and contrast classical conditioning with operant conditioning.

5.   Apply classical and operant conditioning models to learning situations.

6.   Describe the applications of operant conditioning to behavior modification.

7.   Discuss the arguments for and against the use of punishment and external reward to control behavior.

8.   Summarize the behavioral views of superstition, insight, and separation anxiety.

Chapter Outline

I.   Introduction

    A.   Learning is any relatively permanent change in behavior that occurs because of experience.

    B.   The **behaviorist** view is that learning, especially conditioning, is the most important influence on behavior.

    C.   Basic learning, called **conditioning**, involves associations between environmental stimuli and responses.

II. Classical Conditioning

    A.   New Reflexes from Old. Pavlov's original experiment on salivation in dogs demonstrates how classical conditioning works.

        1.   Food is an **unconditioned stimulus (US)** because animals react naturally to food by salivating before any learning has taken place.

        2.   The original salivary reflex is the **unconditioned response (UR)**.

        3.   Learning occurs when some **neutral** or **conditioned stimulus (CS)** is regularly paired with the unconditioned stimulus.

        4.   When the original stimulus is removed, the dog will salivate in response to the neutral stimulus presented alone -- a **conditioned response (CR)**.

B.   Classical conditioning is the process by which a previously neutral stimulus acquires the capacity to elicit a response through association with a stimulus that already elicits a similar response. It is also called *Pavlovian* or *respondent conditioning*.

C.   Principles of Classical Conditioning include the following.

    1.   **Extinction** is weakening and eventual disappearance of a learned response. In classical conditioning, it occurs when the CS is repeatedly presented without the US.

    2.   After a time period following extinction, the response can reappear in **spontaneous recovery**.

    3.   **Higher-order conditioning** takes place when a neutral stimulus becomes a conditioned stimulus through association with an already established conditioned stimulus.

    4.   **stimulus generalization** occurs when a stimulus that resembles the CS elicits the CR.

    5.   If a stimulus is different enough from the original CS, different responses will occur in **stimulus discrimination** when a stimulus similar to the CS fails to evoke the CR.

D.   What is Actually Learned in Classical Conditioning?

    1.   The CS must precede the US in order for learning to occur.

    2.   Many psychologists now contend that classical conditioning is not merely an association between two stimuli, but information conveyed by one stimulus about another. The CS must reliably predict the US in order for learning to occur.

III.   Classical Conditioning in Real Life

A.   Learning to Like. The pairing of products with music, attractive people, etc. in marketing is a common application of classical conditioning.

B.   Learning to Fear. A phobia is an acquired, irrational fear of a specific object or situation. Watson and Rayner's famous case of Little Albert involved pairing a loud noise (US) with a white rat (CS).

    1.   **Counterconditioning**, a treatment for phobia, involves the process of pairing a CS with a stimulus that elicits a response that is incompatible with an unwanted CR.

C.   Accounting for Taste. Taste aversion can be learned when various foods or odors are paired with nausea-inducing stimuli.

    1.   Unlike most classical conditioning, taste aversion occurs after a long delay in the presentation of the CS because aversion to bad food has survival value and is probably biologically primed.

D.   Reacting to Medical Treatments. Nausea resulting from chemotherapy may generalize to many aspects, or even mental images, of the medical situation. Placebos may act as conditioning stimuli for real drugs and provide reduced pain and anxiety

IV. Operant Conditioning

   A. **Operant conditioning** (also called *instrumental conditioning*) is the process by which a response becomes more likely to occur or less so, depending on its consequences. In contrast to classical conditioning, which involves reflexive responses, operant conditioning involves complex responses.
      1. In classical conditioning, the response is reflexive. In operant conditioning, the animal or person produces the response.
      2. The Birth of Radical Behaviorism. Thorndike's *law of effect* states that:
         a. Behaviors followed by pleasant consequences tend to recur.
         b. Behaviors followed by unpleasant consequences tend not to recur.
   B. The Consequences of Behavior. A response ("operant") can lead to one of three consequences:
      1. A neutral consequence does not alter the response.
      2. **Reinforcement** is the process by which a stimulus or event strengthens or increases the probability of the response that it follows.
      3. **Punishment** is the process by which a stimulus or event weakens or decreases the probability of the response that it follows.
   C. Primary and Secondary Reinforcers and Punishers.
      1. **Primary reinforcers**, such as food, satisfy a biological need.
      2. **Primary punishers**, such as extreme heat, are stimuli that are inherently punishing.
      3. **Secondary reinforcers** and **secondary punishers** acquire their ability to influence behavior through associations with primary reinforcers and punishers.
   D. Positive and Negative Reinforcers and Punishers.
      1. **Positive reinforcement** is a reinforcement procedure in which a response is followed by the presentation of, or increase in intensity of, a reinforcing stimulus; as a result, the response becomes stronger or more likely to occur.
      2. **Negative reinforcement** is reinforcement procedure in which a response is followed by the removal, delay, or decrease in intensity of an unpleasant stimulus; as a result, the response becomes stronger or more likely to occur.
      3. **Positive punishment** involves presenting something unpleasant following an undesired response, making the response less likely.
      4. **Negative punishment** involves removing something pleasant following an undesired response, making the response less likely.
   E. Principles of Operant Conditioning
      1. **Extinction** is the weakening and eventual disappearance of a learned response. In operant conditioning, it occurs when a response is no longer followed by a reinforcer. At first, there is a

spurt of responding, followed by a decrease in responding. After a period of time, the response may reappear, a phenomenon known as *spontaneous recovery*.

2. Immediate Versus Delayed Consequences. Different effects may be seen for immediate versus delayed consequences. The sooner a reinforcer or punisher follows a response, the greater its effect.

3. Stimulus Generalization and Discrimination. **Stimulus generalization** is the tendency for a response that has been reinforced (or punished) in the presence of one stimulus to occur (or be suppressed) in the presence of other, similar stimuli.

4. **Stimulus discrimination** is the tendency of a response to occur in the presence of one stimulus but not in the presence of other, similar stimuli that differ from it on some dimension.

5. A **discriminative stimulus** signals when a particular type of response is likely to be followed by a certain consequence. The discriminative stimulus exerts **stimulus control** over the response.

6. Learning on Schedule. Reinforcers can be delivered according to different schedules.

    a. In **continuous reinforcement**, every response is rewarded.

    b. **Intermittent (partial) schedules of reinforcement** involve reinforcing only some responses.

        i. **Ratio schedules** deliver a reinforcement after a certain number of responses have occurred.

        ii. **Interval schedules** deliver a reinforcement if a response is made after the passage of a certain amount of time since the last reinforcement.

        iii. Intermittent reinforcement schedules can also be *fixed* (constant) or *variable*.

        iv. Learning curves describe the characteristic patterns of response produced by different schedules of reinforcement.

7. **Shaping** is the rewarding of **successive approximations**, behaviors that are ordered in terms of increasing similarity or closeness, to a desired response. Shaping can be used to establish complex responses.

V. Operant Conditioning in Real Life

    A. **Behavior modification**, or *applied behavioral analysis*, is the application of conditioning techniques to teach new responses or reduce or eliminate maladaptive or problematic behavior.

    B. The Pros and Cons of Punishment

        1. When Punishment Works.

            a. Punishment can eliminate self-destructive behavior if it is applied immediately following the behavior.

            b. Mild punishers are as effective as strong ones.

        c.   Punishment can deter criminals from repeating offenses; consistency is more important than severity.

    2.   When Punishment Fails.

        a.   People often administer punishment inappropriately or mindlessly.

        b.   The recipient of punishment often responds with anxiety, fear, or rage.

        c.   The effectiveness of punishment is often temporary, depending heavily on the presence of the punishing person or circumstances.

        d.   Most misbehavior is hard to punish immediately.

        e.   Punishment conveys little information about appropriate behavior.

        f.   An action intended to punish may instead be reinforcing because it brings attention.

        g.   Punishment should only be used when:

            i.   it does not involve physical abuse.

            ii.   it is accompanied by information about appropriate behavior.

            iii.   it is followed by reinforcement of desired behaviors.

C.   The Problems with Reward.

    1.   **Extrinsic reinforcers** are not inherently related to the activity being reinforced. Examples are money, prizes, and praise.

    2.   **Intrinsic reinforcers** are inherently related to the activity being reinforced, such as enjoyment of the task and the satisfaction of accomplishment.

    3.   Extrinsic reinforcement can undermine intrinsic reinforcement.

    4.   The short-term effectiveness of extrinsic reinforcers should be balanced with the long-term effectiveness of intrinsic reinforcers.

VI.   The World as the Behaviorist Views It

A.   Superstition

    1.   Superstitions can arise if a response is rewarded coincidentally.

    2.   The response may be intermittently reinforced, making it resistant to extinction.

    3.   Superstitions may persist because attention may be paid only to confirming evidence, and because they are reinforced by the agreement of others.

B.   Insight

    1.   **Insight** is a form of problem solving that that appears to involve the sudden understanding of how elements of a situation are related or can be reorganized to achieve a solution.

    2.   The behaviorist views insight as the result of mentally combining previously learned responses.

VII.   Behaviorism: Myths and Realities

   A.   The learning perspective helps to explain how behaviors can be the result
         of patterns of reinforcement.
   B.   Skinner maintained that thoughts and feelings are themselves behaviors
         that can be reinforced or punished.
   C.   Biology places limits on what an organism can learn.

Chapter Summary

1._____ is any relatively permanent change in behavior that occurs because of
experience. One basic kind of learning is called 2._____, and it is this kind of
learning, behaviorists say, that is the basis for the most important explanations about
human behavior.

Russian physiologist Ivan Pavlov discovered a kind of learning now known as
3._____ conditioning. In his original experiments, Pavlov paired a neutral stimulus
with food, which is called the 4._____ stimulus because it elicits a response (in this
case, salivation) without any learning. This response to the presentation of food is
called the 5._____ response. After repeated pairings with food, the neutral, or
6._____, stimulus was presented alone. Even though the food was no longer
present, the dog still salivated -- a 7._____ response. In order for classical
conditioning to be effective, the conditioned stimulus must 8._____ the unconditioned
stimulus.

After conditioning has taken place, the conditioned response will disappear if the
neutral stimulus is presented by itself repeatedly. This procedure is called
9._____. Curiously, the response may reappear at a later time, a phenomenon known
as 10._____.

If the CS-US connection is already learned, one can add another layer to learning by
pairing a new neutral stimulus with an established CS, a procedure known as
11._____ conditioning. Also, animals and humans may make a CR to stimuli that are
similar to an established CS. This is known as stimulus 12._____, which contrasts
with stimulus 13._____, in which neutral stimuli are different enough from the CS to
elicit different responses from the CR.

The classical conditioning model can be used to account for a variety of phenomena,
including taste aversion and phobias. It is also the reason why advertisers associate
attractive people or pleasant music with their products in marketing efforts.

The famous case of "Little Albert" is an illustration of how classical conditioning
procedures can be used to produce phobia. In this (unethical) experiment, John
Watson used a 14._____ as an unconditioned stimulus and a 15._____ as a
conditioned stimulus. The reversal of a phobia was accomplished some years later

with another subject, using the technique of 16._____. This procedure involves pairing the conditioned stimulus with another stimulus that elicits a response that is 17._____ with the fear response.

While classical conditioning always involves reflexive and instinctual responses, 18._____ conditioning involves responses that produce effects on the environment. In other words, the 19._____ of certain responses affect the likelihood of the recurrence of those responses.

There are two kinds of consequences, pleasant and unpleasant. When a pleasant stimulus is presented following a desired response, 20._____ occurs, and the likelihood of repeating the response 21._____. When an unpleasant stimulus follows an undesired response, 22._____ has taken place, and the frequency of the response 23._____. Both of these procedures are termed 24._____ because the consequence is presented after the response. However, we can also affect behavior by removing an unpleasant stimulus in order to increase a desired response, or by removing a pleasant stimulus in order to decrease an undesired response. These operations are called 25._____ and 26._____, respectively. These terms are confusing, but they can be clearer if one remembers that the words, "positive" and "negative" refer to whether the consequence is 27._____ or 28._____, and the terms "reinforcement" and "punishment" refer to whether the frequency of the response 29._____ or 30._____.

Reinforcers like food, that satisfy biological needs are called 31._____ reinforcers. 32._____ reinforcers, like money, gain their reinforcement value from being repeatedly paired with the reinforcers that satisfy biological needs. Punishers can also be categorized in this way.

When a response has been learned but stops occurring because reinforcement has been removed, 33._____ has taken place. When the reinforcement is first withdrawn, there is usually a 34._____ of responding, followed by a gradual decline in the rate of response. The sooner a reinforcer or punisher follows a response, the greater its effect.

As in classical conditioning, an animal or human may respond to stimuli that were not present during the original learning, but which resemble the original stimuli. As in classical conditioning, this phenomenon is known as stimulus 35._____. If the new stimuli are different enough from the original stimuli, then stimulus 36._____ will occur. In the learning environment, a stimulus that signals the availability of a consequence is called a 37._____ stimulus. This stimulus is said to exert 38._____ over the response.

The procedure in which each and every target response is reinforced is called 39._____ reinforcement. However, one does not have to reinforce every response in order to build or to maintain a response. In fact, partial reinforcement makes a response more resistant to 40._____. Therefore, it is important to resist reinforcing a response intermittently if you want to get rid of it.

Reinforcement can be applied according to several different 41._____, each of which produces a characteristic pattern of responding. 42._____ schedules deliver a reinforcer after a certain number of responses have occurred, and the reinforcement is contingent on the number of responses. 43._____ schedules deliver a reinforcer after the passage of some amount of time since the last reinforcer, thus the reinforcement is contingent on the timing of responses. The number of responses or the interval between responses can be either 44._____ (occurring in a predictable pattern) or 45._____. Different schedules of reinforcement produce different characteristic patterns of response, which are described by learning 46._____.

Because complex behaviors are not usually produced spontaneously, they must often be built using a procedure called 47._____. In this procedure, the person or animal is first rewarded for making 48._____ to the target behavior. For example, if you want to get a rat to press a bar for food, you might first reinforce it for coming closer to the bar, then for touching the bar, etc.

The use of operant techniques to affect behavior in real-world settings is known as 49._____. Punishment works to eliminate self destructive behavior if it is applied 50._____ following the behavior. Contrary to popular belief, mild punishers are as effective as strong ones, and thus the 51._____ of punishment is more important that its severity.

Although punishment can be a powerful technique for controlling behavior, it is not without its problems. Physical punishment can be inappropriately applied and the person being punished may have negative 52._____ reactions, which can create more problems. The effects of punishment are sometimes temporary, depending heavily on the presence of the punishing person, and much misbehavior is difficult to punish easily, since that person cannot always be present. The 53._____ given by this person can also be inadvertently reinforcing. Finally, punishment conveys little or no information about appropriate alternative behaviors. Therefore, if punishment is to be used, it should be accompanied by the opportunity for, and reinforcement of, appropriate alternative responses.

Rewarding appropriate behaviors seems like a better option than punishment. However, it is not without its own problems. Often, a person will work for 54._____ rewards, like money or praise. At other times, the person works for self-applied, or 55._____, reinforcers. Research has demonstrated that intrinsic motivation may decrease when extrinsic rewards are applied. Therefore, there is a trade-off between the short-term effectiveness of 56._____ rewards and the long-term effectiveness of 57._____ rewards.

The behaviorist view of superstitious behavior is that a coincidental 58._____ has followed the behavior at some time. Recall that a behavior does not have to be rewarded every time; superstitious behaviors are not. They may persist because they are rewarded 59._____, which makes them highly resistant to extinction. Superstition may persist because the person only pays attention to 60._____ evidence, and because the superstition is reinforced by other people.

Behaviorists are also interested in 61._____, which is a sudden realization about how to solve a problem. While this phenomenon appears to be antithetical to the behaviorist view of learning as a trial-and-error process, behaviorists argue that insight really reflects the use of previously learned responses to solve problems. It merely requires mentally combining these responses in new ways.

Multiple Choice Self-Test

1.   A cat associates food with the sound of an electric can opener. What kind of learning is this?
a.   classical conditioning
b.   operant conditioning
c.   social learning
d.   consequential learning

2.   On a trip to the dentist, Jason notices that he cringes when he hears the sound of the dentist's drill in the waiting room. In classical conditioning terms, the sound of the drill is:
a.   an unconditioned stimulus.
b.   a conditioned stimulus.
c.   an unconditioned response.
d.   a conditioned response.

3.   The sound of a dentist's drill may be associated with the pain of the drill. In classical conditioning terms, the drill is:
a.   an unconditioned stimulus.
b.   a conditioned stimulus.
c.   an unconditioned response.
d.   a conditioned response.

4.   In classical conditioning terms, cringing at the sound of a dentist's drill is:
a.   an unconditioned stimulus.
b.   a conditioned stimulus.
c.   an unconditioned response.
d.   a conditioned response.

5.   In her animal learning lab, Mary has trained a rabbit to blink at the sound of a buzzer by repeatedly pairing the buzzer with a puff of air to the rabbit's eye. If Mary wants to achieve higher-order conditioning, she will:
a.   present the buzzer alone repeatedly.
b.   present the buzzer alone intermittently.
c.   pair another neutral stimulus with the buzzer.
d.   present the buzzer alone several times, wait a day, and present the buzzer alone again.

6. In her animal learning lab, Mary has trained a rabbit to blink at the sound of a buzzer by repeatedly pairing the buzzer with a puff of air to the rabbit's eye. If she now repeatedly presents the buzzer alone, the rabbit will:
a. blink very quickly the first few times.
b. gradually stop blinking at the sound of the buzzer.
c. continue to blink at the sound of the buzzer for several hundred trials, then stop.
d. abruptly stop blinking after the first few trials.

7. On Monday, Mary got a rabbit to blink at the sound of a buzzer by pairing the buzzer with a puff of air to the rabbit's eye. On Tuesday, she got it to stop blinking at the sound of the buzzer by removing the air puff. If she waits a day and presents the buzzer alone, the rabbit will:
a. blink at first, but stop blinking in fewer trials than the previous day.
b. continue to blink for more trials than the previous day.
c. become conditioned to some other aspect of the environment.
d. do nothing.

8. Billy works on his father's farm. When it is lunchtime, his father rings a large bell in order to tell everyone that lunch is ready. Billy has noticed that he always feels happy when the bell rings, as it has been associated with taking a break from work and with eating. One night, the bell is damaged in a thunderstorm. The next day at lunchtime, Billy's father uses a cowbell instead, and Billy notices that he does not feel happy as usual. In other words, he has displayed:
a. negative reinforcement.
b. punishment.
c. stimulus generalization.
d. stimulus discrimination.

9. Hank is trying to condition his lab rat to salivate at the sound of a buzzer by pairing it with food. There is a short in the electrical wire, however, and the buzzer only works 50% of the time. The rat will:
a. not learn anything.
b. easily learn the association.
c. respond only sporadically with salivation.
d. salivate more than if the buzzer had worked all the time.

10. Hank is trying to condition his lab rat to salivate at the sound of a buzzer by pairing it with food. There is a short in the wire that controls the food delivery mechanism, however, and it only works 50% of the time. The rat will:
a. not learn anything.
b. easily learn the association.
c. respond only sporadically with salivation.
d. salivate more than if the food mechanism had worked all the time.

11.   Ethan and his ex-girlfriend, Jane, used to take long walks together in the woods every day. Their relationship turned sour in the fall, and they often argued on their walks. Eventually the relationship ended. A year later, Ethan notices that he feels sad whenever he smells rotting leaves, a smell that was frequently present on their walks during the breakup. A classical conditioning expert would say that:

a.   the smell of the leaves has acted as an unconditioned stimulus.
b.   the smell of the leaves has acted as a conditioned stimulus.
c.   Ethan has been inadvertently rewarded for feeling sad.
d.   the sad feeling is an example of spontaneous recovery.

12.   Hunter goes to a psychologist because he has an irrational fear of being left in the house alone. The psychologist teaches him a relaxation technique, and directs Hunter to imagine scenes of being alone in the house while he is very relaxed. The psychologist is using a procedure called:

a.   negative reinforcement.
b.   biofeedback.
c.   operant conditioning.
d.   counterconditioning.

13.   In the famous case of Little Albert, the white rat was the:
a.   unconditioned stimulus.
b.   punishment.
c.   discriminative stimulus.
d.   conditioned stimulus.

14.   When we engage in "trial-and-error learning," we are learning through:
a.   the consequences of our actions.
b.   conditioned fear.
c.   an association between conditioned and unconditioned stimuli.
d.   insight.

15.   Operant conditioning is to classical conditioning as:
a.   voluntary is to involuntary.
b.   free will is to determined.
c.   stimulus is to response.
d.   consequence is to association.

16.   Little Pierpont throws a temper tantrum at the grocery store and won't stop until his father buys him some candy. How has Pierpont manipulated his father's "candy buying" behavior?
a.   He has positively reinforced it.
b.   He has negatively reinforced it.
c.   He has positively punished it.
d.   He has negatively punished it.

17. Burton's father catches him drinking and takes the car away from him for a week. What procedure has his father used to try to get Burton to stop drinking?
a. negative reinforcement
b. positive punishment
c. negative punishment
d. spontaneous recovery

18. Ann's poodle, "Crackers," will stand on its hind legs if commanded because doing so earns the dog a treat. Ann trained her dog by using:
a. punishment.
b. counterconditioning.
c. reinforcement.
d. classical conditioning.

19. Mr. Sillypenny decided to make a concerted effort to encourage his son to practice playing the piano. Every time his son began to practice, Mr. Sillypenny said, "That's a good boy; you'll be in Carnegie Hall some day." However, his son seemed to practice less and less often as time went by. If nothing else has changed, then Mr. Sillypenny's comment is a:
a. positive punishment.
b. discriminative stimulus.
c. negative punishment.
d. positive reinforcement.

20. A poker chip is a:
a. primary reinforcer.
b. discriminative stimulus.
c. negative reinforcer.
d. secondary reinforcer.

21. Most students are happy when they get a good grade on a test. This is because a good grade is a:
a. primary reinforcer.
b. unconditioned stimulus.
c. secondary reinforcer.
d. discriminative stimulus.

22. A rat learns to press a bar for food. Later, an experimenter decides to do extinction trials, so that the food is no longer delivered when the rat presses the bar. When the extinction trials first begin, the rat will:
a. slow down its bar pressing.
b. speed up its bar pressing.
c. continue bar pressing at the same rate.
d. stop bar pressing.

23. Barnabus tried to start his car on a cold, snowy morning. At first, he could hear the motor click when he turned the ignition key, but after several turns of the key, the motor remained silent. Barnabus gave up trying to start his car and went into the house to call a taxi. What type of learning is illustrated here?
a. counterconditioning
b. positive reinforcement
c. positive punishment
d. extinction

24. Most students take notes in class, but do not take notes when listening to their roommates. What process accounts for this?
a. stimulus generalization
b. stimulus discrimination
c. intermittent reinforcement
d. conditioned stimulus

25. Tina has decided to punish her daughter for using sexual slang words. If Tina wants this punishment to be maximally effective, she should:
a. use physical punishment.
b. use guilt and shame as punishment.
c. put her daughter on a token economy.
d. teach her daughter the correct words and reward their use.

26. Nine-year-old Bea loves to read. She read 35 books two summers ago. This summer, her school started a summer reading program, in which children receive certificates and free pizza coupons for every 10 books they read. What is most likely to happen for Bea?
a. She will not love reading as much as she used to.
b. She will love reading more than ever.
c. She will read more books.
d. She will stop reading.

27. Beatrice is trying to train her dog to obey commands like, "speak," "sit," and "heel." She rewards the dog each time the command is correctly obeyed. In operant conditioning terms, these commands are:
a. schedules of reinforcement.
b. shaping.
c. discriminative stimuli.
d. intermittent reinforcement.

28. Geraldo is trying to toilet train his two-year-old son. He begins by praising the boy for sitting on the toilet at Geraldo's direction without fussing. Then, he stops praising the boy for this behavior, instead praising him only for sitting on the toilet without being told to do so. Finally, he withdraws this praise for merely sitting on the toilet, instead praising the boy only for using the toilet properly. What process is taking place?

a. reinforcement of successive approximations
b. stimulus discrimination
c. intermittent reinforcement
d. a variable-ratio schedule of reinforcement

29. Artemus is 10-year-old Sam's stepfather. He takes care of the boy at home during the day while Sam's mother works. Artemus is concerned about Sam's frequent cursing and wants to eliminate this behavior. However, he does not feel comfortable punishing Sam because he is not Sam's real father. Instead, he tells Sam's mother when she comes home from work if Sam has cursed that day, and she administers punishment if he has. What is Sam most likely to learn?

a. that he gets punished when he curses
b. that his stepfather has no control over any of his behavior
c. that cursing brings rewards
d. that he gets punished when his mother comes home

30. Alonzo can never predict when his mail will arrive. Sometimes the mail truck comes to his home early in the morning, while on other days the mail does not arrive until late in the evening. Alonzo therefore checks his mailbox periodically throughout the day and evening. Alonzo is being reinforced on a:

a. VI schedule.
b. VR schedule.
c. FR schedule.
d. FI schedule.

True-False Self-Test

T   F   1.   A change in behavior must be absolutely permanent in order to say that learning has taken place.

T   F   2.   A conditioned stimulus was always neutral before learning took place.

T   F   3.   A previously extinguished behavior can return even if no new learning has taken place.

T   F   4.   A stimulus that is similar to a conditioned stimulus can elicit a similar response.

T   F   5.   A neutral stimulus must reliably predict an unconditioned stimulus in order for classical conditioning to occur.

T   F   6.   People and animals can be conditioned to avoid certain foods, even though the unconditioned stimulus is presented long after the conditioned stimulus.

T   F   7.   Phobias are acquired through operant conditioning.

T   F   8.   Counterconditioning is similar to punishment.

T   F   9.   Operant conditioning involves the pairing of neutral and instinctive stimuli.

T   F   10.   Reinforcement always involves pleasant stimuli as consequences.

T   F   11.   Negative reinforcement increases the probability of a response.

T   F   12.   Punishment is usually an effective manipulator of behavior.

T   F   13.   Money is a good example of a secondary reinforcer.

T   F   14.   Extinction can be either a classical or an operant process.

T   F   15.   Shaping involves both extinction and reinforcement.

T   F   16.   Stimulus discrimination inhibits adaptive learning.

T   F   17.   Continuous schedules of reinforcement are more resistant to extinction than intermittent schedules.

T   F   18.   Ratio schedules of reinforcement are more resistant to extinction than interval schedules.

T   F   19.   In order for a phobia to affect behavior, an individual must remember the original conditioning event.

T   F   20.   A person who receives a paycheck every month is being reinforced on a FI schedule.

T   F   21.   Mild punishers, such as a spray of water in the face, are not as effective as severe punishers, such as electric shock.

T	F	22.	Animals being reinforced on FI schedules show more variability in their response rates than animals on other schedules.
T	F	23.	Shaping improves the speed of learning on complex tasks.
T	F	24.	Punishment is sometimes accompanied by unwanted emotional side effects.
T	F	25.	Punishment should always be accompanied by reinforcement of the desired behavior.
T	F	26.	In operant conditioning, the terms "positive" and "negative" refer to whether a stimulus is pleasant or unpleasant.
T	F	27.	Negative attention always acts as a punisher.
T	F	28.	Extrinsic reinforcement builds intrinsic reinforcement over time.
T	F	29.	The behaviorist views insight as covert trial-and-error learning.
T	F	30.	The term shaping is synonymous with the reward of successive approximations.

Key Terms

behaviorism An approach to psychology that emphasizes the study of observable behavior and the role of the environment as a determinant of behavior.

conditioning A basic kind of learning that involves associations between environmental stimuli and the organism's responses.

unconditioned stimulus (US) The classical-conditioning term for a stimulus that elicits a reflexive response in the absence of learning.

unconditioned response (UR) The classical-conditioning term for a reflexive response elicited by a stimulus in the absence of learning.

conditioned stimulus (CS) The classical-conditioning term for an initially neutral stimulus that comes to elicit a conditioned response after being associated with an unconditioned stimulus.

conditioned response (CR) The classical-conditioning term for a response that is elicited by a conditioned stimulus; it occurs after the conditioned stimulus is associated with an unconditioned stimulus.

classical conditioning The process by which a previously neutral stimulus acquires the capacity to elicit a response through association with a stimulus that already elicits a similar response. Also called *Pavlovian* and *respondent conditioning*.

extinction The weakening and eventual disappearance of a learned response; in classical conditioning, it occurs when the conditioned stimulus is no longer paired with the unconditioned stimulus.

spontaneous recovery The reappearance of a learned response after its apparent extinction.

higher-order conditioning In classical conditioning, a procedure in which a neutral stimulus becomes a conditioned stimulus through association with an already established conditioned stimulus.

stimulus generalization After conditioning, the tendency to respond to a stimulus that resembles one involved in the original conditioning. In classical conditioning, it occurs when a stimulus that resembles the CS elicits the CR.

stimulus discrimination The tendency to respond differently to two or more more similar stimuli; in classical conditioning, it occurs when a stimulus similar to the CS fails to evoke the CR.

counterconditioning In classical conditioning, the process of pairing a conditioned stimulus with a stimulus that elicits a response that is incompatible with an unwanted conditioned response.

operant conditioning The process by which a response becomes more likely to occur or less so, depending on its consequences.

reinforcement The process by which a stimulus or event strengthens or increases the probability of the response that it follows.

punishment The process by which a stimulus or event weakens or reduces the probability of the response that it follows.

primary reinforcer A stimulus that is inherently reinforcing, typically satisfying a physiological need; an example is food.

primary punisher A stimulus that is inherently punishing; an example is electric shock.

secondary reinforcer A stimulus that has acquired reinforcing properties through association with other reinforcers.

secondary punisher A stimulus that has acquired punishing properties through association with other punishers.

positive reinforcement A reinforcement procedure in which a response is followed by the presentation of, or increase in intensity of, a reinforcing stimulus; as a result, the response becomes stronger or more likely to occur.

negative reinforcement A reinforcement procedure in which a response is followed by the removal, delay, or decrease in intensity of an unpleasant stimulus; as a result, the response becomes stronger or more likely to occur.

extinction The weakening and eventual disappearance of a learned response; in operant conditioning, it occurs when a response is no longer followed by a reinforcer.

stimulus generalization In operant conditioning, the tendency for a response that has been reinforced (or punished) in the presence of one stimulus to occur (or be suppressed) in the presence of other, similar stimuli.

stimulus discrimination In operant conditioning, the tendency of a response to occur in the presence of one stimulus but not in the presence of other, similar stimuli that differ from it on some dimension.

discriminative stimulus A stimulus that signals when a particular response is likely to be followed by a certain type of consequence.

stimulus control Control over the occurrence of a response by a discriminative stimulus.

continuous reinforcement A reinforcement schedule in which a particular response is always reinforced.

intermittent (partial) schedule of reinforcement A reinforcement schedule in which a particular response is sometimes but not always reinforced.

shaping An operant-conditioning procedure in which successive approximations of a desired response are reinforced.

successive approximations In the operant-conditioning procedure of shaping, behaviors that are ordered in terms of increasing similarity or closeness to the desired response.

behavior modification The application of conditioning techniques to teach new responses or reduce or eliminate maladaptive or problematic behavior.

extrinsic reinforcers Reinforcers that are not inherently related to the activity being reinforced. Examples are money, prizes, and praise.

intrinsic reinforcers Reinforcers that are inherently related to the activity being reinforced, such as enjoyment of the task and the satisfaction of accomplishment.

insight A form of problem solving that that appears to involve the sudden understanding of how elements of a situation are related or can be reorganized to achieve a solution.

Suggested Research Projects

1.   Select a behavioral problem that is occurring on your campus, such as long lines in the cafeteria, students not studying until the night before the test, lack of attendance at nonrequired campus functions, etc. Describe the problem in operant terms, i.e., what are the reinforcers, punishers, discriminative stimuli, etc. Using operant principles, devise a plan to remedy the problem.

2.   Think of a habit that you would like to get rid of. Describe the habit in operant terms. Chart the occurrence of the undesired response over some time period. For example, if you want to quit smoking, keep a log of how many cigarettes you smoke, as well as the circumstances, such as eating or getting out of class, that accompany the response (these are discriminative stimuli). Then, using operant principles (such as punishing the behavior or rewarding incompatible behaviors), devise a behavioral plan to change your habit.

Suggested Readings

Kohn, A. (1999). *Punished by rewards: The trouble with gold stars, incentive plans, A's, praise, and other bribes.* An examination of what the author believes are misapplications of behaviorism.

Skinner, B. F. (1948). *Walden two.* New York: Macmillan. A novel about the application of behavioral technology in a community.

Watson, D. L., & Tharp, R. G. (1996). *Self-directed behavior: Self-modification for personal adjustment* (7th ed.). Monterey, CA: Brooks/Cole. Suggestions for changing one's own behavior through the application of learning principles.

CHAPTER 6

Social and Cognitive Learning

Learning Objectives

After reading and studying this chapter, you should be able to:

1.   Compare and contrast social-cognitive learning theory with behaviorism.

2.   Describe the process of observational learning.

3.   Explain how cognitive factors influence learning.

4.   Describe the sources of self-efficacy.

5.   Describe the various factors involved in gender development.

6.   Describe the various factors involved in moral development.

7.   Compare and contrast social-cognitive and behavioral theories of moral development.

8.   Discuss the successes and criticisms of the learning perspective.

Chapter Outline

I.   Introduction

    A.   **Social-cognitive learning theories** emphasize how behavior is learned and maintained through the interaction between individuals and their environments, an interaction strongly influenced by such cognitive processes as observations, expectations, perceptions, and motivational beliefs.

II.   Beyond Behaviorism. Social learning theorists emphasize four phenomena:

    A.   **Latent learning**, a form of learning that is not immediately expressed in an overt response; it occurs without obvious reinforcement.
        1.   A good deal of learning remains latent until circumstances allow or require it to be expressed.
        2.   Latent learning involves gaining knowledge about responses and their consequences.
    B.   **Observational learning** is a process in which an individual learns new

responses by observing the behavior of another (a model) rather than through direct experience; in behaviorism, it is called *vicarious conditioning.*

    1.   Behaviorists explain observational learning in stimulus-response terms. But social learning theorists also try to take into account the thought processes of the learner.

    2.   Observational learning explains why children sometimes imitate the behavior of adults and behaviors that they see on television.

C.   The Power of Perceptions.

    1.   Two people can experience the same event and have entirely different interpretations of the event.

    2.   Observing aggressive behavior in media may lead some, but not all viewers to be more aggressive, but aggressive people may also be attracted to violent media.

    3.   The cognitive processes of perception and interpretation, along with other personality dispositions intervene between what we see, what we learn, and how we respond.

D.   Motivating Beliefs.

    1.   Social-cognitive learning theorists maintain that our learned habits, beliefs, and goals exert their own effects on behavior.

    2.   **Motivation** is a process within a person or animal, which causes movement toward a goal or away from an unpleasant situation.

    3.   **Locus of control** is a general expectation about whether the results of a person's actions are under his or her control (internal locus) or beyond the person's control (external locus).

         a.   These expectations can create a **self-fulfilling prophecy**, an expectation that comes true because of the tendency of the person holding it to act in ways that bring it about. These expectations are formed by the person's experience with effort and success or lack of success.

         b.   People with an *external locus of control* tend to believe that they are victims of situational influences.

         c.   An *internal locus of control* is strongly related to achievement and health benefits.

         d.   An internal locus of control may reflect only the experience of middle-class people.

    4.   A second important motivating belief is *explanatory style* -- a characteristic way of explaining one's successes and failures.

         a.   *Pessimistic explanatory styles*, which are associated with depression, attribute failures to internal, stable, and global characteristics.

         b.   *Optimistic explanatory styles*, which are associated with achievement, resilience, and health, attribute failures to external and unstable factors that are limited in impact.

    5.   A third important motivating belief is **self-efficacy**, a person's belief that he or she is capable of producing desired results, such as

mastering new skills and reaching goals. Self-efficacy affects task performance, commitment to goals, persistence, career choice, problem solving ability, health, and ability to handle stress. Self-efficacy is acquired from four sources:

    a.   Having experiences in mastering new skills and overcoming obstacles.

    b.   Having successful and competent role models.

    c.   Getting feedback and encouragement from others.

    d.   Learning how to read and manage your own physiological state.

    e.   People with high self-efficacy interpret failure as a learning opportunity.

6.   Self-efficacy is also related to how one thinks about goals.

    a.   **Performance goals** are goals framed in terms of performing well in front of others, being judged favorably, and avoiding criticism. Setting performance goals works against self-efficacy.

    b.   **Mastery goals** are goals framed in terms of increasing one's competence and skills. People who set these goals feel greater intrinsic pleasure at an accomplishment.

III.   Learning the Rules of Gender

A.   *Sex* refers to anatomical and physical attributes of males and females. *Gender* refers to human attributes that are culturally and psychologically defined as more appropriate for one sex than the other.

B.   **Gender identity** is the fundamental sense of being male or female; it is independent of whether the person conforms to the social and cultural rules of gender. **Gender typing** is the process by which children learn the abilities, interests, personality traits, and behaviors associated with being masculine or feminine in their culture.

C.   Limitation of Behavioral Explanations

    1.   Early learning theories, which emphasized reinforcement and punishment of "sex-appropriate" and "sex-inappropriate" behavior, and imitation, assumed that a child is a passive participant in his or her upbringing.

    2.   Gender typing usually begins as soon as a child is born.

    3.   But children seem to act out gender stereotypes no matter what their parents do.

    4.   Boys and girls tend to segregate in themselves into single-sex play groups.

    5.   Children select whom they will imitate.

        a.   Children are unlikely to imitate a same-sex parent's nontraditional behavior.

        b.   Reinforcement works only when certain people administer it.

        c.   Parents often reinforce children's gender-typed preferences.

6.	Researchers in the biological tradition believe that gender-typed behavior has a biological basis, but social-cognitive theorists believe that gender typing results from:
	a.	subtle and unintended reinforcers.
	b.	the development of children's cognitive understanding of gender.
	c.	the specific situations the child is in.
D.	Hidden Reinforcers.
	1.	Parents and teachers often communicate subtle gender messages without an awareness that they are doing so.
	2.	These messages reflect adults' gender-typed beliefs and expectations, which are unwittingly transmitted to their children by rewarding different behavior in boys and girls.
E.	Gender Schemas. A **gender schema** is a mental network of knowledge, beliefs, metaphors, and expectations about what it means to be male or female. Once they develop gender schema, children change their behavior to conform to it. Gender schemas:
	a.	are learned early in life and affect preference for playmates, toys, and styles of play.
	b.	seem to be more rigid for boys than for girls.
	c.	can change throughout life as they accommodate to new experiences.
F.	Gender in Social Context
	1.	Some situations evoke gender-typed behavior, while others do not.
		a.	People adjust their behavior to situations.
		b.	Many people report exploring cross-gendered kinds of behaviors by middle age.
		c.	People are more likely to attribute behavior to sex when the group contains only one female (or male).
		d.	When women are not tokens, or a small percentage of a group, they are perceived as being diverse.

IV.	Learning to be Moral

A.	Morality involves kindness, fairness, responsibility, empathy, consideration, conscience, and good intentions.
B.	Behavioral and Cognitive Theories
	1.	Behaviorism overlooks the importance of developing cognitive categories of right and wrong that can be applied to new situations.
	2.	Kohlberg's cognitive theory (which was based on moral reasoning, not behavior) involved 3 levels:
		a.	preconventional morality -- based on punishment, direction of authority, and desire to obey or disobey.
		b.	conventional morality -- based on trust, caring, and loyalty.
		c.	postconventional ("principled") morality -- based on principles of justice.

3. From the social-cognitive perspective, Kohlberg's theory has three main limitations:
   a. It tends to overlook educational and cultural influences on moral reasoning. It sometimes confuses verbal sophistication with morality.
   b. People's moral reasoning is often inconsistent across situations.
   c. Moral reasoning is often unrelated to moral behavior.
4. Gilligan's criticism was that women tend to base moral decisions on compassion and care, while men base moral decisions on abstract principles such as law and justice. However, research indicates that people of both sexes use both bases.

V. Social-Cognitive Learning Theories

A. Social learning theories emphasize:
   1. the power of observational learning.
   2. children's internalization of parents' moral standards.
   3. the acquisition of conscience.
B. Moral Emotions.
   1. The capacity for moral feeling seems to be inborn.
   2. *Moral sense* develops out of a child's attachment to parents.
   3. *Empathy*, the ability to feel bad about another person's unhappiness or pain, is essential for internalizing morality:
      a. Infants exhibit general distress at another person's misery.
      b. *Shame*, a wound to the self concept at having done something wrong, and *guilt*, remorse for not living up to one's own standards, also regulate moral behaviors.
C. Parental Lessons. Children internalize moral standards as much from how parents act as from what they teach.
   1. **Power assertion** is a method of correcting a child's behavior in which the parent uses punishment and authority. It is associated with:
      a. a lack of moral feeling and behavior in children.
      b. poor self-control.
      c. an inability to internalize moral standards.
   2. **Induction** is a method of correcting a child's behavior in which the parent appeals to the child's own abilities, sense of responsibility, and feelings for others. Induction is associated with:
      a. children's guilt when they hurt others.
      b. internalized standards of right and wrong.
      c. confessing misbehavior rather than lying.
      d. accepting responsibility for behavior.
      e. thoughtfulness.
   3. Punishments accompanied by explanations, consistent discipline, affection, and high parental expectations are also essential.

D.   The Larger Culture.
       1.   Moral expectations vary across cultures.
       2.   The most altruistic cultures are those in which children are
             assigned tasks like preparing food and caring for younger children.

VI.   Essay Two: Evaluating the Learning Perspective

       A.   Contributions of this Perspective
             1.   The recognition that we all influence others, and in turn are
                   influenced by others, every day of our lives, whether we know it or
                   not.
             2.   The understanding that merely naming a behavior does not explain
                   it.
             3.   A wide range of practical applications, for example, setting goals is
                   most likely to improve performance when:
                   a.   the goal is specific.
                   b.   the goal is challenging but achievable.
                   c.   The goal is framed in terms of getting what you want rather
                         than avoiding what you do not want.
             4.   Social learning research findings are applicable to solving personal
                   and social problems:
                   a.   Self-efficacy can be acquired and improved.
                   b.   Health habits can be improved by raising self-efficacy and
                         internal locus of control, and by providing positive models.
       B.   Limitations and Misuses of this perspective:
             1.   There is a tendency to study one influence on learning at a time,
                   but behaviors are caused by complex interactions.
             2.   Environmental reductionism, the tendency to attribute all
                   behavior to situational factors, ignores biological attributes that are
                   known to affect behavior, such as physical characteristics of the
                   body, biological preparedness to learn a particular task, and
                   instinctive drift, the tendency of an organism to revert to
                   instinctive behavior over time; it can interfere with learning.
             3.   The error of assuming that if something is learned, it can easily be
                   changed.
             4.   Oversimplification in applying learning techniques.

Chapter Summary

Social-cognitive learning theory holds that most learning is acquired through the
1._____ between individuals and their environments. Its proponents agree with
2._____ that people are subject to the laws of classical and operant conditioning, but
add that observations, perceptions, motivational beliefs, and expectations also affect
learning.

For instance, Tolman demonstrated that an organism can learn in the absence of reinforcement and without an overt response, a phenomenon that he called 3._____ learning. 4._____ learning involves watching others as the basis for the acquisition of behavior. The person one learns from is called a 5._____. If that person is reinforced or punished for some response, an observer may acquire the response through 6._____ conditioning, although the observer may not exhibit the response for some time. Even very young children seem to have a propensity for observing and imitating others.

Two people may observe the same situation and have different 7._____of it. This explains why observational learning does not produce the same results in everybody. Beliefs are learned through experience, and in turn, they also exert their own influences on interpretations and behavior, sometimes overcoming the effects of rewards and punishers. 8._____, a process within a person (or animal) that causes movement toward a goal, is powerfully affected by beliefs.

Researchers have described some types of beliefs that have pervasive influences on behavior. Rotter concluded that people develop generalized 9._____ about which situations and acts will be rewarded. A person with an internal 10._____ expects rewards and punishments to depend on his or her behavior, while a person with an 11._____ locus of control feels like he or she is at the mercy of fate, luck, chance, or other forces outside of the self. These expectations can create a 12._____, in which a person acts in such a way as to confirm his or her expectations. An internal locus of control is strongly related to achievement, but critics have argued that an internal sense of control reflects the experience of middle-class people, who have often been rewarded for hard work, in sharp contrast to poor and minority peoples.

People also have a propensity for assigning responsibility for events to themselves or the environment. 13._____ style is the typical way in which a person accounts for negative events. People with a 14._____ style tend to explain these events as 15._____ (being their own fault), 16._____ (lasting for an indefinite period), and 17._____ (affecting everything). In contrast, people with an 18._____ style see negative events as more 19._____ (not their own fault), 20._____ (temporary), and 21._____ (not affecting them in a global way). The latter type of style is associated with 22._____ and health.

23._____ is the fundamental belief that one is competent. It affects a wide variety of behaviors, including persistence, health habits, and career choice. According to Bandura, it is acquired from four sources: experiences in 24._____new skills and overcoming obstacles, having successful and competent 25._____encouragement from others, and learning how to read and manage one's 26._____ state. Occasional failure is important to the development of self efficacy, but only if it is interpreted 27._____.

People who set 28._____ goals want to increase their competence and skills. Therefore, they are not as bothered by failures (if they have learned something), as people who set 29._____ goals, who tend to take failure more personally.

While sex is a biological distinction, 30._____, the cultural attributes assigned to males and females, is a 31._____ distinction. Social-cognitive learning theorists are interested in several associated areas, including the development of 32._____ (the fundamental sense of oneself as male or female) and 33._____ (the process of learning what it means to be "masculine" or "feminine").

While behavioral theories depict children as passive participants in the gendering process, we now know that children selectively imitate adults of the same sex, and that they respond differentially to same-sex and other-sex reinforcement. Although parents may be very egalitarian in their views, they may subtly reinforce gender stereotyped behaviors. Early in their lives, children acquire beliefs about which behaviors are gender appropriate and which are not. These beliefs, called gender 34._____, regulate behavior. For instance, five-year-old children tend to be strongly self-critical if they behave in a cross-gendered fashion.

Gender-typed behavior is more salient in some situations than in others. Social learning theorists make an important distinction between the acquisition of gendered behavior in childhood and its 35._____ in adulthood. People tend to attribute behavior to a person's sex when there are very few or only one person of that sex in a group.

Social learning theorists are also interested in the study of 36._____, which is described as kindness, fairness, responsibility, and good intention. Behavioral theories overlook the importance of developing cognitive categories of right and wrong that can be applied to new situations. Kohlberg outlined a stage theory of moral development based on a cognitive model. The first level is called 37._____ morality, in which a person behaves in a certain way in order to avoid being punished or because of his or her own desires. 38._____ morality is based on trust, caring and loyalty, and 39._____ morality is based on higher principles, such as justice and duty. Social-cognitive learning theorists have been critical of this model. For instance, it has been argued that Kohlberg's stages reflect 40._____ sophistication rather than moral development. It does not take into account actual moral 41._____ or inconsistencies in moral behavior across 42._____.

Gilligan theorized that women tend to base moral decisions on compassion and care, and that these could be as moral as decisions based on 42._____ principles such as justice. A good deal of research, however, has revealed that most people take both compassion and justice into account. Later social-cognitive theories have emphasized the development of morality as being based on empathy, shame, guilt, and attachment to the caregiver. The capacity for morality seems to be inborn, as evidenced by empathic behaviors exhibited by even very young children. Empathy seems to develop in predictable ways.

According to social-cognitive learning theorists, children internalize moral standards as much from their parents' behaviors as from their lessons. 44._____ assertion by parents, which controls the behavior of children through punishment, is associated with a lack of moral feeling. On the other hand, 45._____, in which a parent appeals to the child's resources, affection for others, and responsibility, tends to have a positive impact on the development of moral feelings. Punishments are only effective when they are accompanied by 46._____ about why the behavior was inappropriate. Morality also appears to be positively influenced by consistent discipline, parental affection, high parental standards, and requiring children to behave in helpful ways.

The learning perspective has been quite useful in many circumstances. People will inevitably be influenced by their environments, and so we would do well to design those environments so that this influence is positive. Learning researchers tend to study one influence at a time, and this does not realistically reflect actual environments, as there are almost always a complex variety of influences on any given behavior.

The benefits of learning research have included the development of programs for raising self-efficacy, the finding that goals are most helpful when they are demanding but realistic, and the use of learning interventions to change health habits. Like other perspectives, however, the learning perspective has its dangers, including environmental 47._____, the tendency to explain every behavior by situational influences. It has been well demonstrated that all organisms are biologically prepared to learn some responses more easily than others. Animals and humans tend to gravitate toward these types of behaviors, even if they are rewarded for incompatible responses. This is a phenomenon known as 48._____.

People who advocate egalitarianism and social change are drawn to the learning perspective because of its assertion that human behavior is malleable. This gives them hope that inequalities can be rectified by changes in environments. Some biological psychologists disagree, especially with regard to gender differences. However, even if there are biologically based average differences between the sexes, they should never be used to restrict the opportunities of any individual.

People sometimes try to apply learning theories in oversimplified ways. Despite these problems, learning theorists are probably correct in their belief that society does not take as much advantage as it could of what we have learned in this area.

Multiple Choice Self-Test

1. Albert Bandura's ideas about self-efficacy differ from the behaviorist view of behavior in that:
a. behaviorists predict that self-efficacy is unrelated to failure.
b. Bandura predicts that behaviorists are incapable of developing a strong sense of self-efficacy.
c. behaviorists predict that repeated failures will extinguish response efforts.
d. behaviorists predict that repeated failures will increase response efforts.

2. Which of the following has been shown to positively affect self-efficacy?
a. attempting tasks that have a low degree of challenge.
b. learning how to manage one's own physiological state.
c. having others confront one's shortcomings.
d. attempting tasks that have a very high degree of challenge.

3. When child rearing takes the form of threats, physical punishment, and depriving the child of privileges, it can be described as:
a. power assertion.
b. totalitarianism.
c. positive punishment.
d. negative punishment.

4. Maureen is only 9 months old. She sees her older brother stub his toe and then try to hide his tears. Maureen is likely to:
a. laugh.
b. display direct aggression.
c. exhibit distress at her brother's pain.
d. inhibit her own sense of pain.

5. Betty's parents told her that the members of her family perform poorly in college because "they are too active to sit still and study." After hearing this, Betty performs poorly during her first semester at college. What does this situation seem to illustrate?
a. genetic determination of attention span
b. self-fulfilling prophecy
c. authoritarian parenting
d. classical conditioning

6. Social-cognitive learning theorists believe that most human learning is acquired through:
a. punishment, challenge, and mistakes.
b. social functions.
c. reinforcement.
d. observation, beliefs, and expectations.

7. Arlene, an adult, throws a temper tantrum at a car dealership when they don't have the car she wants. In contrast to behaviorists, social learning theorists would point out that:
a. Arlene was probably reinforced for temper tantrums at some time.
b. Arlene may have been punished for keeping quiet as a child.
c. the reinforcement for temper tantrums may have generalized inappropriately.
d. the behavior may be affected by Arlene's having chosen to go to this car dealer.

8. Behaviorism is to social-cognitive learning theory as:
a. direct influence is to interactions.
b. part is to whole.
c. black is to white.
d. science is to belief system.

9. Social learning theory holds that trial-and-error learning is:
a. impossible.
b. unlikely.
c. inefficient.
d. latent.

10. Dee watches her friend make a paper airplane. Two years later, Dee's sister asks Dee to make a paper airplane. Dee is able to do so, despite the fact that she has never done so before. What kind of learning has Dee exhibited?
a. operant
b. latent
c. semantic
d. induction

11. When children view violence on television:
a. they inevitably become more aggressive afterwards.
b. their activity level increases, and they become aggressive if they are rewarded for doing so.
c. they become more likely to increase aggressive behavior.
d. aggression is actually decreased.

12. Which of the following is TRUE?
a. violent movies cause viewers to be violent.
b. people with aggressive personalities tend to like violent television.
c. there is no link between violent media and violent behavior.
d. there is a link between violent television, but not violent video games, and violent behavior.

13. Greg and Rick watch an adventure movie together. Greg is excited at the hero's courage and cunning, but Rick is disgusted by the hero's violence. Greg stays in the movie theater while Rick walks out. In explaining these differences in behavior, social learning theories would emphasize differences in Greg's and Rick's:
a. perceptions of the movie events.
b. histories of reinforcement.
c. masculine socialization.
d. number of hero models in their lives.

14. According to social-cognitive learning theory, theoretical constructs like confidence, goal-setting, and motivation are:
a. unscientific because they cannot be observed.
b. of limited value.
c. necessary for complete explanations of behavior.
d. impossible to measure.

15. Dean believes that his friend, Helen, is angry with him. He asks her about it, but she says (truthfully) that she is not angry. Unsatisfied, he asks her again, and then again. By this time, she answers (truthfully again) that she IS angry. This scene illustrates:
a. latent learning.
b. operant conditioning.
c. masculine socialization.
d. self-fulfilling prophecy.

16. People who rely on psychics, horoscopes, and lucky numbers exhibit:
a. an internal locus of control.
b. an external locus of control.
c. self-efficacy.
d. a pessimistic explanatory style.

17. Jawan exhibits an external locus of control. This may be somewhat adaptive for him if:
a. he has some useful psychological skills.
b. he is a member of an oppressed minority.
c. he has adequate role models.
d. he has a high degree of self-efficacy.

18. John's girlfriend has just broken up with him. According to Martin Seligman, John is most likely to become depressed if he explains this event in terms of:
a. his poor judgment in choosing her.
b. her irresponsible behavior in their relationship.
c. the mistakes he made in their relationship.
d. his being unlovable.

19. In comparison with a characteristic like poor athleticism, low intelligence is more:
a. global.
b. stable.
c. internal.
d. external.

20. If you want to gain a greater sense of self-efficacy during your college years, you will set goals that emphasize:
a. mastery.
b. performance.
c. achievement.
d. competition.

21. In mainstream United States culture, emotional inexpressiveness is usually a characteristic of:
a. sex.
b. gender.
c. low social class.
d. critical density.

22. Six-year-old Reuben has a solid sense of gender identity, so he knows that:
a. boys are active and girls are passive.
b. men are physically stronger than women.
c. his mother takes care of children better than his father.
d. he is male and his sister is female.

23. According to social-cognitive theory, Girls acquire "feminine" personality characteristics through the process of:
a. sex differentiation.
b. hormonal secretion.
c. gender socialization.
d. cross-gender modeling.

24. On Halloween, Chris is supposed to wear a costume to school, and so his mother suggests that he dress as a girl. Chris does not feel comfortable with this because of his:
a. gender schema.
b. gender identity.
c. sex differentiation.
d. self-efficacy.

25. Which of the following is TRUE?
a. Power assertion is the best way to build morality in children.
b. Moral expectations vary across cultures.
c. Kohlberg's theory was based largely in behaviorism.
d. Post-conventional reasoning invariably leads to moral behavior.

26. The major criticism of Kohlberg's theory of morality is that:
a. there are no identifiable stages.
b. cognitive categories are not clearly identified.
c. it overlooks educational influences on moral behavior reasoning.
d. there is no place for altruistic behavior.

27. A child who comforts a sad friend shows:
a. fairness.
b. responsibility.
c. empathy.
d. principle.

28. Cross-cultural research indicates that giving children household chores is associated with:
a. positive psychological characteristics.
b. a sense of lost childhood.
c. no identifiable effect.
d. measurable gains in IQ.

29. When 5-year old Arnie throws a temper tantrum and breaks a plate, his parents discipline him by making him clean up the mess, and they explain that they believe that he can learn better ways of managing his anger for his own good. His parents are using:
a. transduction.
b. deception.
c. induction.
d. meta-correction.

30. Compared to the average boy, the average girl has:
a. less rigid gender schemas.
b. more rigid gender schemas.
c. higher levels of gender identity.
d. more biologically-based gendering.

True-False Self-Test

T F 1. Unlike "gender," the term "sex" refers to the biologically based characteristics associated with maleness and femaleness.

T F 2. Parents who use induction methods typically provide their children with explanations of prohibitions.

T F 3. Social-cognitive theorists do not acknowledge the power of reinforcement and punishment to affect behavior.

T F 4. Kohlberg only investigated moral reasoning, not actual behavior.

T F 5. Young children readily copy the actions of an adult who is behaving in a fashion contrary to typical gender roles.

T	F	6.	According to social learning theory, people influence environments.
T	F	7.	Learning can remain latent for indefinite periods of time.
T	F	8.	A rat will not learn a maze without being reinforced for doing so.
T	F	9.	In general, observation of aggressive television models is associated with increased aggression in children.
T	F	10.	People tend to develop generalized expectancies that guide a great deal of their behavior.
T	F	11.	An external locus of control is associated with positive psychological characteristics in middle-class people.
T	F	12.	Optimistic explanatory style has positive effects on physical health.
T	F	13.	Pessimists tend to view negative events as highly unstable.
T	F	14.	Gilligan maintained that women tend to base moral decisions on higher principles than most men.
T	F	15.	The observation of successful models may help to build self-efficacy.
T	F	16.	Setting performance goals is the best way to increase one's confidence and skills.
T	F	17.	"Male" and "female" are gender terms.
T	F	18.	A boy with a secure gender identity will behave in sex-"appropriate" ways.
T	F	19.	Gender schemas can change throughout the lifespan.
T	F	20.	Power assertion is associated with a lack of moral feeling in children.
T	F	21.	Social-cognitive learning theorists dispute the assumption that moral behaviors are the same across situations.

T   F   22.   Parental induction is associated with negative psychological outcomes in children.

T   F   23.   In general, power assertion seems to be the most effective parenting technique.

T   F   24.   Social-cognitive learning theorists have developed techniques for raising self-efficacy.

T   F   25.   Social-cognitive learning theory does not account for biologically-based behaviors.

T   F   26.   Induction is associated with poor self-control in children.

T   F   27.   Moral expectations vary across cultures.

T   F   28.   Grades positively affect a child's intrinsic motivation.

T   F   29.   Parents should never punish children.

T   F   30.   Explaining the reason for punishments to a child is rarely necessary.

Key Terms

Social-cognitive learning theories Theories that emphasize how behavior is learned and maintained through the interaction between individuals and their environments, an interaction strongly influenced by such cognitive processes as observations, expectations, perceptions, and motivational beliefs.

latent learning A form of learning that is not immediately expressed in an overt response; it occurs without obvious reinforcement.

observational learning A process in which an individual learns new responses by observing the behavior of another (a model) rather than through direct experience; in behaviorism, it is called *vicarious conditioning.*

motivation A process within an person or animal, which causes movement toward a goal or away from an unpleasant situation.

self-fulfilling prophecy An expectation that comes true because of the tendency of the person holding it to act in ways that bring it about.

locus of control A general expectation about whether the results of a person's actions are under his or her control (internal locus) or beyond the person's control (external locus).

self-efficacy A person's belief that he or she is capable of producing desired results, such as mastering new skills and reaching goals.

performance goals Goals framed in terms of performing well in front of others, being judged favorably, and avoiding criticism.

mastery goals Goals framed in terms of increasing one's competence and skills.

gender identity The fundamental sense of being male or female; it is independent of whether the person conforms to the social and cultural rules of gender.

gender typing The process by which children learn the abilities, interests, personality traits, and behaviors associated with being masculine or feminine in their culture.

gender schema A mental network of knowledge, beliefs, metaphors, and expectations about what it means to be male or female.

power assertion A method of correcting a child's behavior in which the parent uses punishment and authority.

induction A method of correcting a child's behavior in which the parent appeals to the child's own abilities, sense of responsibility, and feelings for others.

instinctive drift The tendency of an organism to revert to instinctive behavior over time; it can interfere with learning.

Suggested Research Projects

1.   A frequent topic of conversation is "the difference between men and women." Assemble one group of all males, one group of all females, and one group of both males and females, and hold general discussions on this topic. What gender schemas do you discover? Are there differences in gender schemas among groups? What do you attribute these differences to?

2.   Take a negative life event (like a car accident, an unwanted pregnancy, a relationship break-up, the attainment of a low grade point average, etc.) and make a list of possible interpretations for the event. Identify each interpretation using Seligman's three dimensions: stable-unstable, internal-external, global-specific.

Suggested Readings

Bem, S. L. (1993). *The lenses of gender: Transforming the debate on sexual inequality*. New Haven, CT: Yale University Press. A discussion of the psychological, historical, and cultural roots of gender stereotyping.

Seligman, M. E. P. (1995). *What you can change... and what you can't: The complete guide to successful self-improvement: Learning to accept who you are*. San Francisco: Fawcett. A leading cognitive psychologist applies findings from years of research to suggest strategies for healthy mental functioning.

CHAPTER 7

Thinking and Reasoning

Learning Objectives

After reading and studying this chapter, you should be able to:

1. Define key cognitive terms: concept, proposition, schema, nonconscious process.

2. Distinguish inductive reasoning from deductive reasoning.

3. Apply dialectical reasoning to an argument.

4. Distinguish divergent thinking from convergent thinking.

5. Discuss the importance of creativity for psychological functioning.

6. Describe the stages of Piaget's theory.

7. Discuss the criticisms and later extensions of Piaget's theory.

8. Identify cognitive biases in arguments.

9. Discuss the research on mental rigidity and its antidotes.

10. Describe some recent research findings on animal cognition.

Chapter Outline

I.   The Elements of Cognition

    A.   Functions of thinking
        1.   Allows the person to go beyond the present.
        2.   Allows for the manipulation of mental representations of objects, situations, and activities.
        3.   Simplifying and summarizing information aids problem solving.
    B.   A **Concept** is a mental category that groups objects, relations, activities, abstractions, or qualities having common properties.
        1.   **Basic concepts** are concepts that have a moderate number of instances and that are easier to acquire than those having few or many instances.
        2.   A **prototype** is an especially representative example of a concept.

3. A **proposition** is a unit of meaning that is made up of concepts and expresses a single idea.
4. A **cognitive schema** is an integrated network of knowledge, beliefs, and expectations concerning a particular topic or aspect of the world.
5. A **mental image** is a mental representation that mirrors or resembles the thing it represents; mental images can occur in many and perhaps all sensory modalities.

II. How Conscious is Thought?

A. **Subconscious processes** are mental processes occurring outside of conscious awareness but accessible to consciousness when necessary.
B. **Nonconscious processes** are mental processes occurring outside of and not available to conscious awareness. Intuition and insight are examples of nonconscious processes.
C. Conscious processes are needed for deliberate choices, unexpected events, or when events cannot be handled automatically.
D. Usually much of our thinking is conscious, but it still may be mindless; in other words, we may act out of habit without analyzing our behavior.

III. Reasoning and Creativity

A. Formal Reasoning. **Reasoning** is the drawing of conclusions or inferences from observations, facts, or assumptions.
B. In *formal reasoning problems*, the information needed for a solution is specified clearly and there is a single correct answer.
   1. An **algorithm** is a problem-solving strategy guaranteed to produce a solution even if the user does not know how it works.
   2. **Deductive reasoning** is a form of reasoning in which a conclusion follows necessarily from certain premises; if the premises are true, the conclusion must be true.
      a. Deductive reasoning often takes the form of a *syllogism*, a simple argument consisting of two premises and a conclusion.
   3. **Inductive reasoning** is a form of reasoning in which the premises provide support for a certain conclusion, but it is still possible for the conclusion to be false.
      a. Science depends heavily on inductive reasoning.
C. Informal Reasoning. In *informal reasoning problems*, there may be no clearly correct solution.
   1. Informal reasoning often calls for a **heuristic**, a rule of thumb that suggests a course of action or guides problem solving but does not guarantee an optimal solution.
   2. **Dialectical reasoning** is a process in which opposing facts or ideas are weighed and compared, with a view to determining the best solution or resolving differences.

D. Creative Thinking. When rules and strategies have been successful in the past, a person develops a **mental set**, a tendency to solve new problems using procedures that worked before on similar problems.

E. Creativity involves going beyond present knowledge and habit to produce new solutions.

    1. Less creative people rely solely on **convergent thinking**, thinking aimed at finding a single correct answer to a problem.

    2. **Divergent thinking** is mental exploration of unconventional alternatives in solving problems; by breaking mental sets, it tends to enhance creativity.

F. Creativity is strongly associated with:

    1. nonconformity.

    2. curiosity.

    3. persistence.

IV. The Development of Thought and Reasoning

A. Piaget's Stages: How Children Think. Piaget proposed that thought involves adaptation to new observations and experiences, and that it takes two forms:

    1. **assimilation** -- In Piaget's theory, the process of absorbing new information into existing cognitive structures.

    2. **accommodation** -- In Piaget's theory, the process of modifying existing cognitive structures in response to experience and new information.

    3. Piaget's proposed four stages of cognitive development.

        a. The sensory-motor stage (birth – age 2) involves:

            i. learning through concrete actions.

            ii. coordinating sensory information with bodily movements.

            iii. attaining **object permanence**, the understanding that an object continues to exist even when you cannot see or touch it. This is the beginning of the child's capacity to use mental imagery and other symbolic systems.

        b. In the preoperational stage (ages 2-7),:

            i. children show accelerated use of symbols and language.

            ii. Piaget believed that children cannot perform **operations** -- In Piaget's theory, mental actions that are cognitively reversible.

            iii. Piaget believed that preoperational children cannot reason or perform in the mind, and that they engage only in **egocentric thinking** , seeing the world from only your own point of view; the inability to take another person's perspective.

iv. Piaget believed that preoperational children could not grasp the concept of **conservation** The understanding that the physical properties of objects -- such as the number of items in a cluster or the amount of liquid in a glass -- remain the same even when their form or appearance changes.

c. In the concrete operations stage (ages 7-12), children become able to:

i. understand conservation, reversibility, and cause and effect, identity, and serial ordering.

ii. perform some mental operations such as mathematics.

d. The formal operations stage (age 12 - adulthood) includes:

i. abstract reasoning.

ii. comparison and classification of ideas.

iii. reasoning about situations they have not experienced firsthand and future possibilities.

iv. systematic problem solving.

v. logical conclusions based on premises common to their culture and experience.

4. Research has called into question some of Piaget's theory.

a. Stage changes are not sweeping or clear-cut.

b. Children can understand far more than Piaget gave them credit for. There is some evidence of earlier object permanence, use of symbols, and perspective taking than Piaget proposed.

c. Preschoolers are not as egocentric as Piaget proposed.

i. They show perspective taking and the beginnings of developing a **theory of mind**, a system of beliefs about the way your own mind and other people's minds work, and of how people are affected by their beliefs and feelings; it emerges at age 4 or 5.

B. Beyond Piaget: How Adults Think

1. Reflective judgment involves:

a. questioning assumptions.

b. evaluating evidence.

c. relating evidence to theory or opinion.

d. considering alternative interpretations.

e. reaching reasonable and plausible conclusions that can be defended.

f. reassessing conclusions in the face of new information.

2. King & Kitchener have identified 7 stages in the development of reflective thinking.

a. In the two *prereflective* stages, the person assumes that correct answer exists and can be known through the senses with no distinction between knowledge and belief.

        b.   In the three *quasi-reflective* stage, the person recognizes that some things cannot be known with certainty, but has no way of dealing with this knowledge.

        c.   In the last two stages, the person becomes capable of *reflective* judgment, meaning that he or she:

            i.   understands that some judgments are more valid than others.

            ii.   is willing to consider evidence from a variety of sources and reason dialectically.

            iii.   able to defend conclusions as representing the best understanding of an issue based on currently available evidence.

    3.   Reflective judgment is not usually developed until middle or late 20's, if at all. Support for reflective thinking can help build this skill.

V.   Barriers to Reasoning Rationally

    A.   Obstacles to rational reasoning include the need to be right and mental laziness.

    B.   The Hindsight Bias. The **hindsight bias** is the tendency to overestimate one's ability to have predicted an event once the outcome is known; the "I knew it all along" phenomenon.

        1.   When we are sure that we knew something all along, we are less willing to find out what we need to know in order to make accurate predictions in the future.

    C.   Exaggerating the Improbable. The **availability heuristic** is the tendency to judge the probability of a type of event by how easy it is to think of examples or instances.

    D.   Avoiding Loss. People tend to have an *aversion to loss*, a tendency to avoid or minimize risks or losses.

    E.   The **confirmation bias** is attending only to evidence that confirms beliefs.

    F.   The Need for Cognitive Consistency. **Cognitive dissonance** is a state of tension that occurs when a person simultaneously holds two cognitions that are psychologically inconsistent, or when a person's belief is incongruent with his or her behavior.

        1.   The state of tension is uncomfortable and motivates a person to reduce it, especially:

            a.   when you need to justify a choice or decision that you freely made.

            b.   when your actions violate your self concept.

            c.   when you put a lot of effort into a decision, only to find that the results were less than you hoped for. **Justification of effort** is the tendency of individuals to increase their liking for something that they have worked hard or suffered to attain; a common form of dissonance reduction.

    G.   Overcoming Our Cognitive Biases. People are not equally irrational in all situations.

      1.   Cognitive biases diminish when:
          a.   people have expertise in what they are doing.
          b.   decisions have serious consequences.
      2.   Understanding biases helps to reduce or eliminate them.

VI.   Animal Minds

    A.   Animal Intelligence. **Cognitive ethology** is the study of cognitive processes in nonhuman animals. Animals may be capable of:
       1.   using tools.
       2.   basic mathematical reasoning.
    B.   Animal Language. *Language* is the ability to combine elements that are themselves meaningless into an infinite number of utterances that convey meaning. To qualify as language, a communication system must:
       1.   use a combination of sounds, gestures, or symbols that are *meaningful*, not random.
       2.   permit *displacement*, communication about objects and events that are not present here and now, but rather are displaced in time and space.
       3.   have a grammar (syntax) that permits *productivity*, the ability to produce and comprehend an infinite number of new utterances.
          a.   By these criteria, no nonhuman species has its own language.
          b.   Researchers have tried to teach language to primates and appeared to have done so, but skeptics point out that they overinterpreted the animals utterances. However, researchers have demonstrated that some animals can acquire language.
    C.   Thinking About the Thinking of Animals.
       1.   On one side of the argument are those who worry about *anthropomorphism*, the tendency to falsely attribute human qualities to nonhuman beings.
       2.   On the other side are those who warn about *anthropocentrism*, the tendency to think, mistakenly, that human beings have nothing in common with other animals.

Chapter Summary

Thinking allows a person to go beyond the present and to mentally manipulate internal representations of objects, activities, and situations. These representations allow us to simplify and summarize information.

1._____ are the building blocks of thought. Those that have a moderate number of instances are called 2._____, which are easier to acquire than those having few or many instances. A 3._____ is an especially representative example of the concept.

Concepts may be linked together in complicated networks called 4._____. We can represent the world in our minds by using mental images.

We can handle a good deal of information and perform many complex tasks because a portion of mental processing takes place outside of our awareness. 5._____ processes can be brought into consciousness when necessary, while 6._____ processes remain outside of awareness but nevertheless affect behavior. Intuition is an example of this kind of process. Fully conscious processing is only needed when automatic processing is inadequate, as when a person must make a deliberate choice or handle an unexpected situation.

7._____ is purposeful mental activity that involves operating on information in order to reach conclusions. In formal reasoning problems, the information needed for a solution is specified and there is a single correct answer. An 8._____ is a problem-solving strategy guraranteed to produce a solution. In 9._____ reasoning, if the premises are true, the conclusion must be true. This kind of reasoning often takes the form of a 10._____, a simple argument consisting of two premises and a conclusion. Science depends heavily on 11._____ reasoning, in which the premises support a conclusion, but it is still possible for the conclusion to be false.

In informal reasoning problems, there may be no clearly correct solution. These problems often call for a 12._____, a rule of thumb that suggests a course of action. 13._____ reasoning is a process in which opposing facts or ideas are weighed and compared. Less creative people rely on 14._____ thinking, which is aimed at finding a single correct answer, rather than 15._____ thinking, which is mental exploration of unconventional alternatives in solving problems by breaking mental sets.

Jean Piaget was a pioneer in the study of cognitive development. He proposed that mental functioning depends on 16._____ to new observations and experiences, which takes two forms, 17._____, the process of absorbing new information into existing cognitive structures, and 18._____, the modification of existing cognitive structures in response to new information.

Piaget proposed four stages of cognitive development. During the 19._____ stage, the infant learns only through concrete actions. The major development in this stage is the sense of 20._____, which is the understanding that objects continue to exist even though they cannot be seen. This is the beginning of thought, the child's capacity for using 21._____ .

Normal children aged 2 to 7 are in the 22._____ stage, in which the use of language and symbols accelerates. Piaget mistakenly believed that children at this stage could not reason, and that they are 23._____, or incapable of taking another person's perspective.

During the 24._____ stage (ages 7 to 12), children come to acquire the concept of 25._____, the notion that physical properties do not change when their form or appearance changes. They learn mental operations and can understand cause and effect.

Around age 12, children enter the 26._____ stage, where they become capable of 27._____ reasoning. They can now compare and classify ideas and imagine multiple possibilities. They also become capable of searching systematically for solutions to problems.

Piaget's critics have argued that changes from one stage to the next are not as clear-cut or sweeping as he proposed, and that there is some situational specificity to cognitive ability. Research findings have demonstrated that some aspects of object permanence, perspective taking, and use of symbols develop earlier in life than Piaget suggested. Moreover, there is evidence that children begin to develop a 28._____ , a system of beliefs about the way their minds and those of others work, by age 4 or 5.

29._____ involves the abilities to evaluate and integrate evidence, relate evidence to theory, and reach and defend conclusions. King and Kitchener have demonstrated that people can reach the stage of formal operations without having acquired these skills. They described stages of development in this area, the earliest of which are the 30._____ stages, when people believe that answers always exist and can be known, and they cannot distinguish between belief and evidence. In the 31._____ stages, people recognize that some things cannot be known with certainty but have no way of dealing with this knowledge.

When a person becomes capable of reflective judgment, he or she is willing to consider evidence from different sources, see inquiry as an ongoing process, and make coherent and defensible judgments. Most people do not show evidence of reflective judgment until they are in their middle or late 32._____, if at all. However, this set of skills can be improved when students practice and are encouraged in the right direction.

Obstacles to rational reasoning include mental laziness, the need to be right, and several cognitive biases that hinder problem solving. For example, there is also a tendency to use one's ability to explain past events as evidence that one can predict future events. This kind of distortion is known as 33._____ bias. People sometimes exaggerate the probability of rare events. This bias in cognitive processing, called the 34._____ heuristic, is the tendency to judge probability on the basis of how easy it is to think of examples of events. People are also biased toward making decisions that minimize or avoid 35._____. They are less likely to take risks in order to gain something. Another cognitive distortion, called the 36._____ bias, is the result of selectively attending to evidence that confirms one's belief, while ignoring other evidence.

People become uncomfortable when their behavior does not conform to their beliefs or when they hold two incompatible beliefs. This cognitive 37._____ motivates a person to reduce discomfort by changing beliefs or behaviors, or by making excuses. People tend to be especially motivated to reduce this tension when they think that their decisions are freely chosen, important, and irrevocable, when their actions violate their self-concepts, and when they have put a lot of effort into something that has had a disappointing outcome. A person who has worked hard to achieve a goal may overvalue that goal in order to reduce dissonance, a phenomenon called 38._____.

39._____ is the study of cognitive processes in nonhuman animals. One question in this area is whether animals' communication systems constitute true 40._____, the ability to combine meaningless utterances into those that convey meaning. In order to qualify, the communication system must have symbols that are 41._____, not random, permit 42._____, communication about objects and events not present, and have a grammar that permits 43._____, the ability to produce novel utterances. By these criteria, no nonhuman species has language, but there have been some successful attempts to have animals learn language from humans. On one side of the argument are those who worry about 44._____, the inclination to falsely attribute human qualities to nonhumans. On the other side are those who warn against 45._____, the mistaken belief that humans and animals have nothing in common.

Multiple Choice Self-Test

1. We need internal representations in order to:
a. solve even the simplest problem.
b. simplify and summarize the amount of data we receive so that we can deal with the information.
c. experience pleasure or pain.
d. carry out reflex actions.

2. "Flowers," "work," and "difficult" are all examples of:
a. concepts.
b. operations.
c. symbols.
d. qualities.

3. The statements "All cows eat grass" and "Holsteins are types of cows" are:
a. propositions.
b. concepts.
c. symbols.
d. schemas.

4. Practiced basketball players can make shots without thinking about them. However, if you asked them to tell you about their shooting techniques, they could readily describe them because their shooting is a/an:
a. internal conscience process.
b. conscious process.
c. subconscious process.
d. nonconscious process.

5. Byron is taking a multiple choice test in algebra. He gets to an especially difficult question. He has no idea how to solve it, but he has a strong feeling that choice 'C' is the correct answer. If he is accessing information that is beneath the surface of awareness, then Byron is engaged in:
a. conscientious processing.
b. conscious processing.
c. nonconscious processing.
d. subconscious processing.

6. Edie is faced with the following simple problem: "X" is an integer; "X" is less than 9; "X" is greater than 7. Her understanding that X=8 is the result of:
a. dialectical reasoning.
b. inductive reasoning.
c. deductive reasoning.
d. divergent reasoning.

7. Jan overhears a conversation in which a person is describing a communication device that has no visual mode and can reach more than one person at a time. Jan believes that the person is talking about a radio. She comes to this conclusion through the process of:
a. dialectical reasoning.
b. inductive reasoning.
c. deductive reasoning.
d. divergent reasoning.

8. Andy is listening to a debate about the legalization of certain drugs. Each debater presents various arguments and pieces of evidence in support of her position, and Andy decides whether he thinks that legalization would be beneficial through the process of:
a. dialectical reasoning.
b. inductive reasoning.
c. deductive reasoning.
d. divergent reasoning.

9. Creative people are especially good at using:
a. divergent thinking.
b. convergent thinking.
c. well-established problem solving methods.
d. highly organized thinking.

10. Billie's old car, which has two high beams and two low beams, has developed a problem. When she turns the low beams on, nothing happens. When she turns the high beams on, all four headlights come on. Billie is upset because she does not want to pay to have the car fixed, but then she realizes that she can leave the switch on "high" all the time if she disconnects the high beams. Her innovative solution involves:
a. divergent thinking.
b. convergent thinking.
c. well-established problem solving methods.
d. highly organized thinking.

11. Armand is balancing his checkbook. Because all of his entries in the checkbook are correct and his arithmetic is accurate, he can follow the prescribed series of steps and come up with the correct balance. This process involves:
a. divergent thinking.
b. convergent thinking.
c. well-established problem solving methods.
d. highly organized thinking.

12. Alvie goes to a zoo and sees a puma for the first time. Even though he has never seen nor heard of pumas before, it is easy for him to understand that a puma is a large cat through the process of:
a. accommodation.
b. assimilation.
c. conservation.
d. representation.

13. Ariel is a young child who has learned about different kinds of animals in school. She thinks of mammals as small animals like cats and dog, but she has to change her thinking when her teacher tells her that cows are also mammals. Ariel changes her ideas about mammals through the process of:
a. accommodation.
b. assimilation.
c. conservation.
d. representation.

14. Object permanence is the beginning of:
a. dialectical reasoning.
b. abstract thought.
c. concrete operations.
d. the use of mental imagery.

15. Karen watches as her mother rolls a lump of clay into a long, skinny tube. According to Piaget, if Karen knows that there is no more clay than there was before, she is at least in which stage?
a. sensory-motor.
b. preoperational.
c. concrete operations.
d. formal operations.

16. According to Piaget, the ability to understand abstract proverbs like "a stitch in time saves nine" and "the early bird gets the worm" depends on one's being at least in which stage?
a. sensory-motor.
b. preoperational.
c. concrete operations.
d. formal operations.

17. Which of the following is NOT a criticism of Piaget?
a. Changes from one stage to another are not clear-cut.
b. Changes from one stage to another are not sweeping.
c. Preoperational children are capable of perspective taking.
d. Children actively interpret their worlds.

18. Inga believes that there is a single answer for every question. Kitchener and King would label her cognitive level:
a. reflective.
b. prereflective.
c. postreflective.
d. quasi-reflective.

19. Bart is talking to a friend who believes that the 1969 moon landing was an elaborate hoax staged by the government to get Americans to give up more tax dollars. Bart realizes that he cannot know with absolute certainty that this is not true, so he feels that he should accept this hypothesis as a possibility. Kitchener and King would place Bart in the stage of:
a. critical thinking.
b. reflective judgment.
c. prereflective thinking.
d. quasi-reflective thinking.

20. Which of the following is TRUE?
a. All mammals have true language.
b. Some animals have learned language from humans.
c. All primates, but not other mammals, have true language.
d. Many animals, including some mammals, have true language.

21. Antoinette loses her keys and decides to mentally review her day's activities, and then retrace her steps, looking for her keys on the way. Her strategy is:
a. a heuristic.
b. an algorithm.
c. a confirmation bias.
d. a loss aversion.

22. People are more afraid to fly on planes than to drive cars, even though the likelihood of dying in a car accident is much greater than that of dying in an airplane crash. This irrational fear could be due to:
a. an algorithm.
b. loss aversion.
c. attribution bias.
d. the availability heuristic.

23. Donyel is a middle manager in a corporation. He is upset because he has had to pay a fine to the bank for overdrawing his corporate checking account. His boss tells him not to worry about it because it is "the cost of doing business." The difference between Donyel's and his boss's reaction can be explained by:
a. the availability heuristic.
b. loss aversion.
c. attribution bias.
d. confirmation bias.

24. On a popular talk show, 30-year-old identical twin brothers are reunited after having been separated at birth. To everyone's surprise, they have very similar jobs, got married in the same year, and performed at the same level in college, where they majored in the same discipline. It is easy to believe that all of these behaviors are genetically based, but to do so would be to fall victim to:
a. attribution bias.
b. perceptual set.
c. cognitive dissonance.
d. confirmation bias.

25. When his car doesn't start, Maximillian checks the spark plugs first, since he did so the last several times the car would not start, and each time it enabled him to solve the problem. Now he checks the spark plugs because of:
a. confirmation bias.
b. the availability heuristic.
c. mental set.
d. prereflective judgment.

26. Dr. Hampton gives a lecture on responsible drinking at a college's orientation for first-year students, then he goes out and gets drunk with friends. The next day, one of his colleagues asks him how he can do these two things, and Dr. Hampton says that they offered him so much money to give the lecture that he could not turn it down. He believes this in order to reduce his:
a. cognitive dissonance.
b. mental set.
c. reflective judgment.
d. biopsychosocial discomfort.

27. Arnie works very hard on his poetry so that he can win the "poetry slam" competition. Dottie is a naturally gifted poet who writes her poems in a few minutes on the day of the competition. They tie for first place. According to cognitive dissonance theory, what will be their reactions?
a. Arnie will value winning more than Dottie will.
b. Dottie will value winning more than Arnie will.
c. Arnie will value winning more if he thinks Dottie is a better poet than he is.
d. Dottie will value winning more if she thinks that Arnie is a harder-working poet than she is.

28. Little two-year-old Kimery believes that the moon follows her when she is riding in the car. She is engaging in:
a. concrete operations.
b. assimilation.
c. her theory of mind.
d. egocentric thinking.

29. Dan wears his favorite sweater to class on test day and gets an "A" even though he didn't study very hard. He begins to call it his "lucky sweater" and wears it to every test, not seeming to notice it when he does poorly. Dan's persistent belief that his sweater is lucky is a result of:
a. the availability heuristic.
b. loss aversion.
c. confirmation bias.
d. cognitive dissonance.

30. The study of cognitive processes in nonhuman animals is called:
a. cognitive anthropomorphism.
b. comparative anthropocentrism.
c. cognitive ethology.
d. rational zoology.

True-False Self-Test

T   F   1.   Thinking can free a person from the immediate confines of the present.

T   F   2.   Symbols are a type of representational thought.

T   F   3.   Propositions are made up of schemas.

T   F   4.   Riding a bicycle is a subconscious process for most adults.

T   F   5.   Science makes extensive use of deductive reasoning.

T   F   6.   Most people cannot reason dialectically until their middle twenties.

T   F   7.   Creative thinking is strongly related to divergent thinking.

T   F   8.   Piaget's theory of cognitive development has never been challenged.

T   F   9.   One always changes one's schemas in the process of assimilation.

T   F   10.   Object permanence appears during the concrete operations stage.

T   F   11.   The biggest advances in the ability to grasp cause-and-effect relationships occur in the preoperational stage.

T   F   12.   Dialectical reasoning is only possible in the formal operations stage.

T   F   13.   Most 3- and 4-year-olds are capable of perspective taking.

T   F   14.   Many adults never reach the reflective reasoning stages.

T   F   15.   The quasi-reflective stage precedes the prereflective stage.

T   F   16.   Reflective judgment skills can be developed, to an extent, through education.

T   F   17.   Algorithms exist for most human problems.

T   F   18.   Cognitively, benefits and losses are usually viewed similarly.

T F 19. People tend to overestimate the likelihood of rare events when they hear about these events more often than they hear about commonplace events.

T F 20. Being able to explain the past leads one to overestimate the ability to predict the future.

T F 21. If a person behaves in ways that are inconsistent with personal values, cognitive dissonance will result.

T F 22. People are particularly motivated to reduce dissonance if they have not put much effort into a task.

T F 23. We often justify our effort by decreasing our liking for something we have worked hard to achieve.

T F 24. Cognitive biases diminish when people have expertise in what they are doing.

T F 25. Understanding a bias can help to reduce or eliminate it.

T F 26. Humans have sometimes been able to teach language to animals.

T F 27. Displacement is always present in a true language.

T F 28. Saying that your dog is in love with you is anthropocentric.

T F 29. A penguin is a prototypical bird.

T F 30. Intuition is a nonconscious process.

Key Terms

concept A mental category that groups objects, relations, activities, abstractions, or qualities having common properties.

basic concepts Concepts that have a moderate number of instances and that are easier to acquire than those having few or many instances.

prototype An especially representative example of a concept.

proposition A unit of meaning that is made up of concepts and expresses a unitary idea.

cognitive schema An integrated network of knowledge, beliefs, and expectations concerning a particular topic or aspect of the world.

mental image A mental representation that mirrors or resembles the thing it represents; mental images can occur in many and perhaps all sensory modalities.

subconscious processes Mental processes occurring outside of conscious awareness but accessible to consciousness when necessary.

nonconscious processes Mental processes occurring outside of and not available to conscious awareness.

reasoning The drawing of conclusions or inferences from observations, facts, or assumptions.

algorithm A problem-solving strategy guaranteed to produce a solution even if the user does not know how it works.

deductive reasoning A form of reasoning in which a conclusion follows necessarily from certain premises; if the premises are true, the conclusion must be true.

inductive reasoning A form of reasoning in which the premises provide support for a certain conclusion, but it is still possible for the conclusion to be false.

heuristic A rule of thumb that suggests a course of action or guides problem solving but does not guarantee an optimal solution.

dialectical reasoning A process in which opposing facts or ideas are weighed and compared, with a view to determining the best solution or resolving differences.

mental set A tendency to solve new problems using procedures that worked before on similar problems.

convergent thinking Thinking aimed at finding a single correct answer to a problem.

divergent thinking Mental exploration of unconventional alternatives in solving problems; by breaking mental sets, it tends to enhance creativity.

assimilation In Piaget's theory, the process of absorbing new information into existing cognitive structures.

accommodation In Piaget's theory, the process of modifying existing cognitive structures in response to experience and new information.

object permanence The understanding that an object continues to exist even when you cannot see or touch it.

operations In Piaget's theory, mental actions that are cognitively reversible.

egocentric thinking Seeing the world from only your own point of view; the inability to take another person's perspective.

conservation The understanding that the physical properties of objects -- such as the number of items in a cluster or the amount of liquid in a glass -- remain the same even when their form or appearance changes.

theory of mind A system of beliefs about the way your own mind and other people's minds work, and of how people are affected by their beliefs and feelings; it emerges at age 4 or 5.

hindsight bias The tendency to overestimate one's ability to have predicted an event once the outcome is known; the "I knew it all along" phenomenon.

availability heuristic The tendency to judge the probability of a type of event by how easy it is to think of examples or instances.

confirmation bias The tendency to look for or pay attention only to information that confirms one's own belief.

cognitive dissonance A state of tension that occurs when a person simultaneously holds two cognitions that are psychologically inconsistent, or when a person's belief is incongruent with his or her behavior.

justification of effort The tendency of individuals to increase their liking for something that they have worked hard or suffered to attain; a common form of dissonance reduction.

cognitive ethology The study of cognitive processes in nonhuman animals.

Suggested Research Projects

1. Collect one week's worth of "letters to the editor" from your local newspaper. Identify premises, conclusions, and biases. Construct counterarguments and make use of dialectical reasoning in evaluating the letter writers' claims.

2. You can illustrate the influences on creativity with a simple exercise. Take two groups of people and give them an idea-production task, such as generating a list of uses for a paper clip or planning a hypothetical vacation that can cost only a certain amount of money. Give them a time limit. In one group, try to create some of the conditions for creative thought that are described in your chapter. In the other group, try to undermine these factors. Which group produced the richer ideas? Which group produced the greater number of ideas?

Suggested Readings

Adams, J. (1991). *Conceptual blockbusting*. New York: Norton. A guide to creative problem solving.

Griffin, D. R. (1994). *Animal minds*. Chicago: University of Chicago Press. The author presents the case for a continuum of consciousness, with many non-human vertebrates showing parallels to human conscious function.

CHAPTER 8

Memory

Learning Objectives

After reading and studying this chapter, you should be able to:

1. Explain the concept of memory as a reconstructive process.

2. Discuss the relationship between reconstructed memories and eyewitness testimony.

3. Describe the various ways that psychologists measure memory.

4. Compare and contrast the various models of memory.

5. Define the three types of memory found in the three-box model.

6. Explain the organization of long-term memory.

7. Explain the serial position effect.

8. Describe some methods of improving memory.

9. Compare and contrast theories of forgetting.

10. Discuss the hypotheses about childhood amnesia.

11. Discuss the relationship between memory and narrative.

12. Discuss the advantages and disadvantages of the cognitive perspective.

Chapter Outline

I.   Reconstructing the Past

    A.   *Memory* refers to the capacity to retain and retrieve information, and to the structures that account for this capacity.
        1.   Memory confers competence and a sense of identity.
    B.   The Manufacture of Memory. Memory is not like a video camera. It is a reconstructive process.
        1.   **source amnesia** The inability to distinguish what you originally experienced from what you heard or were told.

C. The Fading Flashbulb. "Flashbulb memories" are vivid recollections of unusual events, but they are not always complete or accurate.
D. The Conditions of Confabulation. Because memory is reconstructive, it is subject to *confabulation* – confusing an event that happened to someone else with one that happened to you, or believing that you remember something that never happened. Confabulations are likely when:
1. You have thought about the imagined event many times.
2. The image of the event contains a lot of details.
3. The event is easy to imagine.
4. You focus on your emotional reactions to the event rather than on what actually happened.

II. Memory and the Power of Suggestion

A. The Eyewitness on Trial. Eyewitness testimony is not always reliable.
1. Errors are especially likely to occur when the suspect's ethnicity differs from that of the witness.
2. Accounts are influenced by leading questions, suggestive comments, and misleading information.
B. Children's Testimony.
1. There are two extreme views in the controversy about children reporting abuse:
a. Children always lie.
b. Children never lie.
2. Extremists on either side are wrong.
3. Research findings have demonstrated that children:
a. recollect accurately most of what they have observed or experienced.
b. will sometimes say something happened when it did not.
c. can be influenced to report an event in a certain way.
4. Children's suggestibility is influenced by:
a. age. Preschoolers' memories are more vulnerable to suggestion than school-aged children's or adults' memories.
d. pressure to conform to an interviewer's expectations.
C. Memory Under Hypnosis. **Hypnosis** is a procedure in which the practitioner suggests changes in the sensations, perceptions, thoughts, feelings, or behavior of the subject, who cooperates by altering his or her normal cognitive functioning accordingly.
1. Hypnosis has many uses in treating psychological and medical problems, but does not increase the accuracy of memory.
2. Under hypnosis, the tendency to confuse fact and speculation is increased by a desire to please the hypnotist and by the hypnotist's encouragement of fantasy and reporting of detailed images.
3. Hypnosis boosts the amount of information recalled, but also the amount of errors.
4. Hypnosis cannot be used to produce a re-experience of long-ago events.

III.   In Pursuit of Memory

    A. Measuring Memory. **Explicit memory** is conscious, intentional recollection of an event or an item of information. It is measured by:

        1. **recall** The ability to retrieve and reproduce from memory previously encountered material.

        2. **recognition** The ability to identify previously encountered material. Recognition is superior to recall.

    B. **Implicit memory** is unconscious retention in memory, as evidenced by the effect of a previous experience or previously encountered information on current thoughts or actions. It is measured by:

        1. **priming**, a method for measuring implicit memory in which a person reads or listens to information and is later tested to see whether the information affects performance on another type of task.

        2. **relearning method**, a method for measuring retention that compares the time required to relearn material with the time used in the initial learning of the material.

IV.   Models of Memory

    A. The information-processing model likens the mind to a highly complex computer.

        1. Information-processing models include:

            a. Encoding: the conversion of information into a form that can be received by the brain.

            b. Storing the material over time.

            c. Retrieving or recovering stored material.

        2. In storage, information may be represented as *cognitive schemas* – mental networks of knowledge, beliefs, or expectations.

        3. In most information-processing models, storage takes place in three systems:

            a. *sensory memory*, which retains incoming sensory information for a second or two.

            b. *short-term memory*, which holds a limited amount of information for a brief period.

            c. *long-term memory*, storage for up to decades.

    B. **Parallel distributed processing (PDP)** is an alternative to the information-processing model of memory, in which knowledge is represented as connections among thousands of interacting processing units, distributed in a vast network and all operating in parallel. It is also referred to as *connectionist* model.

V. The Three-Box Model of Memory

    A. **Sensory memory** is a memory system that momentarily preserves extremely accurate images of sensory information. It is the entryway of memory.

        1. Visual images (icons) remain for up to half a second in a visual subsystem.

        2. Auditory images remain in an auditory subsystem for up to a second or two.

        3. **Pattern recognition** is the identification of a stimulus on the basis of information already contained in long-term memory. It occurs during the transfer from sensory to short-term memory.

    B. Short-term Memory: Memory's Scratch Pad. **Short-term memory (STM)** is a limited-capacity memory system involved in the retention of information for brief periods; it is also used to hold information retrieved from long-term memory for temporary use.

        1. Information not transferred from STM to long-term memory is lost.

        2. Because it holds information from long-term memory for temporary use, STM is also known as *working memory*.

        3. Estimates of the capacity of STM range from 2 to 20 items.

        4. A **chunk** is a meaningful unit of information; it may be composed of smaller units. Grouping items into chunks increases the capacity of STM.

    C. Long-term memory: Final Destination. **Long-term memory** (LTM) is the memory system involved in the long-term storage of information. There appears to be no practical limit to the capacity of LTM.

        1. Organization in Long-term Memory. Information is organized by:

            a. *semantic categories*.

            b. **network models**, models of long-term memory that represent its contents as a vast network of interrelated concepts and propositions.

            c. the way that words sound or look. *Tip-of-the-tongue (TOT)* states are examples of this kind of organization.

            d. familiarity, relevance, or association with other information.

        2. The Contents of Long-term Memory.

            a. **Procedural memories** are memories for the performance of actions or skills ("knowing how").

            b. **Declarative memories** are memories of facts, rules, concepts, and events ("knowing that"); they include:

                i. **semantic memories**, memories of general knowledge, including facts, rules, concepts, and propositions.

                ii. **episodic memories**, memories for personally experienced events and the contexts in which they occurred.

3. From Short-term to Long-term Memory: A Riddle. The three-box model can account for the **serial position effect** -- the tendency for recall of the first and last items on a list to surpass recall of items in the middle of the list.
   a. The *primacy effect* (better recall for items at the beginning of the list) may be due to the "emptiness" of STM, which makes transfer to LTM easier for early items.
   b. The *recency effect* (better recall for items at the end of the list) may be due to items remaining in STM at recall.
   c. However, recency is still seen when testing occurs later.

VI. How We Remember

A. Effective Encoding. Some encoding takes place automatically; other information requires *effortful encoding*. For the latter, you should:
   1. select the main points.
   2. label concepts.
   3. associate the information with personal experiences or with material you already know.
   4. rehearse the information until it is familiar.
B. *Rehearsal* is the review or practice of material.
   1. **Maintenance rehearsal** is rote repetition of material in order to maintain its availability in memory. It usually only maintains information in STM.
   2. **Elaborative rehearsal** is the association of new information with already stored knowledge and analysis of the new information to make it memorable. It is also called *elaboration of encoding*.
   3. **Deep processing** is the processing of meaning, rather than simply the physical or sensory features of a stimulus.
C. **Mnemonics** are strategies and tricks for improving memory, such as the use of a verse or formula.
   1. Mnemonics can be easily memorized rhymes, formulas, visual images, word associations, chunking strategies, or stories to help make the material more meaningful.
D. To improve memory:
   1. encode elaborately.
   2. use distributed instead of massed learning sessions.
   3. monitor your learning.
   4. overlearn the material.

VII. Why We Forget

A. Decay. The **decay theory** is the theory that information in memory eventually disappears if it is not accessed; it applies more to short-term than to long-term memory.
B. Replacement. Another theory holds that new information entering memory can wipe out old information.

C. Interference. Interference theory holds that similar items of information interfere with one another in storage or retrieval.
   1. **Retroactive interference** is forgetting that occurs when recently learned material interferes with the ability to remember similar material stored previously.
   2. **Proactive interference** is forgetting that occurs when previously stored material interferes with the ability to remember similar, more recently learned material.
D. **Cue-dependent forgetting** is the inability to retrieve information stored in memory because of insufficient cues for recall.
   1. A mental or physical state can act as a retrieval cue. **State-dependent memory** is the tendency to remember something when the rememberer is in the same physical or mental state as during the original learning or experience.
E. **Psychogenic amnesia** occurs when no organic causes are present and there is a partial or complete loss of memory for threatening information or traumatic experiences.
   1. The psychodynamic view is that this material is *repressed* and can be retrieved when the anxiety associated with the memory is removed.
   2. However, traumatic events are more likely to be remembered than forgotten.

VIII. Autobiographical Memories

A. Childhood Amnesia: The Missing Years. **Childhood (infantile) amnesia** is the inability to remember events and experiences that occurred in the first two or three years of life. Freud thought that this was another instance of repression. Cognitive explanations include:
   1. Lack of a sense of self. Cognitive self-recognition may be necessary for the establishment of autobiographical memory.
   2. Impoverished encoding.
   3. A focus on the routine by children.
   4. Different ways of thinking about the world. Later schemas may not be useful for reconstruction of early events.
B. Memory and Narrative: The Stories of Our Lives
   1. Narratives (stories) provide unifying themes to organize and give meaning to life events.
   2. Narratives rely on memory, but also on interpretation and imagination.
   3. Old people remember more from adolescence and early adulthood than from midlife, a phenomenon known as *reminiscence bump*.

IX. Memories and Myths

A. Memories are subject to distortion, and a person's confidence in his or her memory is not a good guide to its accuracy.

B.   People can and do forget troubling memories, which can return.

X.   Essay Three: Evaluating the Cognitive Perspective

A.   Contributions of This Perspective. Cognitive research has produced:
1.   innovative methods for exploring the "black box" of the mind.
2.   an understanding of how cognition affects behavior and emotion.
3.   findings of tremendous social and legal relevance.
4.   strategies for improving mental abilities from infancy to old age.
B.   Misuses and Misunderstandings of This Perspective. Critics of the cognitive perspective argue that the cognitive perspective relies on metaphor for models of the mind. Misuses of this perspective include:
1.   Cognitive reductionism, the tendency to reduce all behavior to mental processes.
2.   Errors of cause and effect that occur when people overlook the fact that the mind and the body, thoughts and circumstances, interact.
3.   Cognitive relativism, the assumption that all thoughts, memories, and ideas should be taken equally seriously.

Chapter Summary

While it is common to think of memory as functioning like a tape recorder, research has demonstrated that memory is a 1._____ process. People alter incoming information in order to make sense of it, and they cannot separate the original experience from the added information. 2._____ amnesia is the inability to distinguish original experiences from what you heard or were told.

Most people report that they have very vivid memories of some events, but even these so-called 3._____ memories are subject to distortion. Because memory is reconstructive, it is subject to 4._____, confusing an event that happened to someone else with what happened to you, or believing that you remember something that never happened.

Eyewitness testimony is not always reliable. Errors are especially likely when the witness is of a different 5._____ than the suspect. Our reconstructions of past events are also influenced by the manner in which we are questioned about them. Children's memories of abuse have aroused great controversy. Research has revealed that these memories are neither always reliable or always wrong and children's suggestibility is influenced by age and interviewer pressure.

6._____ is a procedure where a practitioner suggests changes in psychological processes to a cooperative subject. While it has been helpful in treating some psychological or medical problems, it does not increase the accuracy of memory.

If we want to test for conscious memory of an event or item of information, called 7._____ memory, we can either ask the person to recall the information, or we can have them identify the information in a 8._____ task. Recall is usually more difficult.

Some material is stored outside of conscious awareness in 9._____ memory. Assessing this kind of memory sometimes involves measuring how fast the person learns the material a second or third time. This technique is known as the 10._____ method. We can also measure this same type of memory through 11._____, in which a person has an opportunity to make responses in the form of implicitly memorized material.

Some cognitive psychologists liken the memory system to the functioning of a computer. These 12._____ models depict memory in terms of inputs and outputs, and organizing of information. In these models, the first process of memory is 13._____, in which incoming information is converted into a form that the brain can process and store. Next comes the process of 14._____, which allows the material to be maintained over time. Finally, memories are recovered through the process of 15._____.

When information is first encountered, it is stored for a very brief period of time in 16._____ memory. Then, some of this material may be processed further in 17._____ memory for a short time. This is also called 18._____ memory because it is the site of information retrieved for temporary use from relatively permanent memory. Information that makes its way into 19._____ memory may be maintained indefinitely, and there appears to be no practical limit to the amount of material that can be stored here.

The computer model of memory is useful, but its critics have noted that the brain has pattern recognition functions that are far more sophisticated than those of any computer. Some cognitive scientists use a 20._____ processing, or connectionist, model, which depicts the system as a neural net of interconnected processing units.

According to the information-processing, or three-box, model, information from sensory memory is first transferred to short-term memory (STM). This material can be maintained through rehearsal, and either transfers to long-term memory (LTM) or decays and is lost. The capacity of STM has usually been reported as 7 items plus or minus 2. However, estimates range from 2 to 20 items. STM can be enlarged if one groups items into bigger units called 21._____.

Items in STM that are meaningful in some way enter LTM relatively easily. LTM is organized and indexed. Most theorists describe several different kinds of information. 22._____ memories are memories for the performance of actions or skills. Specific pieces of information, such as facts and events, are stored in 23._____ memory, which has two types, 24._____ (general knowledge), and 25._____ (internal representations of personally experienced events).

When given a list of things to remember, people tend to remember the items that are presented at the beginning and the end of the list, a phenomenon called the 26._____ effect. Theoretically, the 27._____ effect (the tendency to recall early items) is due to STM being empty at the beginning of the task. The 28._____ effect (the tendency to recall later items) may be due to the presence of these items remaining in STM at the time of the recall. However, this effect persists even if the recall task is not undertaken immediately.

Long-term retention of material usually requires review and practice of information. There are two strategies used in this process. 29._____ involves rote repetition of the material. 30._____, a more effective strategy, involves relating the new material to information that is already stored in LTM. Deep processing refers to internalizing the meaning, not just the content, of materials.

31._____ are formal devices for encoding, storing, and retaining information. They often include chunking or strategies that make the material more meaningful. It is also helpful to encode elaborately, to use distributed instead of 32._____ learning sessions, and to make use of 33._____, which involves continuing to study material that has already been learned.

There are several different theories of forgetting. The 34._____ theory is that material that is not used merely fades away. 35._____ theory holds that some items impede the retention of others. When new information gets in the way of one's ability to recall old information, the interference is termed 36._____. 37._____ interference occurs when old information inhibits the ability to remember new material. A very common type of forgetting is 38._____ forgetting, in which contextual cues from the original learning situation are no longer present to aid us in retrieving the specific information we are looking for. When the retrieval cue is one's mood or physical state, the memory is said to be 39._____. At other times, memories for traumatic events may be lost, a phenomenon called 40._____ amnesia.

Theories of memory and forgetting have been applied to 41._____, the inability to recall information from the first few years of life. Freud believed that this phenomenon is due to repression, but cognitive scientists tend to emphasize the theoretical necessity of a cognitive sense of self for the formation of autobiographical types of memory. Others believe that early childhood information-processing strategies may be so markedly different from later ones that no recall cues exist.

We are frequently telling stories to ourselves and others, and these narratives provide unifying themes to organize, interpret, and give meaning to our memories. One interesting phenomenon is 42._____, the tendency for old people to remember more from adolescence and early adulthood than from midlife. All memories are subject to distortion, and a person's confidence in his or her memory is not a good guide to its accuracy. Sometimes people forget troubling memories that may return later in their lives.

Like all other viewpoints, the cognitive perspective has its critics. One major objection is that cognitive models of the mind are all based on 43._____, like computers and memory boxes, without enough attention to empirical validation of these models. On the positive side, cognitive findings have given us innovative approaches to exploring the "black box" of the mind, an understanding of how cognition affects behavior, and strategies for improving mental abilities.

The cognitive perspective can also be misunderstood and misused. One of the greatest dangers is cognitive 44._____, the tendency to see all behavior as being caused only by cognitive factors. Because cognitive research has produced powerful findings, there is also a tendency to make errors about cause and effect. And because cognitive research has demonstrated that emotional factors influence one's acceptance or rejection of arguments, there is the danger of cognitive 45._____, which involves failing to think critically and seeing two sides of any argument as having equal merit.

Multiple Choice Self-Test

1.   Mr. T. believes that he won a ukelele playing contest at age 6. Actually, he came in fourth, but he heard his parents tell their friends that he won so many times that he incorrectly remembers winning. His memory distortion is called:
a.   source amnesia.
b.   storage inhibition.
c.   proactive interference.
d.   childhood amnesia.

2.   Research on memory indicates that the process of storing and recalling information is essentially:
a.   reconstructive.
b.   iconic.
c.   undistorted.
d.   empirical.

3.   Memories that are produced through age regression hypnosis can best be understood as:
a.   accurate reproductions of childhood events.
b.   imagination.
c.   distorted reproductions of childhood events.
d.   willful fabrication.

4.   Dejuan can name all fifty state capitols in alphabetical order. This information is stored in:
a.   procedural memory.
b.   implicit memory.
c.   explicit memory.
d.   priming.

5. "Flashbulb" memories:
a. are highly accurate.
b. are always distorted.
c. are sometimes distorted.
d. rarely involve emotion-arousing events.

6. One can test for explicit memory through:
a. recall and recognition.
b. relearning and priming.
c. relearning and recognition.
d. recall and priming.

7. Abby gets hundreds of letters a day. The 25th letter she read yesterday was about disreputable dog groomers. Although she had no recollection of the letter, she found herself bringing up the subject of disreputable dog groomers yesterday at lunch, probably because of:
a. the serial position effect.
b. implicit memory.
c. retroactive interference.
d. explicit memory.

8. The view of the mind as a computer is most popular in the:
a. neural net model.
b. information-processing model.
c. data-entry model.
d. parallel distributed processing model.

9. Eddie is able to remember the names of the Great Lakes by remembering that the word "homes" contains the first letter of each lake. This strategy is a:
a. mnemonic device.
b. pneumatic device.
c. automatic device.
d. autonomic device.

10. Leigh stops at a phone booth to call a friend, looks up the friend's phone number in the telephone book, closes the book, and makes the call, but her friend's line is busy. Leigh will probably have to look up the number again if she tries to call again after a minute or two because of:
a. the limits of sensory memory.
b. proactive interference.
c. the limits of short-term memory.
d. parallel distributed processing.

11. Estelle sees her friend across a crowded room and instantly recognizes her friend's face. This recognition occurs:
a. in sensory memory.
b. in short-term memory.
c. during the transfer of information from short-term memory to long-term memory.
d. during the transfer of information from sensory memory to long-term memory.

12. Cathy is going grocery shopping. She remembers that she wants to buy figs, bread, and ice by remembering the word "FBI." She has combined her three items of memory into one:
a. icon.
b. sensory unit.
c. working memory.
d. chunk.

13. Long-term memory is best described as a(n):
a. warehouse with many boxes.
b. elaborate network.
c. semantic web.
d. pile of collected items.

14. Declarative memories include:
a. procedural and semantic memories.
b. procedural and episodic memories.
c. semantic and episodic memories.
d. procedural, semantic, and episodic memories.

15. George has listed 9 errands that he needs to complete during the day, but he leaves the list on his desk when he leaves the house. He decides to do the errands from memory. Which item is he most likely to forget?
a. the fourth item
b. the second item
c. the eighth item
d. the ninth item

16. Theorists usually account for the recency effect by saying that recently presented items are more easily remembered because they remain in short-term memory during recall. What finding disputes this suggestion?
a. The primacy effect is more powerful than the recency effect.
b. Items in the middle of the list are more easily recalled than items at the end of the list.
c. Recent studies have shown that the recency effect does not really exist.
d. The recency effect is seen even when the recall task takes place much later.

17. In studying for her anatomy test, Kim forms an image of a hippopotamus going to college in order to remember that the hippocampus is the site of learning and memory. Her study strategy makes use of:
a. elaborative rehearsal.
b. maintenance rehearsal.
c. the absurdity principle.
d. deep processing.

18. Morris is a golfer who is excellent at the putting part of the game. However, he practices his putting every day in order to make use of:
a. elaborative rehearsal.
b. deep processing.
c. overlearning.
d. procedural overestablishment.

19. The capacity of short-term memory is:
a. 4 items.
b. 7 items, plus or minus 2.
c. 2-20 items.
d. virtually limitless.

20. Matt has moved 12 times in the past 15 years. He cannot remember most of the addresses or phone numbers from his old residences because he has not had to use them in some time. Therefore, they have most likely been forgotten because of:
a. proactive interference.
b. motivated forgetting.
c. retroactive interference.
d. decay.

21. Dana loves to play racquetball in the winter and tennis in the summer. Although she is an excellent racquetball player, the first time she plays racquetball each year, she makes frequent shots to a point about two and a half feet up the wall (which makes for a very bad racquetball shot). She never had this problem until she started playing tennis in the summertime. The failure of Dana's procedural memory in racquetball is most likely due to:
a. decay.
b. proactive interference.
c. retroactive interference.
d. neural volley.

22. Anita always drinks three cups of coffee before her 8 a.m. class. On the day of the test, she oversleeps a little, has no time for coffee, and barely makes it to class. She does poorly on the test, but curiously remembers a good deal of the information when she is having coffee after the test is over. Apparently, her memory was:
a. state-dependent.
b. overgeneralized.
c. anterograde.
d. retroactive.

23. Some colleges require students to take final exams in different classrooms rather than in the rooms in which their classes were held the entire term. This practice should result in:
a. improved exam performance.
b. increased cue-dependent forgetting.
c. decreased state-dependent memory.
d. no difference in exam performance.

24. To say that a person is angry only because he or she interprets an event as disrespectful to the self reflects:
a. cognitive reductionism.
b. the biopsychosocial model.
c. cognitive relativism.
d. logical reasoning.

25. Frank believes that the 1986 space shuttle disaster never really happened, that it was staged in order to deflect attention away from President Reagan. His position is absurd since a hoax of this magnitude could never be perpetrated, but Frank argues by proposing a large number of hypothetical events that are so unlikely as to be nearly impossible. His friend Ernest accepts Frank's position because he knows of other cases where a person who was telling the truth was not believed. Ernest has committed the error of:
a. cognitive reductionism.
b. confusion of cause and effect.
c. cognitive relativism.
d. cognitive discursive bias.

26. Eighty year old Mabel can tell elaborate stories about her high school days but can't seem to recall much about her 50s. This phenomenon is:
a. midlife amnestic disorder.
b. reminiscence bump.
c. the recency effect.
d. narrative storage selectivity.

27. Sol thinks that he got a school perfect-attendance award in the third grade, when actually it was his childhood friend, Greta. Sol's distortion is called:
a. interference.
b. psychogenic amnesis.
c. overlearning.
d. confabulation.

28. Dr. Kovaleski sees a robbery when he stops at his local convenience store. He gets a good look at the robber and is later asked to identify this perpetrator in a lineup. Under what circumstances is Dr. Kovaleski most likely to make an error in identifying the robber?
a. the robber is much shorter than Dr. Kovaleski.
b. Dr. Kovaleski rehearsed his image of the robber before the lineup.
c. the robber and Dr. Kovaleski are of very different ethnicities.
d. the robber is a woman.

29. Criticisms of the cognitive include all of the following EXCEPT:
a. findings from cognitive psychology have yielded little useful information.
b. cognitive psychology relies too heavily on metaphor.
c. all thoughts and opinions are not equally valid.
d. cognitive psychologists sometimes confuse cause and effect.

30. Elijah can't remember any of the Spanish he learned because he hasn't spoken Spanish in 20 years. His forgetting is due to:
a. delay.
b. proactive interference.
c. retroactive interference.
d. parallel distributed processing.

True-False Self-Test

T   F   1.   Memory operates like a tape recorder.

T   F   2.   Source amnesia often arises from psychological trauma.

T   F   3.   Hypnosis is a reliable method of recovering lost memories from early childhood.

T   F   4.   Flashbulb memories are not always accurate.

T   F   5.   People alter information as it is being stored in memory.

T   F   6.   Cognitive schemas affect memory.

T   F   7.   Answers to trivia questions are stored in implicit memory.

T   F   8.   One way of testing implicit memory is through priming.

T   F   9.   One can assess explicit memory with recall tasks.

T   F   10.   The information-processing model of memory emphasizes networks of association.

T   F   11.   The capacity of long-term memory is virtually limitless.

T   F   12.   The parallel distributed processing model holds that knowledge is represented in relatively distinct procedural, semantic, and episodic forms.

T   F   13.   Sensory memory is the entryway to memory.

T   F   14.   A good deal of material in short-term memory decays and is quickly lost.

T   F   15.   The construction of chunks increases the capacity of short-term memory.

T   F   16.   It is easier to remember words from the middle of a list than from either the beginning or the end of a list.

T   F   17.   Maintenance rehearsal is the most effective learning method.

T   F   18.   Mnemonics usually involve deep processing.

T   F   19.   Most forgetting occurs soon after the initial learning.

T   F   20.   Cue-dependent forgetting is relatively common.

T   F   21.   Emotional states sometimes provide recall cues.

T   F   22.   Cognitive theory holds that childhood amnesia may be the result of infants' undeveloped cognitive sense of self.

T   F   23.   To give both sides of an argument equal merit is to commit the error of cognitive reductionism.

T   F   24.   One important critical thinking skill to build in students is cognitive relativism.

T   F   25.   Confabulation sometimes occurs because memory is reconstructive.

T   F   26.   Chunking is a powerful memory tool.

T   F   27.   Cognitive psychology emphasizes the role of interpretations in emotional reactions.

T   F   28.   Eyewitness testimony can be strongly influenced by the use of leading questions.

T   F   29.   Children are more likely to make false reports of abuse if they think that the adult questioning them wants to hear these reports.

T   F   30.   Emotional intensity may cause a child to confuse reality and fantasy.

Key Terms

source amnesia The inability to distinguish what you originally experienced from what you heard or were told.

hypnosis A procedure in which the practitioner suggests changes in the sensations, perceptions, thoughts, feelings, or behavior of the subject, who cooperates by altering his or her normal cognitive functioning accordingly.

explicit memory Conscious, intentional recollection of an event or an item of information.

recall The ability to retrieve and reproduce from memory previously encountered material.

recognition The ability to identify previously encountered material.

implicit memory Unconscious retention in memory, as evidenced by the effect of a previous experience or previously encountered information on current thoughts or actions.

priming A method for measuring implicit memory in which a person reads or listens to information and is later tested to see whether the information affects performance on another type of task.

relearning method A method for measuring retention that compares the time required to relearn material with the time used in the initial learning of the material.

parallel distributed processing (PDP) An alternative to the information-processing model of memory, in which knowledge is represented as connections among thousands of interacting processing units, distributed in a vast network and all operating in parallel.

sensory memory A memory system that momentarily preserves extremely accurate images of sensory information.

pattern recognition The identification of a stimulus on the basis of information already contained in long-term memory.

short-term memory (STM) In the three-box model of memory, a limited-capacity memory system involved in the retention of information for brief periods; it is also used to hold information retrieved from long-term memory for temporary use.

chunk A meaningful unit of information; it may be composed of smaller units.

long-term memory (LTM) In the three-box model of memory, the memory system involved in the long-term storage of information.

network models Models of long-term memory that represent its contents as a vast network of interrelated concepts and propositions.

procedural memories Memories for the performance of actions or skills ("knowing how").

declarative memories Memories of facts, rules, concepts, and events ("knowing that"); they include semantic and episodic memories.

semantic memories Memories of general knowledge, including facts, rules, concepts, and propositions.

episodic memories Memories for personally experienced events and the contexts in which they occurred.

serial position effect The tendency for recall of the first and last items on a list to surpass recall of items in the middle of the list.

maintenance rehearsal Rote repetition of material in order to maintain its availability in memory.

elaborative rehearsal The association of new information with already stored knowledge and analysis of the new information to make it memorable.

deep processing In the encoding of information, the processing of meaning, rather than simply the physical or sensory features of a stimulus.

mnemonics Strategies and tricks for improving memory, such as the use of a verse or formula.

149

decay theory The theory that information in memory eventually disappears if it is not accessed; it applies more to short-term than to long-term memory.

retroactive interference Forgetting that occurs when recently learned material interferes with the ability to remember similar material stored previously.

proactive interference Forgetting that occurs when previously stored material interferes with the ability to remember similar, more recently learned material.

cue-dependent forgetting The inability to retrieve information stored in memory because of insufficient cues for recall.

state-dependent memory The tendency to remember something when the rememberer is in the same physical or mental state as during the original learning or experience.

amnesia (psychogenic) When no organic causes are present, the partial or complete loss of memory for threatening information or traumatic experiences.

childhood (infantile) amnesia The inability to remember events and experiences that occurred in the first two or three years of life.

Suggested Research Projects

1.   Ask some family members or friends to write detailed accounts of some event that was mutually experienced. Look for discrepancies in the accounts.

2.   Keep a "forgetting and remembering" journal for several weeks. Write down instances in which you have forgotten something and try to discover any memory principles that might be involved, such as the serial position effect or retroactive interference. You should also write down unusual instances of remembering, like suddenly remembering a school classmate whom you had long forgotten. Try to explain the sudden remembering with memory principles, such as contextual cuing.
    (Source: Terry, W.S. (1984). A "forgetting journal" for memory courses. *Teaching of Psychology, 11*, 111-112.)

Suggested Readings

Anderson, J. R. (2000). *Learning and memory: An integrated approach*. New York: Wiley. A description of the interactions between what we learn and what we remember.

Samuel, D. (1999). *Memory: How we use it, lose it, and can improve it*. New York: NYU Press. An integration of memory theory with practical applications for improving one's memory.

CHAPTER 9

The Social Context

Learning Objectives

After reading and studying this chapter, you should be able to:

1.   Describe the field of social psychology.

2.   Discuss research findings on the power of social roles.

3.   Describe the effects of the presence or absence of social groups on conformity and groupthink.

4.   Explain the social factors that decrease an individual's sense of responsibility.

5.   Describe the conditions under which independent action is most likely to take place.

6.   Discuss attribution theory and the research surrounding it.

7.   Compare and contrast friendly and coercive persuasion.

8.   Summarize the important research on work motivation.

9.   Compare and contrast the effects of cooperative and competitive situations.

Chapter Outline

I.   Roles and Rules

    A.   **Social norms** are rules that regulate human life, including social conventions, explicit laws and implicit cultural standards.

    B.   A Social **role** is a given social position that is governed by a set of norms for proper behavior.

        1.   Role behavior is regulated by norms and sometimes laws.

        2.   Role violation often carries penalties.

        3.   Gender roles contain different norms for women than for men, however the requirements of social roles can change with changing social and economic conditions.

        4.   Role requirements can cause a person to behave in ways that violate personal standards.

    C.   The Obedience Study. Milgram's study illustrates the power of roles.

1. Subjects were led to believe that they were inflicting painful and perhaps fatal electric shocks.
2. About 2/3 of subjects delivered the highest shock level at the urgings of the experimenter, who was in the role of authority.
3. Subjects were more likely to disobey the experimenter:
   a. when the experimenter left the room.
   b. when the victim was right there in the room.
   c. when two experimenters issued conflicting demands.
   d. when the person ordering them on was an ordinary man.
   e. when the subject worked with peers who refused to go further.
4. Milgram's experiment demonstrated that aggressive behavior may sometimes lie more in the role than the person.
5. Criticisms of Milgram's experiment – some critics believe that:
   a. it is unethical to put subjects into a position where they might suffer emotional pain.
   b. certain personality traits, like hostility and rigidity, increase obedience to authority.
   c. Milgram's comparison of the study's participants to Nazis is not warranted.

D. The Prison Study. Haney, Banks, and Zimbardo's experiment assigned roles of prisoner and guard to college students:
   1. "Prisoners" developed negative emotional and physical reactions.
   2. Some "guards" became sadistic.
   3. The experiment has been criticized as unscientific. Haney and Zimbardo contend that it contributes to the understanding of real prisoners and guards.

E. The Power of Roles. Demands for obedience can be dangerous. People follow orders when they would rather not because of the following factors:
   1. Having a strong respect for authority.
   2. Routinizing the task.
   3. Wanting to be polite.
   4. Becoming entrapped. **Entrapment** is a gradual process in which individuals escalate their commitment to a course of action to justify their investment of time, money, or effort.

II. Individuals in Groups

A. Group Pressures.
   1. Conformity is taking action or adopting attitudes under real or perceived group pressure. Asch conducted experiments in which confederates made incorrect judgments about the length of lines.
      a. Only 20% of subjects were independent on every trial.
      b. 1/3 of subjects conformed over half the time.
      c. Conformity reflects cultural norms.
      d. Reasons for conformity include:
         i. identification with the group.

ii.   a wish to be liked.

iii.   belief that the group is more knowledgeable than the self.

iv.   desire for personal gain or avoidance of loss.

v.   Some groups' low tolerance for nonconformity.

2.   **Groupthink** is the tendency in close-knit groups for all members to think alike for the sake of harmony and to suppress dissent. Symptoms of groupthink include:

    a.   an illusion of invulnerability.

    b.   self-censorship.

    c.   direct pressure on dissenters to conform.

    d.   an illusion of unanimity.

3.   Features of groups that are vulnerable to groupthink:

    a.   members' feeling that they are part of a tightly connected team.

    b.   feelings of being under pressure from outside forces.

    c.   Presence of a strong, directive leader.

4.   Groupthink can be counteracted by encouraging the expression of doubt and dissent by group members.

D.   Peers have powerful influences on behavior. Children's behavior can depend critically on situations.

1.   Peer acceptance is critically important to most children. Peer rejection is traumatic.

2.   Peer support for academic achievement may be a factor in average differences in test scores among ethnicities.

3.   Peer group identification is essential for survival of the next generation.

4.   Ages 16-24 are critical for the formation of *generational identity*.

E.   The Anonymous Crowd. **Diffusion of responsibility** is the tendency of members in organized or anonymous groups to avoid taking responsibility for actions or decisions because they assume that others will do so.

1.   *Bystander apathy* reflects diffusion of responsibility.

2.   In work settings, *social loafing,* doing less than one's share of a group's work, is encouraged by situations in which:

    a.   individuals are not held accountable for the work they do.

    b.   people feel that hard work will duplicate other's efforts.

    c.   workers feel that others are getting a "free ride."

    d.   the work is uninteresting.

3.   Social loafing is decreased when:

    a.   job challenge is increased.

    b.   each group member has a different and important job.

4.   Conformity can induce people to take part in either collective violence or collective kindness.

5.   In extreme cases of diffusion of responsibility, people can experience deindividuation, in which they lose their sense of individuality.

       a.   In some legal cases, there have been arguments that people should be held less responsible for their crimes because of deindividuation.

F.   The Conditions of Independent Action. Dissent and *altruism*, the willingness to take selfless or dangerous action on behalf of others are in part a consequence of deeply held moral values and conscience. Also affecting these decisions are situational influences such as when:

1.   the situation increases the chances that you will perceive the need for intervention or help.

2.   the situation makes it more likely that you will take responsibility.

3.   the cost benefit ratio supports your decision to get involved.

4.   you have an ally.

5.   you become entrapped.

III.   Social Influences on Beliefs

A.   **Social cognition** is an area in social psychology concerned with social influences on thought, memory, perception, and other cognitive processes.

B.   Attributions. **Attribution theory** is the theory that people are motivated to explain their own and others' behavior by attributing causes of that behavior to a situation or disposition.

1.   A *situational attribution* identifies the cause of the action as something in the situation or the environment.

2.   A *dispositional attribution* identifies the cause of the action as something in the person.

3.   The **fundamental attribution error** is the tendency, in explaining other people's behavior, to overestimate personality factors and underestimate the influence of the situation.

4.   People are likely to overlook situational attributions when:

       a.   they are in a good mood and not likely to think about people's motives critically.

       b.   they are distracted and preoccupied.

5.   The fundamental attribution error is more common in Western, individualistic cultures than in cultures with more of a group orientation.

6.   When it comes to explaining one's own behavior, people often reveal the **self-serving bias**, the tendency, in explaining one's own behavior, to take credit for one's good actions and rationalize one's mistakes.

7.   Attributions are also affected by the **just-world hypothesis**, the notion that many people need to believe that the world is fair and justice is served; that bad people are punished and good people rewarded.

8.   Happy couples tend to make situational attributions for partners' lapses and dispositional attributions for positive behaviors;

unhappy couples do the opposite. But attributions can change over time.
    C.   Processes of Persuasion: Friendly Techniques.
        1.   The **validity effect** is the tendency of people to believe that a statement is true or valid simply because it has been repeated many times.
        2.   Attractiveness of the communicator increases acceptance.
        3.   Fear can cause people to resist arguments that are in their own best interest. Fear increases acceptance only if it is moderate and accompanied by information about how to avoid danger.
    D.   Coercive Techniques. Persuasion techniques become coercive when they suppress and individual's ability to reason, think critically, and make personal choices in his or her best interest. The key processes in *coercive persuasion* (sometimes called *brainwashing*) are:
        1.   the person is put under physical or emotional distress.
        2.   the person's problems are reduced to one simple explanation, which is repeatedly emphasized.
        3.   the leader offers unconditional love, acceptance, and attention.
        4.   a new identity based on the group is created.
        5.   the person is subjected to entrapment.
        6.   the person's access to information is severely controlled.

IV.   Social Influences on Motivation

    A.   McClelland and associates speculated that some people have a **need for achievement**, a learned motive to meet personal standards of success and excellence in a chosen area (abbreviated *nAch*).
        1.   McClelland used the **Thematic Apperception Test (TAT)** a personality test that asks respondents to interpret a series of drawings showing ambiguous scenes of people, scored for various motives such as the needs for achievement, affiliation, or power.
        2.   People with high nAch:
            a.   tell stories about working hard.
            b.   foresee devastation if they are unsuccessful.
            c.   are more likely to start their own businesses.
            d.   set high personal standards.
            e.   prefer to work with capable colleagues rather than with people who are merely friendly.
        3.   Many psychologists have criticized the idea that achievement depends entirely on achievement motive. Type and conditions of work are also important factors.
    B.   The Conditions of Work. Motivation to work is highest when:
        1.   the work provides a sense of meaningfulness.
        2.   employees have control over many aspects of their work.
        3.   tasks are varied rather than repetitive.
        4.   the company maintains clear and consistent rules.
        5.   employees have supportive relationships at work.

6.   employees receive useful feedback about their work.
7.   the company offers opportunities for employees' growth and development.

C.   Other effects on motivation:
1.   Work motivation is not related to money, but is related to *incentive pay*.
2.   When the proportion of men and women in an occupation changes, so does motivation. As job segregation changes, so do motivations.
3.   When people have few opportunities to advance, they tend to emphasize motivations other than achievement.
4.   Most companies have a "glass ceiling" that prevents minorities and women from advancing beyond a certain level.

D.   Competition and Cooperation
1.   Competition:
a.   often decreases work motivation.
b.   causes insecurity and anxiety.
c.   causes jealousy and hostility.
d.   can have a negative effect on achievement.
2.   Cooperation is built by promoting interdependence in reaching mutual goals; it is associated with:
a.   liking others in the group and cooperating groups.
b.   higher motivation, performance, and achievement.
c.   better problem solving, satisfaction, and participation.
3.   Motivation and reduced risk of groupthink are associated with:
a.   clarity of purpose.
b.   member's autonomy.
c.   prompt feedback on performance.
d.   a physical environment that allows for informal meetings.
e.   rewards to individuals for group performance.

V.   The Question of Human Nature

A.   For psychologists in the sociocultural perspective, the task is to identify the conditions that make positive behaviors likely to occur.

Chapter Summary

While psychologists of other perspectives generate explanations of human behavior based on qualities within the 1._____, social and industrial/organizational psychologists stress the influences of situational sources, including the impact of the presence of others.

Social 2._____ are rules and conventions that guide social interactions. Social 3._____ are social positions that carry with them norms, and sometimes laws, that prescribe the people's behavior. These prescriptions can influence a person to behave in ways that contradict personal values or sense of self.

The power of roles was demonstrated in the 1960s in two major studies. Milgram designed a study in which subjects were led to believe that they were giving painful electric shocks to others. Surprisingly, over 2/3 of the subjects were completely willing to obey an experimenter who directed them to deliver even fatal shocks. In subsequent experiments, Milgram manipulated several variables to investigate the conditions under which people were likely to disobey. He found that the physical closeness of both the experimenter and the 4._____ had an effect, as well as the presence of conflict within the group of experimenters and or the group of subjects. When the person giving the orders was not placed in an authoritative role, the amount of obedience 5._____. While Milgram convincingly demonstrated the power of the role of the authority, these experiments have been criticized as being 6._____.

Another major study was Haney, Banks, and Zimbardo's prison experiment, where college students were given the roles of prisoners and guards. Subjects in these studies took on characteristics of the roles, with the prisoners developing emotional and physical symptoms, and the guards sometimes displaying sadistic behaviors. Critics of this study maintain that the experimental setup was too 7._____ to be of value, but the authors countered that these subjects were enacting roles just as real prisoners and guards do.

Social psychologists have pointed out several factors in obedience: fear of negative consequences, respect for authority, a wish to be liked, and a desire for personal gain. Good manners are norms that facilitate obedience to authorities. In addition, when a person complies with small requests, increasingly larger and larger requests may be harder to resist because the person has already committed to a course of action and has become 8._____.

9._____ is taking action or taking on attitudes as the result of some perceived group pressure. In a series of experiments by Asch, subjects were asked to match lines according to their length. Confederates in the experiments gave wrong answers. It was found that 1/3 of subjects conformed to the group's incorrect estimation over half of the time. Conformity is affected by identification with the group, the wish to be accurate, personal gain motivation, and the desire to be liked.

When groups are close, they tend to reason similarly and suppress dissent, a phenomenon called 10._____, which is associated with risky decision making. Janis proposed that the following factors are involved: the desire to preserve harmony in the group and agree with the leader, the avoidance of disagreement or embarrassment, and the avoidance of outside information. These tendencies tend to work against critical thinking or expression of one's misgivings. Groupthink can be counteracted by encouraging these activities.

Peers can have powerful influences on behavior. Peer support, or lack of it, for academic achievement is a factor in the aptitude test score differences among different 11._____. Ages 16-24 appear to be critical in the formation of 12._____identity.

There have been striking incidents in which large groups of people have failed to act to help a person in distress. 13._____ occurs when group members are inactive due to the belief that someone else will take responsibility. When a group of people notices that someone needs help, but nobody offers it, the people exhibit a type of this phenomenon called 14._____. In work groups, the tendency to allow others to work harder is called 15._____, which is encouraged by conditions in which group members are not held accountable, when work is uninteresting, and when workers feel that efforts will duplicate those of their coworkers. Work environments in which jobs are important and interesting, and in which individual and group performance is evaluated, are associated with greater motivation. In extreme instances, people lose their senses of self in situations and then behave mindlessly, a phenomenon known as 16._____.

Although there are strong demands for obedience and conformity, people have sometimes been able to resist these pressures. Independent action is more likely when the person sees the need for action, decides to take responsibility, has an ally, weighs the cost of doing nothing, feels competent, and/or becomes entrapped in intervening.

17._____ is an area of psychology concerned with social influences on processes such as thought, memory, and perception. 18._____ is the theory that people are motivated to explain the causes of their own and others behavior. These explanations are either 19._____, identifying the cause by appeal to something in the environment, like social pressure, or 20._____, explaining the cause as something within the person, such as a character trait. The 21._____ is the tendency to overestimate personality factors in assigning causes to others' behavior. It is more common in Western cultures that emphasize the individual as opposed to cultures with more of a group identity.

People also make errors in assigning causes to their own behavior, such as the 22._____, the tendency to take credit for one's successes and rationalize one's mistakes. Attributions are also affected by the 23._____, the notion that good things happen to good people and that bad things happen to bad people. People in happy couples tend to make 24._____ attributions for their partners' relationship mistakes and 25._____ attributions for their positive behaviors. People in unhappy couples tend to do the opposite.

Change in attitudes can be accomplished by mere repetition of communication. The existence of this 26._____ effect is the reason why advertisers repeat their messages over and over. Attitudes can also be affected by arguments from admired or attractive people. Extreme fear is not a very good motivator, but moderate fear can be useful if it is accompanied by information about avoidance of danger.

The term "brainwashing" is used to describe what social psychologists call 27._____ persuasion. Several techniques can be used to strip an individual of his or her identity and suppress the ability to reason. These include the infliction of physical or emotional distress, the definition of personal problems in simplistic terms with promised solutions, unconditional acceptance by a leader, group-based individual identity, entrapment, and restricted access to information.

McClelland and his associates speculated that some people have a strong 28._____, a drive to meet high standards of success. They measured this need by having people interpret ambiguous drawings on the 29._____Test. These people dream of work success and see failure as a devastating consequence.

While some psychologists believe that motivation is internal, social psychologists tend to focus on situational forces that encourage or suppress motivation. In work settings, motivation has been demonstrated to be related to many aspects of the job itself, but also to job flexibility, feedback, appreciation, and chances for advancement. Work motivation is not affected by money, but it is related to 30._____, in which people get raises in salary that are tied directly to their work.

Competition in the workplace may undermine motivation and achievement, as it fosters feelings of insecurity, anxiety, jealousy, and hostility. On the other hand, an atmosphere of 31._____ tends to increase performance and satisfaction. Work teams perform best when the group has a clear purpose, members have autonomy, feedback on performance is prompt, and individuals are rewarded for team performance.

Multiple Choice Self-Test

1. In Dr. Dare's discussion-oriented general psychology course, males talk a great deal more than females. In explaining this phenomenon, a social psychologist would emphasize:
   a. connections between male hormones and behavior.
   b. childhood experiences that encourage males to dominate conversation.
   c. power differences between professor and student.
   d. aspects of the situation that encourage males to talk.

2. Lauren visits a friend and has dinner with the friend's family. At Lauren's house, family members get up and leave the table when they are finished eating. When Lauren does so at her friend's house, she gets some strange looks from the family. Her friend later tells her that a person has to ask to be excused at their house. Lauren has discovered a difference in:
   a. norms.
   b. roles.
   c. obedience.
   d. conformity.

3.   "Authority," "son," "teammate," "subordinate," and "partner" are all examples of:
a.   norms.
b.   roles.
c.   conventions.
d.   entrapment.

4.   In Milgram's obedience study, subjects were less likely to inflict dangerous shocks when:
a.   they did not hear the victim's reactions.
b.   the experimenter wore a white lab coat instead of a suit.
c.   the experimenter was close by.
d.   two experimenters issued different demands.

5.   In Milgram's obedience study, subjects who were willing to inflict dangerous shocks were:
a.   sadistic.
b.   masochistic.
c.   influenced by a powerful situation.
d.   no different from other subjects.

6.   The Milgram studies have been criticized as being:
a.   artificial.
b.   unethical.
c.   unscientific.
d.   illogical.

7.   In the Prison Study, the guards:
a.   sometimes acted sadistically.
b.   all acted the same.
c.   complained about their roles.
d.   developed emotional symptoms.

8.   The Prison Study has been criticized for:
a.   not being relevant to social psychology.
b.   being artificial.
c.   confusing cause and effect.
d.   being overly reductionistic in its explanations.

9.   Obedience is more likely when:
a.   the authority is disliked.
b.   the authority issues conflicting orders.
c.   people fail to think critically.
d.   disadvantages to compliance are obvious.

10.   Alvin is asked to act as a faculty advocate for a student who is bringing a sexual
        harassment complaint against a faculty member. He thinks that he will just have
        to advise the student and attend a hearing, but the case goes on for years, with
        Alvin spending large amounts of time in helping the student pursue justice. If he
        had known at the beginning how much work this would entail, he would not have
        agreed to be the advocate. However, he does not quit midway into the task
        because of:
a.   closure.
b.   compliance.
c.   norms.
d.   entrapment.

11.   Conformity in an individual is most likely when:
a.   the individual has high status in the group.
b.   the individual knows a good deal about the issue compared with others.
c.   the individual identifies with the group.
d.   the group's tolerance for nonconformity is low.

12.   Compared with group-oriented cultures, people from Western, individualistic
        cultures are more likely to:
a.   have many social norms.
b.   demand conformity to group ideologies.
c.   make the fundamental attribution error.
d.   think in terms of situational influences for others' behavior.

13.   Groupthink can be counteracted by:
a.   emphasizing the shared goals of group members.
b.   encouraging dissent and the expression of doubt.
c.   applying pressure from outside groups.
d.   the presence of a strong leader.

14.   For a social psychologist, one of the most powerful ways to improve minority
        achievement test scores is:
a.   increasing peer support for behaviors related to achievement.
b.   strong negative consequences for poor performance.
c.   teacher's rewarding minority students who achieve.
d.   increasing generational identity.

15.   Research has demonstrated that relationship satisfaction is associated with:
a.   clearly defined gender roles.
b.   the tendency to make situational attributions for partners' mistakes.
c.   the tendency to make dispositional attributions for partners' mistakes.
d.   alternation of power positioning between partners.

16. Esther works in a fast food restaurant. The shift manager insists that someone clean up the parking lot each night, but the manager never assigns this task to a specific person. Because Esther hates this job, she tries to look busy at the end of the night so that someone else will do it. Esther exhibits:
a. self-serving bias.
b. low need for achievement.
c. altruism.
d. social loafing.

17. Bill is a powerful university president who surrounds himself with like-minded people. One of his subordinates is given the task of drafting a racial harassment policy for the college. This subordinate drafts an inadequate policy. At a meeting with his senior staff, the president expresses his satisfaction with the policy and nobody on the staff disagrees, so the policy is adopted. The next year, the college finds itself in several lawsuits as a result of this policy. The failure of the staff to make a better decision was most likely the result of:
a. the principle of least interest.
b. social facilitation.
c. social inhibition.
d. groupthink.

18. A worker is least likely to engage in social loafing when:
a. each group member has a different and important job.
b. supervisors make dispositional attributions for the group's performance.
c. the supervisor encourages dissent and disagreement.
d. job duties require little physical effort.

19. Estee is a corporation head who has 12 people on her senior staff. Sometimes they must make decisions that could result in the loss or gain of millions of dollars. Under which of the following conditions is a risky decision LEAST likely to be made?
a. The group is highly cohesive.
b. Estee encourages disagreement among group members.
c. The group has little access to outside information.
d. There is high group identification in members.

20. Several years ago, a group of fans at a professional football game threw an usher off the upper deck of the stadium. None of these fans had any history of violent behavior. Their action was most likely the result of:
a. groupthink.
b. deindividuation.
c. social loafing.
d. obedience to authority.

21. Dr. Singh decides to penalize the entire class for one student's mistake. An individual student is most likely to complain about this if:
a. there is social loafing by other students.
b. the student knows that others agree with him or her.
c. Dr. Singh has been unfair in other situations.
d. Dr. Singh is usually fair; this is an exception.

22. Zina celebrated her 60th birthday in 1994. Which event is most likely to have influenced the generational identity of her age cohort?
a. the communist scare of the 1950s.
b. the Vietnam War of the 1960s.
c. World War II.
d. the Great Depression of the 1930s.

23. In order to sell its products, McDuffer's company saturates the television market with at least 20 commercials a day. Even if the company's products are not particularly appealing, the commercials will change some people's attitudes toward the products because of the:
a. Zeigarnik effect.
b. principle of least interest.
c. validity effect.
d. deindividuation principle.

24. According to principles of social psychology, which of the following statements would be most helpful in getting people to avoid risky sexual practices?
a. "Sex can kill you or ruin your life."
b. "Sex can be dangerous. Be careful about sexual matters."
c. "Sex can be fatal. Don't mess around."
d. "Sex can be dangerous. If you have sex, use a condom."

25. Which of the following represents the kind of messages used in coercive persuasion?
a. "Low self-esteem derives from many sources. We can help you by listening."
b. "Once you admit your failings, you won't struggle as much."
c. "Once you purge yourself of your hated inner child, all of your problems will disappear."
d. "If you don't get help from us, please get it from someone."

26. Adam tells you that he got a good grade on his Chemistry test because he is smart and studies hard, but that he got a bad grade on his Philosophy exam because the instructor is unfair. Adam seems to be exhibiting:
a. self-serving bias
b. belief in a just world.
c. fundamental attribution error.
d. coercive persuasion.

27. "My father doesn't make a lot of money because he grew up in a poor neighborhood and didn't have the right connections" is what kind of attribution?
a. dispositional.
b. situational.
c. self-serving.
d. achievement motivated.

28. Social psychologists believe that:
a. we should increase coercive persuasion in society.
b. we need to identify conditions that make positive behavior more likely.
c. we can increase workers' motivation to achieve by raising them differently as children.
d. we need to identify mental obstacles to problem solving.

29. You probably act differently in the presence of your parents than in the presence of your friends because of the differences in:
a. attributions.
b. social roles.
c. entrapment.
d. deindividuation.

30. The pressure to conform:
a. is a social problem in every context.
b. is unrelated to groupthink.
c. can lead to either positive or negative behaviors.
d. causes social loafing.

True-False Self-Test

T   F   1.   Entrapment can affect both obedience and independent action.

T   F   2.   A norm is composed of many roles.

T   F   3.   Roles can make a person go against his or her morals.

T   F   4.   Milgram's study demonstrated the power of roles.

T   F   5.   Subjects in Milgram's studies were less likely to deliver shocks to victims they could not see.

T   F   6.   "Prisoners" in the Prison study became depressed and panicked.

T   F   7.   Wanting to be polite makes one less likely to disobey authority.

T   F   8.   Only about 20% of subjects in Asch's experiments were independent on every trial.

T   F   9.   Very few subjects followed Milgram's orders to inflict lethal electric shocks.

T   F   10.   Groupthink can be counteracted by encouraging dissent.

T   F   11.   Relationship happiness is associated with a tendency to make dispositional attributions for positive behaviors.

T   F   12.   Bystander apathy reflects diffusion of responsibility.

T   F   13.   Groupthink often results in risky group decisions.

T   F   14.   Seeking information outside of the group helps to reduce the risk of groupthink.

T   F   15.   Diffusion of responsibility often leads to social loafing in work situations.

T   F   16.   Deindividuation is least likely in small groups.

T   F   17.   Independent action depends wholly on critical thinking.

T   F   18.   Situational factors cause obedience, while individual factors cause independent action.

T   F   19.   Attributions are affected by culture.

T   F   20.   The critical period for formation of generational identity is ages 12 to 16.

T   F   21.   Intense fear is an excellent motivator for attitude change.

T   F   22.   Coercive persuasion usually involves building suspicion of people outside of the group.

T   F   23.   Entrapment is a technique of coercive persuasion.

T   F   24.   Pay is the most important factor in job motivation.

T   F   25.   Competitive work environments have psychological hazards.

T   F   26.   Competition breeds excellence under most circumstances.

T	F	27.	Intergroup hostility can be decreased by making the groups interdependent in reaching mutual goals.
T	F	28.	Employees' individual performance suffers when they are part of a team.
T	F	29.	Individuals should never be rewarded for team performance.
T	F	30.	Achievement is influenced by both individual and situational factors.

Key Terms

norms (social) Rules that regulate human life, including social conventions, explicit laws and implicit cultural standards.

role A given social position that is governed by a set of norms for proper behavior.

entrapment A gradual process in which individuals escalate their commitment to a course of action to justify their investment of time, money, or effort.

groupthink In close-knit groups, the tendency for all members to think alike for the sake of harmony and to suppress dissent.

diffusion of responsibility In organized or anonymous groups, the tendency of members to avoid taking responsibility for actions or decisions because they assume that others will do so.

social cognition An area in social psychology concerned with social influences on thought, memory, perception, and other cognitive processes.

attribution theory The theory that people are motivated to explain their own and others' behavior by attributing causes of that behavior to a situation or disposition.

fundamental attribution error The tendency, in explaining other people's behavior, to overestimate personality factors and underestimate the influence of the situation.

self-serving bias The tendency, in explaining one's own behavior, to take credit for one's good actions and rationalize one's mistakes.

just-world hypothesis The notion that many people need to believe that the world is fair and justice is served; that bad people are punished and good people rewarded.

validity effect The tendency of people to believe that a statement is true or valid simply because it has been repeated many times.

need for achievement A learned motive to meet personal standards of success and excellence in a chosen area (abbreviated *nAch*).

Thematic Apperception Test (TAT) A personality test that asks respondents to interpret a series of drawings showing ambiguous scenes of people; scored for various motives such as the needs for achievement, affiliation, or power.

Suggested Research Projects

1. Illustrate the power of norms for yourself by violating some of them. For example, you can violate gender norms by behaving in a way characteristic of the other sex, such as saying to a friend (if you are male), "Oh, it's soooo good to see you!" or (if you are female) "Hey, how 'bout them Yankees?" If you have a small class, violate a norm by sitting in a different place each class period. Sensitize yourself to other norms and violate the ones that you can without too serious consequences.

2. Construct a questionnaire of work values such as pay, flexibility, appreciation, etc., and ask a group of college students of different majors to rank these values from most to least important. Are there differences between groups? What are some of the individual and situational factors that might influence these differences?

Suggested Readings

Aronson, E. (1999). *The social animal* (8th ed.). New York: Freeman. An interesting presentation of a variety of social psychology topics.

Cialdini, R. (2000). *Influence: Science and practice* (4th ed.). Glenview, IL: Scott Foresman. Basic and applied research on social influence.

Milgram, S. (1974). *Obedience to authority*. New York: Harper & Row. A detailed description of the obedience studies described in the textbook.

Myers, D. G. (1999). *Social psychology* (6th ed.). Boston: McGraw-Hill. A well-written textbook surveying the field of social psychology.

Chapter 10

The Cultural Context

Learning Objectives

After reading and studying this chapter, you should be able to:

1. Describe the areas of cultural and cross-cultural psychology.

2. Discuss the methodological difficulties inherent in studying culture.

3. Describe some general cultural differences in communication styles, time organization, and the concept of the self.

4. Compare and contrast four outcomes of the ethnic identity and acculturation processes.

5. Describe research on cultural conceptions of intelligence.

6. Define social constructionism.

7. Discuss the cultural variations in gender roles.

8. Discuss the functions and dangers of ethnocentrism and stereotyping.

9. Describe the sources of prejudice and bigotry.

10. Discuss the misinterpretations and misuses of the sociocultural perspective.

11. Discuss the issues of IQ testing.

12. Discuss social and cultural factors in psychotherapy.

13. Discuss social and cultural factors in attempts to reduce prejudice.

Chapter Outline

I. The Study of Culture

    A. **Culture** is a program of shared rules that govern the behavior of members of a community or society; and a set of values, beliefs, and attitudes shared by most members of that community.

        1. Every culture includes a system of rules for behavior and social organization.

B. *Cultural psychologists* study the effects of culture on behavior. *Cross-cultural psychologists* compare members of different societies.

C. Both cultural and cross-cultural psychology overlap a great deal with *cultural anthropology*, the study of customs within and across human cultures.

D. Until recently, most Western psychologists have been uninterested in culture and have erroneously assumed that their findings would generalize to other cultures.

E. Culture exerts powerful effects on behavior, sometimes directly conflicting with biological dispositions, as in the cultural pressure for Western women to be very thin.

F. Research difficulties in the study of culture include:
   1. methodological problems in devising studies (the problem of cultural and linguistic equivalence) and selecting samples.
   2. problems in interpreting results. The same behavior may have different meanings across cultures and may persist long after its original function has been abandoned.
   3. the problem of stereotyping. We should not assume that all members of a culture behave in the same way. Cross-cultural findings are also politically and emotionally sensitive.

II. The Rules of Culture

   A. Nonverbal Communication
      1. Some aspects of *body language* and nonverbal signals are universal; some are specific to particular cultures.
         a. *Conversational distance* (how close to stand to another when talking) is one example of cross-cultural variation in nonverbal behavior.
         b. When a nonverbal rule is broken, people are likely to feel uncomfortable.
         c. People from different cultures differ in how attentive they are to body language in contrast to direct verbal communication.
   B. The Organization of Time
      1. **Monochronic cultures** are cultures in which time is organized sequentially; schedules and deadlines are valued over people.
      2. **Polychronic cultures** are cultures in which time is organized horizontally; people tend to do several things at once and value relationships over schedules.
      3. Time organization stems from a culture's economic system, social organization, political history, and ecology.
   C. The Self and Self-identity
      1. Individualism and Collectivism. **Individualist cultures** are cultures in which the self is regarded as autonomous, and individual goals and wishes are prized above duty and relations with others.

2. **Collectivist cultures** are cultures in which the self is regarded as embedded in relationships, and harmony with one's group is prized above individual goals and wishes.
   a. The boundaries between the self and others are more flexible and shifting.
3. Self-definition affects many aspects of individual psychology, including:
   a. which personality traits are encouraged.
   b. how emotions are expressed.
   c. whether relationships or individual freedom are valued more.
4. In collectivist cultures:
   a. the strongest human bond is not usually between husband and wife, but between parent and child or siblings.
   b. child rearing is a communal matter.
5. The collectivism-individual distinction is an average one; there is great overlap and regional differences.

D. Ethnic identity and acculturation. **Social identity** is the part of a person's self-concept that is based on his or her identification with a nation, culture, or ethnic group or with a gender role or other roles in society.
   1. **Ethnic identity** is a person's identification with a religious or ethnic group.
   2. **Acculturation** is the process by which members of groups that are minorities in a given society come to identify with and feel part of the mainstream culture.
   3. For any individual, there are four ways of balancing these two forces.
      a. *Bicultural* people have strong ties both to their ethnicity and to the larger culture.
      b. People who choose *assimilation* have weak feelings of ethnicity but a strong sense of acculturation.
      c. *Ethnic separatists* have a strong sense of ethnic identity but weak feelings of acculturation.
      d. People who feel *marginal* are connected neither to their ethnicity nor to the dominant culture.
   4. The way a person balances ethnic identity and acculturation often changes in response to personal experiences, and to social and historical events.
   5. As groups develop a strong ethnic identity, they often reject the name that was imposed on them by the larger culture, but not all members of the group agree on the group label.

III. Culture and Intelligence

A. The Meanings of Intelligence.
   1. People in all cultures can reason deductively, but differ in the areas in which they will apply this reasoning.

2. Cultures differ in their definition of intelligence.
3. Cultures differ in their encouragement of the development of various human capacities.
4. Cultural beliefs about the origins of intelligence and the reasons for achievement affect skill development.

B. Culture and the Measurement of Intelligence.
1. Two major questions:
   a. Is it possible to design an intelligence test that can be used cross-culturally?
   b. If there are many kinds of intelligence, is it fair to use a test of only the kind of intelligence that is valued by the dominant culture?
2. Intelligence testing began in 1904. French psychologist Alfred Binet designed a test to identify children who would benefit from remedial education.
   a. Binet's test sampled a kind of mental ability and was not intended to be a general measure of intelligence.
   b. Terman revised Binet's test and established norms for American children.
   c. Unlike the French, Americans assumed that IQ tests measured a permanent, inherited trait.
   d. The original American IQ tests favored urban, middle class, and white children by emphasizing the kinds of information and problem-solving abilities valued in the dominant culture.
   e. Test makers responded to criticisms about bias by trying to design tests that were *culture free* or *culture fair*. These attempts met with limited success.
   f. Terman eliminated test items on which boys did worse than girls in his 1937 revision.
3. The dilemma: intelligence tests put some children at a disadvantage, but they also measure skills and knowledge that are useful in the classroom. How can a test eliminate cultural biases while recognizing that biases exist?
4. Proponents of IQ testing maintain that it is useful to identify children who need special help.
5. Critics maintain that testing does more harm than good.

C. Culture and Academic Performance
1. One factor in average cultural group variation in academic performance is cultural beliefs in the origins of intelligence and the reasons for achievement.
2. Asian children performed higher, on average, than American children in mathematical tests despite fewer educational resources. Cultural differences include:
   a. beliefs about intelligence. Americans are more likely to believe that mathematical ability is innate.
   b. standards. American parents have lower standards for their children's performance.

        c.   values. American students do not value education as much as Asian students.

    3.   Stereotypes that portray groups as unintelligent can depress the test performances of people in these groups.

        a.   These people can fall victim to **stereotype threat**, a burden of doubt a person feels about his or her performance, due to negative stereotypes about his or her group's abilities.

    4.   Positive stereotypes can improve performance.

IV.   The Origins of Culture

    A.   Cultural attitudes and traditions reflect history, physical environment, economy, and survival needs.

    B.   Gender and Culture: Themes and Variations. A distinction should be made between biological sex and learned gender. Gender roles differ cross-culturally in:

    1.   the status of women.

    2.   work that is considered appropriate for one sex or the other.

    3.   degree of contact permitted between sexes.

    4.   sexuality, e.g., the value placed on female chastity varies among cultures.

    5.   notions of difference. Some cultures exaggerate presumed differences between men and women; others do not.

    C.   Gender and Culture: Explaining the Differences. Gender roles depend on production and reproduction needs in the culture.

    1.   Rigid ideas about masculinity tend to exist where:

        a.   there is competition for scarce resources.

        b.   enemies must be fought.

        c.   community resources must be protected.

    2.   Honor, Economics, and Male Aggression. U.S. Southerners are more likely than those from other regions to endorse the use of violence for protection. Nisbett traces this difference to the tradition of herding in Southern immigrants.

        a.   This economy is based on aggressiveness and vigilance.

        b.   It fosters a *culture of honor* for even small disputes.

        c.   This cultural tradition continues even though the economy has changed.

    3.   Industrialization and Equality. As countries become more industrialized and urban, gender roles become more modern.

        a.   Industrialization eliminates the traditional reasons for a sexual division of labor.

           i.   Most industrial jobs can be done by either sex.

           ii.   Reproductive technology gives women more choices.

V. Cross-cultural Relations

A. Ethnocentrism and Stereotypes
1. **Ethnocentrism** is the belief that one's own ethnic group, nation, or religion is superior to all others.
    a. Ethnocentric thinking is common in competition.
    b. Such "us-them" thinking encourages **stereotypes** -- summary impressions of a group, in which a person believes that all members of the group share a common trait or traits (positive, negative, or neutral).
    c. Stereotypes are useful in information processing, because they allow us to organize experience, make sense of group differences and predict behavior.
    d. Stereotypes also distort reality because:
        i.   Stereotypes accentuate group differences.
        ii. Stereotypes produce selective perception
        iii. Stereotypes underestimate differences within other groups.
B. Prejudice
1. A *prejudice* is a negative stereotype and a strong, unreasonable dislike or hatred of a group or its individual members.
    a. Prejudices can persist in the absence of evidence.
2. The Origins of Prejudice.
    a. Prejudice bonds people to their group, making them willing to fight for the group.
    b. Prejudices toward unfamiliar outsiders are easy to form in children.
    c. Prejudice serves to ward off feelings of uncertainty and fear.
    d. Prejudice allows people to use a target group as a scapegoat, thus inflating self-esteem.
3. The social roots of prejudice include:
    a. conformity and groupthink.
    b. socialization.
4. Prejudice has economic benefits to groups through justifying discrimination.
5. Prejudice rationalizes conflict and war.
6. The Varieties of Prejudice. Overt attitudes are not necessarily an accurate measure of prejudice.
    a. Underlying hostile feelings often exist even when overt attitudes are stated as nonprejudicial.
    b. Behaviors can show more aggression toward the different group.
    c. People often have prejudiced associations for certain groups.
C. Efforts to Reduce Prejudice. Prejudice is maintained through a cycle of distrust and animosity. Conflict and prejudice are reduced when 4 conditions are met.

1. Both sides must have equal legal status, economic opportunities, and power.
2. Authorities and community institutions must endorse egalitarian norms and provide moral support and legitimacy for both sides.
3. Both sides must have opportunities to work and socialize together, formally and informally.
4. Both sides must cooperate, working together for a common goal.

VI. Can Cultures Get Along?

  A. Cross-cultural psychology has identified the reasons for cultural conflict and has given us some ideas about reducing such conflict.

VII. Essay Four: Evaluating the Sociocultural Perspective

  A. Contributions of This Perspective.
      1. Making psychology more representative and scientific.
      2. Emphasizing the importance of the individual's social context.
      3. Emphasizing the importance of culture in every aspect of human development.
          a. Adolescence is a cultural, not a biological concept.
      4. Increasing psychology's relevance to social life. Cross-cultural psychology helps:
          a. to identify universal social forces that affect behavior.
          b. to reduce misunderstandings in cross-cultural contact.
  B. Misuses and Misinterpretations of This Perspective.
      1. Sociocultural reductionism and reification. One-factor explanations can lead to a denial of individual responsibility.
          a. *Reification* is regarding an intangible object as if it were literal. People often reify culture by citing it as an explanation without specifying its mechanisms.
      2. Stereotyping. There is a danger of exaggerating cultural differences and overlooking within-group variation.
      3. Extreme cultural relativism.
          a. The *absolutist* assumption is that there are universal truths and violations of human rights are to be condemned wherever they occur.
          b. The *relativist* position is that customs and practices can be judged only in the culture's terms.
          c. Understanding the cultural basis of a practice does not mean that it is permanent or proper.
          d. Cultural customs are imbedded in the larger structure of society. We must study the reasons for the existence of customs we find problematic.
      4. Heightened ethnocentrism. No cultural group has always and everywhere been superior to others.

VII.   Making Peace.

   A.   The sociocultural perspective has been helpful in helping companies to appreciate diversity, in developing strategies to reduce prejudice, and in forgiveness and peacemaking.

Chapter Summary

1._____ is a program of shared rules, values, and beliefs that govern the behavior of members of a community or society.   Cultural psychologists study the effects of culture on behavior, while 2._____ psychologists compare members of different societies. The latter field is similar to the field of 3._____.   Researchers in these areas have demonstrated that culture has powerful influences, even on biological processes.

The task of designing adequate research methodology is especially difficult when one is making cultural comparisons. A custom or term in one culture does not always have the same meaning in another culture. Thus there is a problem of cultural and linguistic 4._____. There is the tendency to 5._____ by assuming that all members of a culture are alike. Finally, cross-cultural psychologists must be aware of the political sensitivity of many studies.

People learn cultural rules automatically and conform to them without awareness. Communication by 6._____, the nonverbal signals of body movement, gesture, and gaze, provides information beyond that of verbal language. One important cultural difference is 7._____, the custom that regulates how close or how far apart people normally stand to one another while they are talking. Cultures differ in how much relative attention is paid to verbal vs. nonverbal communications.

Cultures also differ in how people think about and react to time. In 8._____ cultures, people tend to do one thing at a time, emphasize promptness, and adhere to plans. This tendency probably comes from an economic history in which work efforts had to be coordinated. In 9._____ cultures, people do many things at once, and they often change plans spontaneously. These cultures usually have economies based more on natural rhythms than on coordinated work.

While many Western peoples tend to emphasize 10._____, an emphasis on the autonomous self, while other cultures are more centered around the group, an orientation known as 11._____. People from the latter define the "self" as embedded in the community. This basic difference in self-definition has important implications. Individualist cultures emphasize independence, while family cohesiveness and interdependence are more often emphasized by group-oriented peoples. Child rearing is seen as a task for the community, and "privacy" for children is considered totally unimportant.

People develop 12._____ identities based on their ethnic, national, and religious senses of self. Many people tend to struggle with a tension between an 13._____ identity, the identification with their racial group or culture of origin, and

14._____, joining and feeling part of the dominant culture. There are four possible ways for an individual to balance these two forces. When people have strong identifications with both the dominant culture and their ethnicity, they are 15._____. Some people opt for 16._____, in which ethnic identity is not strong, but cultural identification is. In contrast, 17._____ have a strong ethnic identification and weak identification with the dominant culture. Finally, some people feel 18._____, without strong connections to either culture.

Researchers are interested in the development, definition, and measurement of mental abilities cross-culturally. One interesting finding is that most people in every culture are able to reason 19._____, but that they apply this reasoning in different areas, depending on their needs and experiences. Cultures differ in the meaning of "intelligence," and they tend to encourage the development of some intellectual skills, but not others.

French psychologist Alfred Binet created the first intelligence test for children. Although he wanted only to sample a certain kind of mental ability, American researchers began to define intelligence as a 20._____trait. Early versions of American IQ tests favored urban, middle class, and white children.

What set of skills a culture nurtures probably has an effect on the rate of development of a particular skill. Cognitions about the origins of intelligence, standards for performance, and values about education also appear to be important factors in skill development. For instance, Americans are more likely than Asians to believe that mathematical ability is 21._____ and to set lower standards for their children's school performance. Dominant cultural attitudes depicting a group as unintelligent can create a burden of doubt about performance in a group member known as 22._____.

Although many people adhere to the view that there are natural roles and characteristics for males and females, gender arrangements vary across cultures. Although masculinity is associated with power and achievement in many parts of the world, women's status varies across cultures, as do ideas of gender-appropriate work, gender differences in emotional expression, and the amount of socially permitted contact between the sexes. Gender role arrangements appear to be tied to a society's reproduction needs, its economy, and its need to defend itself against other groups. Because production and reproduction are changing, gender roles also appear to be changing. Gender roles are least pronounced in 23._____ societies.

Because people get attached to their cultural group, there is a tendency toward 24._____, the belief that one's own group is superior, especially under the conditions of competition. While this 25._____ helps in information processing, it also leads to distortions in judgment, such as an overattention to differences within the other group, an underattention to similarities within the other group, and a 26._____, where behaviors that do not fit the stereotype are rejected.

When feelings about other groups are unreasonably negative, a person is 27._____. This cognitive and emotional stance allows a person to defend against his or her feelings of being inadequate, afraid, and unsure. Prejudice is maintained through socialization, groupthink, conformity, and other social forces. The greatest prejudice usually occurs when there are 28._____ benefits to discriminating against some group. Overt attitudes are not the only measure of prejudice. Underlying hostile feelings or differences in behavioral tendencies often exist even when the overt attitude is not prejudiced. Prejudice can be reduced under conditions of power equality, institutional support of equality, and opportunities for the two groups to work and socialize together in cooperative ways.

The sociocultural perspective contributes the understanding that behaviors occur in a social, historical, and cultural context, a fact that has been largely ignored by traditional psychology. Research in this area has persuaded most developmental psychologists to abandon the attempt to describe universal stages of development.

Sociocultural research has helped to make psychology more representative and scientific. There are also concerns about the potential misinterpretation and misuse of sociocultural findings. As with any perspective, there is the danger of 29._____, the tendency to view behaviors as being caused by only sociocultural forces. Such a view loses sight of the individual in explanations that overemphasize situational factors. A second concern is that this kind of research may encourage 30._____, the tendency to see all members of a culture as being alike. Sociocultural researchers must be especially careful to avoid this trap, as expectations affect perceptions. Third, there is the danger of extreme cultural 31._____, the nonjudgmental view of harmful behaviors that are socially based. And sociocultural discourse may unintentionally encourage heightened 32._____, the view that one's cultural group is better than others. Despite these concerns, it is undeniable that the sociocultural perspective has produced information in many important areas.

Multiple Choice Self-Test

1.   Cross-cultural psychology is most similar to:
a.   cultural sociology.
b.   cultural anthropology.
c.   archeology.
d.   diplomacy.

2.   Which of the following is FALSE?
a.   Cross-cultural psychology is a young field.
b.   Cultural psychologists face even more methodological obstacles than psychologists in most other fields.
c.   Culture does not influence biological processes.
d.   Cultural pressures sometimes conflict with biological programming.

3.   An African culture and an Asian culture have the same custom. This means:
a   that the cultures must have similar economic needs.
b.   that the cultures must have had some historical contact.
c.   that the cultures are most likely similar in many respects.
d.   nothing by itself; the purpose or meaning of the custom may not be the same for both cultures.

4.   Two groups of public school students, athletes and counter-cultural types, have had a lot of conflict, sometimes escalating into violence. Both groups engage in frequent stereotyping of the other. Which of the following strategies would be best at reducing their mutual prejudice?
a.   Having the two groups sit together in the lunchroom.
b.   Having the two groups work together on a project.
c.   Teaching all of the students about the dynamics of prejudice.
d.   Having the two groups compete to see which can raise more money for charity.

5.   When a cultural rule about nonverbal communication is broken, it tends to make members of that group:
a.   feel uncomfortable.
b.   discuss the impact of the cultural norm.
c.   identify with a different group.
d.   attend more to verbal information.

6.   In most parts of the United States, being an hour late for an appointment would be considered very late. However, this is commonly acceptable in:
a.   monochronic cultures.
b.   achronic cultures.
c.   polychronic cultures.
d.   synchronic cultures.

7.   A culture's way of organizing time probably stems most from its:
a.   economic history.
b.   shared mythology.
c.   history of conflict with other cultures.
d.   religious tradition.

8.   Yoshino emigrated to the U.S. from Japan 30 years ago. She eats mostly American food and follows American traditions. In fact, few people know that she is from a foreign culture because she is so:
a.   bicultural.
b.   ethnic identified.
c.   acculturated.
d.   marginal.

9. Maziar is the son of Iranian immigrants. He enjoys and participates in U.S. culture, but still speaks Farsi at family gatherings and follows many Iranian customs. He is best described as:
a. acculturated.
b. an ethnic separatist.
c. assimilated.
d. bicultural.

10. Chou emigrated to the U.S. from China in the early 1960s. He lives in the "Chinatown" section of a large city, learns very little English, and wants nothing to do with Americans. He is best described as:
a. marginal.
b. bicultural.
c. an ethnic separatist.
d. an ethnic independent.

11. John is an American parent and Ito is a Japanese parent. If they are typical of their cultures, John is more likely than Ito to believe that:
a. people should accommodate to their surroundings.
b. mathematical ability is inborn.
c. language skills are important.
d. achievement is unimportant.

12. Liam emigrated to the United States from Ireland, but now he does not feel like he is a part of either culture. We would describe Liam as:
a. marginal.
b. an ethnic separatist.
c. assimilated.
d. bicultural.

13. DeeDee has heard that boys are better at math than girls. Despite having solid mathematical aptitude, she does not perform as well as she could on mathematics achievement tests. DeeDee has probably been affected by:
a. biological forces.
b. sterotype threat.
c. assimilation.
d. prophetic actualization.

14. Edward is aware of gendered work arrangements in different cultures. He knows that, if he visits traditional ethnic restaurants of 10 different cultures, the sex(es) of the waitpersons will be:
a. male.
b. female.
c. both male and female.
d. variant depending on the culture.

15.   Around the world, male aggressiveness:
a.   must be rewarded in order to appear.
b.   appears to be natural.
c.   is a product of testosterone level.
d.   occurs more in agriculturally based economies.

16.   The major influences on societal gender roles appear to be:
a.   biology and tradition.
b.   parenting and work roles.
c.   production and reproduction.
d.   biology and work roles.

17.   Louis believes that African-Americans are superior to all other peoples. His view is:
a.   separatist.
b.   assimilated.
c.   anthropocentric.
d.   ethnocentric.

18.   Prejudice in a culture will vary in degree over time. Under what condition is prejudice within a culture likely to increase?
a.   poor economic conditions.
b.   war with another country.
c.   increase in leisure time.
d.   integration of political leadership.

19.   The assumption of traditional psychology is that laws of behavior apply to all people everywhere at all times. This erroneous assumption derived from:
a.   relativistic research.
b.   methodological soundness.
c.   a lack of attention to cultural forces.
d.   diversified samples of subjects.

20.   William believes that American males are violent solely because stereotypically violent models are perpetuated by American media. This view reflects:
a.   sociocultural reductionism.
b.   an accurate conclusion based on available evidence.
c.   extreme social relativism.
d.   circular reasoning.

21.   In some cultures, pubescent males must undergo painful circumcision as a passage to manhood. Debra reads about this practice and views it as acceptable since it is culturally based. Her thinking reflects:
a.   sociocultural reductionism.
b.   extreme social relativism.
c.   multicultural tolerance.
d.   stereotype resistance.

22. Traditional IQ tests favored children who were:
a. urban, middle-class, and white.
b. suburban, upper-class, and white.
c. suburban, upper-class, and Asian.
d. rural, upper-class, and white.

23. Which of the following is TRUE?
a. American conceptions of intelligence differ from Binet's definition.
b. Binet created the first intelligence test to identify gifted children.
c. Culture-fair and culture-free IQ tests are now the standard.
d. Terman eliminated test items that favored girls over boys.

24. According to Nesbitt, the Southern United States "culture of honor" is a result of:
a. an agriculturally-based economy.
b. high temperatures that tend to create violence.
c. the low status of Southern culture relative to the rest of the country.
d. the herding economy backgrounds of many Southern immigrants.

25. In order to reduce racial tension in the workplace, Mary Kay, the Chief Executive Officer, transfers white people to departments that have disproportionate numbers of black people. This intervention will:
a. escalate racial tension.
b. reduce racial tension.
c. not reduce racial tension if nothing else is done.
d. reduce racial tension if employees understand the rationale of the intervention.

26. Which of the following BEST illustrates a situation in which cultural pressures often conflict with evolutionary programming?
a. American ideals regarding female body weight.
b. some cultures' high emphasis on athletics.
c. the need to feel healthy at all ages.
d. "blood doping" in Olympic competition.

27. Which of the following is TRUE regarding how children learn their culture's rules about appropriate behavior?
a. Children learn appropriate morals and behaviors through intensive practice and training.
b. People learn their culture's rules effortlessly and often without conscious awareness of the process.
c. Children are biologically predisposed to adopt the behavioral patterns of their biological parents.
d. Children learn a culture's rules slowly because they are treated leniently in most cultures.

28. Jeannie is a middle class American who works with several Arab people. She becomes uncomfortable because they stand too close to her when they talk. They probably do so because:
a. small conversational distance is their cultural norm.
b. they want to intimidate her.
c. they believe that Americans do not hear as well as Arabs.
d. they feel emotionally close to her.

29. When does someone from a "monochronic" society typically arrive for an appointment?
a. a day or two late
b. an hour or so late
c. on time
d. there is no guarantee that he or she will arrive.

30. In a collectivist culture, the strongest human bond is LEAST likely to be between:
a. father and son.
b. husband and wife.
c. brother and sister.
d. mother and daughter.

True-False Self-Test

T   F   1.   Cultural pressures rarely conflict with biological programming.

T   F   2.   The problem of linguistic equivalence is common in cross-cultural research.

T   F   3.   Cultures differ in the attention paid to body language.

T   F   4.   Industrialized cultures generally prescribe much more polarized roles for men and women relative to other kinds of economies.

T   F   5.   Polychronic cultures usually have industrially-based economies.

T   F   6.   Children are given little privacy in collectivist cultures.

T   F   7.   Ethnic identity and acculturation are highly interconnected processes.

T   F   8.   Bicultural people have weak ethnic identities.

T   F   9.   Deductive reasoning is found in all cultures.

T   F   10.   Asians are likely to believe that mathematical skills are the result of hard work.

T   F   11.   The status of women worldwide is not uniformly low.

T   F   12.   In some cultures, men are considered to be the "emotional" sex.

T   F   13.   Rigid concepts of manhood tend to exist in cultures where resources are plentiful.

T   F   14.   Males are more aggressive than females in every culture throughout the world.

T   F   15.   Gender role changes accompany economic and reproductive changes.

T   F   16.   Ethnocentric thinking is common in war.

T   F   17.   Stereotyping causes one to overestimate differences within groups.

T   F   18.   Stereotypes are helpful in information processing.

T   F   19.   Prejudice decreases when the economy of a culture becomes poorer.

T   F   20.   Traditional psychology paid little attention to cultural forces.

T   F   21.   Traditional IQ tests favor suburban people.

T   F   22.   Stereotype threat can depress a person's test performance.

T   F   23.   The "culture of honor" stems from Southern industrialization.

T   F   24.   The "jigsaw classroom" is a prejudice-reduction strategy.

T   F   25.   The support of people in authority is necessary for the reduction of prejudice.

T   F   26.   Conformity and groupthink have no influence on prejudice.

T   F   27.   According to your textbook, the formation of prejudices against cultural groups is an inevitable aspect of what it means to be human.

T	F	28.	Most psychologists today agree that intelligence testing is free of cultural biases.
T	F	29.	The idea that child-rearing is a private family matter is universal in all cultures.
T	F	30.	In the United States, people rely heavily on nonverbal cues rather than the content of verbal language.

Key Terms

culture A program of shared rules that govern the behavior of members of a community or society; and a set of values, beliefs, and attitudes shared by most members of that community.

monochronic cultures Cultures in which time is organized sequentially; schedules and deadlines are valued over people.

polychronic cultures Cultures in which time is organized horizontally; people tend to do several things at once and value relationships over schedules.

individualist cultures Cultures in which the self is regarded as autonomous, and individual goals and wishes are prized above duty and relations with others.

collectivist cultures Cultures in which the self is regarded as embedded in relationships, and harmony with one's group is prized above individual goals and wishes.

social identity The part of a person's self-concept that is based on his or her identification with a nation, culture, or ethnic group or with a gender role or other roles in society.

ethnic identity A person's identification with a religious or ethnic group.

acculturation The process by which members of groups that are minorities in a given society come to identify with and feel part of the mainstream culture.

stereotype threat A burden of doubt a person feels about his or her performance, due to negative stereotypes about his or her group's abilities.

ethnocentrism The belief that one's own ethnic group, nation, or religion is superior to all others.

stereotype A summary impression of a group, in which a person believes that all members of the group share a common trait or traits (positive, negative, or neutral).

Suggested Research Projects

1.   If you live in a large, culturally diverse city, visit several ethnic restaurants and observe the variations in gendered work roles. Do men, women, or both wait tables, work in the kitchen, seat customers, clean up, etc.? How many people who appear to be from outside of the ethnic group work at the restaurant? What conclusions can you tentatively draw from your observations?

2.   Construct some scenarios about behaviors and ask people to judge the behaviors you describe. For example, you might describe a person's behavior and ask people to estimate the person's level of mental health, intelligence, morality, or responsibility for his or her actions. Vary the race, ethnicity, or sex of the person in the story. Do you get different judgments, for instance, about an Asian who does poorly in math compared to a Hispanic who has the same problem, about a woman who cries as the result of work pressure compared with a man who reacts the same way?

Suggested Readings.

Atkinson, D. R., Morten, G., & Sue, D. W. (Eds., 1997). *Counseling American minorities: A cross-cultural perspective* (4th ed.). Boston: McGraw-Hill. A guide for counselors who work with racial and ethnic minority peoples.

Gilmore, D. D. (1990). *Manhood in the making: Cultural concepts of masculinity*. New Haven, CT: Yale University Press. In an anthropological study of the social construction of masculinity in several different cultures, Gilmore concludes that masculinity seems associated with a culture's experience of war and competition for scarce resources.

Hochschild, A. R. (1997). *The second shift*. New York: Avon. The author summarizes research on the sharing of domestic tasks in dual-earner households, and concludes that wives do significantly more domestic work than their husbands.

CHAPTER 11

The Inner Life

Learning Objectives:

After reading and studying this chapter, you should be able to:

1.   Describe the emphases of psychodynamic psychology.

2.   Summarize Freud's theory, including basic motivation, functioning, structure, and development of personality.

3.   Explain similarities and differences in the theories of Freud, Horney, Adler, Jung, Erikson, the object-relations school, and existential psychology.

4.   Describe the goals and processes of psychoanalysis.

5.   Discuss the controversies surrounding psychodynamic psychology and criticisms by researchers of the case study approach.

6.   Discuss the controversy over recovered memories of childhood abuse.

Chapter Outline

I.   Introduction

      A.   Sigmund Freud's theory of **psychoanalysis** emphasizes unconscious motives and conflicts. Psychodynamic approaches are characterized by:
          1.   emphasis on material that is **intrapsychic** -- within the mind (psyche) or self.
          2.   a belief in the primacy of the first five years.
          3.   a belief that psychological development occurs in fixed stages characterized by mental events and unconscious crises that must be resolved.
          4.   a focus on a person's psychic reality as the main influence on behavior.
          5.   a reliance on subjective rather than objective methods of getting at the truth of a person's life.

II.   Freud and Psychoanalysis

      A.   Although Freud has been highly influential, there is much dispute about the lasting significance of his work, reflected in three current attitudes:
          1.   Some see Freud as a genius of history.

2.   Some think that, although some of his ideas have proved faulty, the overall framework and insights of his theory are timeless and brilliant.

3.   Some see Freud's theory as sheer nonsense.

B.   The Structure of Personality.

1.   According to Freud, the personality is a system of three components:

a.   The **id** is the part of the mind containing inherited psychic energy; particularly sexual and aggressive instincts. It contains:

i.   **libido (li-BEE-do)** the psychic energy that fuels the life or sexual instincts of the id.

ii.   the death, or aggressive, instinct.

b.   The **ego** is the part of the mind that represents reason, good sense, and rational self-control; it mediates between id and superego.

c.   The **superego** is the part of the mind that represents conscience, morality, and social standards.

2.   **Defense mechanisms** are methods used by the ego to prevent unconscious anxiety or threatening thoughts from entering consciousness. Defense mechanisms include:

a.   repression, which occurs when threatening unconscious material is blocked from consciousness.

b.   projection, the attribution of unacceptable feelings on to someone else. One target of projection is the *scapegoat*.

c.   reaction formation, the transformation of an uncomfortable feeling to its opposite.

d.   regression, in which a person reverts to previous phase of psychological development.

e.   denial, a refusal to admit that an unpleasant feeling is being experienced.

f.   displacement, a redirection of emotion to other targets. When displacement serves a socially useful purpose, it is called *sublimation*.

g.   acting out, behaving impulsively in reaction to unconscious feelings.

h.   humor, which is used to defend against fear or other uncomfortable feelings.

3.   Neurosis is the result of unhealthy attempts to defend against anxiety.

C.   The Development of Personality

1.   Personality development occurs in *psychosexual* stages, which are the result of the changing expression of sexual energy in different parts of the body. Each stage (except for latency) involves a conflict, and poorly resolved conflicts result in *fixation*, which causes neurosis.

a. The *oral stage* is the first year of life, when the mouth is the focus of sensation. Problems occurring in this stage later result in the adult's constant seeking of oral gratification.

b. The *anal stage* occurs at about ages 2 to 3, when the major issues are toilet training and the control of bodily waste. Fixation in this stage may later result in obsessive neatness and cleanliness (anal retentiveness) or messiness and disorganization (anal expulsiveness).

c. The most crucial stage of development is the *phallic (Oedipal) stage*, which lasts from about ages 3 to 6. Development in this stage involves:

    i. the **Oedipus complex**, a conflict in which a child desires the parent of the other sex and views the same-sex parent as a rival.

    ii. **castration anxiety**, the boy's unconscious fear of castration by the powerful father. Castration anxiety causes the boy to repress his desire for his mother and identify with his father. This is the beginning of superego development.

    iii. penis envy in girls, which is expressed in adulthood as a desire for children.

d. The *latency* stage lasts from about age 5-6 until puberty. Freud thought that this stage is nonsexual, but modern research shows that most latency-age children are curious about sex.

e. The *genital stage* starts at puberty, when mature adult sexuality begins to develop.

2. Freud's own writings reveal that he often formulated his theories and pressured his patients to accept them. An extreme example was his patient "Dora", who resisted sexual advances by her father's friend. Freud reinterpreted her symptoms as repressed desire for sex.

3. Freud left a powerful legacy to psychology.

III. Dissenters and Descendants

A. Psychoanalysis became a nearly religious movement in which Freud punished "heretics" by excluding them from his inner circle.

B. Alfred Adler disagreed with Freud's emphasis on sexual and aggressive instincts. Adler believed that:

1. the prime motive in human behavior is the need for self-improvement that stems from the natural feelings of inferiority that children have.

2. some people develop an **inferiority complex**, an inability to accept one's natural limitations; it occurs when the need for self-improvement is blocked or inhibited.

3. People continue to grow and change throughout life. Development does not stop at the Oedipal phase.

C. Karen Horney challenged Freud's ideas about women. She argued that:
1. when women feel inferior to men, it is because they are socially subordinated to men, not because of some anatomical defect.
2. men may suffer from "womb envy," jealousy around women's ability to bear children.
3. men may unconsciously fear women's sexual power over them, and castration anxiety may be an expression of this fear.
4. the driving force in personality is **basic anxiety**, the feeling of being isolated and helpless in a hostile world; it is the motivating emotion in social relations.

D. Jungian theory. Carl Jung differed from Freud on the nature of the unconscious.
1. He believed that, in addition to the personal unconscious, there is a **collective unconscious**, the universal memories and experiences of humankind, represented in the symbols, stories, and images (archetypes) that occur across all cultures.
2. Jung identified common cultural themes, or **archetypes, (AR-ki-tipes)**, universal, symbolic images that appear in myths, art, stories, and dreams, including the:
   a. *mandala*, the "magic circle" of Eastern religions.
   b. *shadow*, the bestial, evil side of human nature.
   c. *persona*, the public personality.
   d. *anima*, the feminine quality within a man.
   e. *animus*, the masculine quality within a woman.
3. Like Adler and other dissenters, Jung had confidence in the positive part of the ego and believed that people are motivated by goals and desires toward self-fulfillment.

E. Erikson's Psychosocial Theory.
1. Erik Erikson believed that psychosocial events are the most important influences on personality development, and that this development continues in stages throughout one's life, each marked by a different crisis. Erikson's 8 stages are:
   a. trust vs. mistrust, when an infant develops faith that his or her needs can be met.
   b. autonomy (independence) vs. shame and doubt, when a toddler learns to believe in his or her abilities.
   c. initiative vs. guilt, when a child learns to control impulses and energies.
   d. competence vs. inferiority, when a school-age child learns mastery and competence.
   e. identity vs. role confusion, when an adolescent defines the self and plans for the future. This stage involves an identity crisis.
   f. intimacy vs. isolation, when young adults learn to commit to others in relationships.

g.   generativity vs. stagnation, when adults share their work or relationships with younger generations.

h.   ego integrity vs. despair, when older adults strive to accept their lives and deal with their fear of death.

2.   Erikson recognized that social and economic factors affect these stages.

3.   Erikson showed that development is a lifelong process.

4.   Researchers have shown that Erikson's stages are not universal. Findings indicate that:

    a.   identity crises are not limited to adolescence.

    b.   competence is not mastered once and for all in childhood.

    c.   many people are generative throughout their lives.

    d.   women often enter the generativity stage before the identity stage.

F.   Object-Relations Theory. **Object-relations theory** is a psychodynamic approach that emphasizes the importance of the infant's first two years and the baby's formative relationships, especially with the mother.

1.   The infant's attachment is not only to the parent, but also to the infant's evolving perception of the parent.

    a.   The child internalizes a *representation* of the parent.

    b.   Other people are important as *sources of attachment*. The key issue is the balance between independence and connection.

    c.   Early development involves **splitting**, the division of qualities into their opposites, as in the Good Mother versus the Bad Mother; it reflects an inability to understand that people are made up of good and bad qualities.

    d.   Gender roles may be influenced by the tendencies for attachment in girls and the formation of *ego boundaries* in boys.

IV.   Humanist and Existential Psychology

A.   Humanists and existentialists differ from traditional psychodynamic theorists by their focus on free will and choice.

B.   **Humanist psychology** is a psychological approach that emphasizes personal growth and the achievement of human potential rather than the scientific understanding and assessment of behavior. Its chief leaders were Maslow, May, and Rogers.

1.   Abraham Maslow emphasized the side of human nature that involved postive emotions and *peak experiences*, moments of rapture at the attainment of excellence or the experience of beauty. These qualities characterize the *self-actualized* person who strives for meaningful and challenging life.

2.   Carl Rogers was interested in fully functioning individuals who have a *congruence*, or harmony, between their conscious and unconscious selves. Rogers believed that full functioning required

unconditional positive regard, love or support given to another person, with no conditions attached.

    3.   Rollo May was a proponent of **existential psychology**, an approach that emphasizes free will and responsibility for one's actions, and the importance of struggling with the harsh realities of existence, such as the need to find meaning in life and to accept suffering and death.

  C.   Existentialist and humanist psychologists emphasize the role of choice and use of inner resources to construct people's lives.

V.   The Psychodynamic Paradox

  A.   Psychodynamic theorists rely on inference and subjective interpretation, so most psychodynamic assumptions are untestable.

  B.   However, the psychodynamic perspective is able to provide a coherent framework for describing personality and behavior.

  C.   The psychodynamic perspective can explain why people are so defensive about protecting their beliefs.

VI.   Evaluating the Psychodynamic Perspective

  A.   Researchers criticize psychodynamic psychology for being unscientific, a pseudoscience.

  B.   Contributions of This Perspective.

    1.   A willingness to address "big picture" questions such as the reason for universal symbols, the striving to find meaning in one's life, or the irrational nature of psychological energy.

    2.   An imaginative use of qualitative information such as ritual jokes, or literature to explore questions that are difficult to study with the usual methods of scientific psychology.

    3.   An emphasis on self-knowledge, especially the factors below conscious awareness that influence our behavior.

  C.   Misuses and Limitations of This Perspective.

    1.   Psychodynamic reductionism ignores the effects of biology, learning, and culture.

    2.   Violating the principle of falsifiability. Psychodynamic theories are difficult to test.

    3.   Drawing universal principles from the experience of a few, atypical patients represents overgeneralization.

    4.   Basing theories of development on retrospective accounts and fallible memories of patients creates the *illusion of causality*. *Longitudinal* studies often show a different picture from *retrospective* studies, including the areas of:

        a.   recovery from war. Children adopted after World War II tended to adjust well to their new families.

     b.   recovery from abusive or alcoholic parents. A majority of these parents' children do not become abusive or alcoholic themselves.

     c. recovery from sexual abuse. Children who have been abused have more symptoms than nonabused children but most are well adjusted by adulthood.

5.   Relying on subjective methods that are often unvalidated and unreliable. Many clinicians use **projective tests**, psychological tests used to infer a person's motives, conflicts, and unconscious dynamics on the basis of the person's interpretations of ambiguous stimuli.

     a.   These tests may be useful in establishing rapport with a client but have been shown to be unreliable in diagnosing mental illness, determining the better parent in child custody disputes, or distinguishing sexually abused from nonabused children.

     b.   The **Rorschach Inkblot Test** is a projective personality test that asks respondents to interpret abstract, symmetrical inkblots. This test shows poor reliability and validity and should not be used to diagnose psychopathology.

D.   Researchers have begun to study ideas generated by psychodynamic theories using the usual methods of scientific psychology.

Chapter Summary

Psychodynamic psychology has several unique features: an emphasis on the study of unconscious intrapsychic dynamics, a focus on the effects of 1._____ experiences in the formation of adult personality, and a concentration on the individual's symbolic and subjective interpretations of events. 2._____ is widely regarded as the father of psychoanalysis. . He is thought by some to have been the ultimate psychological thinker, but others view him as misguided or even fraudulent.

Freud believed that humans, like animals, are driven by sexual and aggressive 3._____, yet are raised to be social at the same time. As a result, more primitive drives are experienced as threatening. They are often hidden from the conscious mind, but they then emerge in symbolic form.

Freud thought of the personality as a system of three forces. The 4._____ is the instinctual component; it seeks primitive pleasure. The 5._____ attempts to mediate between the biological demands of both libido and the aggressive instincts, and social demands, which are represented by the third component, the 6._____. Freud saw human beings as inevitably in the midst of internal conflict, with the ego always trying to stay in control by balancing the opposing demands of the other two forces.

When the ego feels threatened that the id or the superego will overthrow it, it employs 7._____, which distort reality and allow the ego to avoid psychological discomfort.

These defenses operate unconsciously and function to keep the ego in control, but they can cause emotional problems and self-defeating behavior if they are overused. People tend to develop characteristic styles of defense. When these styles are unhealthy, the person is termed 8._____.

Freud believed that the unconscious was the prime mover in personality. Freud's view was that civilized people and cultures are able to exert ego control over id functions. Thus they are able to control primitive, often destructive, forces in healthy ways.

The personality, according to Freud, develops in a sequence of five predictable stages, each with its own critical psychological issue. If the characteristic problem of each stage is handled well, the child grows up to be a healthy adult. However, if the crisis is not resolved, 9._____ occurs, and 10._____ is the outcome. Freud named these stages, in order from the earliest, 11._____, 12._____, 13._____, and 14._____. The period of 15._____ occurs between the phallic and genital stages. The 16._____ conflict, which occurs during the 17._____ stage, is one of the most controversial aspects of Freud's theory, as he believed that children experience primitive sexual attractions toward their other-sex parent during this stage. He also thought that males and females progress through this stage in different ways, a contention that is frequently argued by many.

Freud's own writings indicate that he formulated his theories and pressured his patients to accept them. In the famous case of the patient 18._____, Freud reinterpreted a girl's symptoms that resulted from sexual advances by her father's friend as repressed desire for sex.

Psychoanalysis became a nearly religious movement that had both its adherents and dissenters. One analyst who disagreed with Freud's emphasis on sex and aggression was 19._____, who saw the prime motivation of personality as a striving for self-improvement. He thought that this striving was a way of dealing with the 20._____ complex of childhood.

21._____ was one of the first to challenge Freud's ideas about women. While Freud suggested that females suffer from 22._____, she argued that it was men's social position that women envied, not their anatomical features. In contrast, she suggested that men suffer from 23._____, a feeling of inferiority that results from an inability to give birth. Men, therefore, unconsciously fear women because of their power. Her theory centers around the person's continuing quest to cope with 24._____, a feeling of being alone and vulnerable in a hostile world.

One of the most important aspects of 25._____'s theory was his conception of the 26._____, a repository of the universal experiences of the human race. This structure contains 27._____, like the Shadow, the Mandala, and the Persona, which predispose people to react in certain ways.

28._____ expanded Freud's theory to encompass the development of the personality through the entire lifespan. Unlike Freud, Erikson believed that 29._____, not psychosexual, events were the most important influences on personality. Among these events are childhood independence and achievement, as well as adult identity formation and relationship development. He recognized that cultures function to inhibit or facilitate movements from one psychosocial stage to the next and showed that development is a lifelong process. Researchers have criticized this theory, pointing out that identity crises are not limited to the period of 30._____ and that many people are generative throughout their lives.

31._____ theory emphasizes relationships as the center of personality development, especially during the period of the first 32._____ years of life. The most important of these relationships involves the child's emotional attachments and reactions to his or her primary caregivers, as well as the child's internal 33._____ of the parent. From these early relationships, the person develops a characteristic style of both interacting with others and experiencing the self. For instance, early development involves 34._____, a separating of positive and negative feelings about the mother. In adulthood, the person must learn to accept and deal with these conflicting feelings in order to be psychologically healthy. As boys and girls both have to deal with their primary relationships with their mothers, some theorists believe that gender roles reflect 35._____ tendencies in girls and the formation of 36._____ in boys.

Humanist and 37._____ psychologists emphasize the free will that comes with being human. A leading theorist in this area, 38._____, emphasized the side of human nature that included positive emotions and 39._____ experiences, moments of rapture at the attainment of excellence or appreciation of beauty. These qualities characterize the 40._____ person, who strives for a meaningful and challenging life.

Another leading theorist, 41._____, was interested in fully functioning individuals who exhibit a 42._____ between their conscious and unconscious selves. He believed that full functioning involved fundamental love and support from others, which he called 43._____ experiences. 44._____ was a proponent of the psychological theory that most emphasizes free will and responsibility, 45._____ psychology. This approach emphasizes the importance of struggling with the harsh realities of life.

Theorists from other perspectives often criticize psychodynamic theories for their reliance on 46._____ data and inference. Since structures like the unconscious and the human spirit are unobservable, little of psychodynamic theory is directly 47._____. At the same time, these theories make intuitive sense and contribute to a sense of a deeper understanding of human personality than learning theory and biological research seem to provide.

Psychoanalysts reject the usual methods of science in favor of their own interpretations of their patients' behaviors. To 48._____ psychologists, this makes psychoanalysis highly suspect, and it has sometimes been labeled a "pseudoscience." Psychodynamic psychologists counter that their approach allows a deeper understanding of people's mental lives. Methodologically, they are willing to examine all aspects of human action, including culture, dreams, and accidental behavior. Psychodynamic psychologists provide explanations for "irrational" behavior, which empirical psychologists have difficulty doing. Explanations based on 49._____ motivations can account for the lack of predictability in human conduct.

Critics of the psychodynamic approach cite its tendency to reduce all behavior to unconscious processes, thus overlooking the importance of biology, learning, culture, and other factors that are known to affect behavior. They also point out that the construction of psychodynamic theories make them impossible to either confirm or disprove. Thus they represent ideologies more than scientific theories, with their appeal based more on popularity than on research evidence.

Psychodynamic psychologists often rely on atypical patient accounts, or 50._____ studies, to illustrate their theories. The findings of small samples are 51._____ to the rest of the population. They also base their theories on patients' memories, which have a great capacity for distortion. The tendency to draw causal inferences from events that occur together is unscientific. These 52._____ studies are not as reliable as following a group of people over a period of years in a 53._____ study, which often shows different results. Some subjective methods have been shown to be invalid and unreliable for the diagnosis of mental illness or other purposes, most notable 54._____ tests, in which individuals are asked to interpret ambiguous stimuli. The most well-known of these tests is the 55._____, which has problems with reliability and validity despite its popularity with therapists. In recent years, empirical psychologists have tried to solve some of these problems by using innovative research methods.

Multiple Choice Self-Test

1.   According to Freud, people who are impulsive and self-centered are too controlled by the:
a.   id.
b.   ego.
c.   superego.
d.   defense mechanism.

2.   A person who is fixated in the anal stage would probably be:
a.   a compulsive smoker or overeater.
b.   excessively sloppy or excessively neat.
c.   sexually dysfunctional or prudish.
d.   self-absorbed.

3.   According to Freud, the sexual drive is fueled by:
a.   repression.
b.   fixation.
c.   projection.
d.   libido.

4.	Andrew is always looking for someone to take care of him. According to Horney, he is looking for protection from his:
a.	basic anxiety.
b.	inferiority complex.
c.	collective unconscious.
d.	ideal self.

5.	"All human beings are searching for ways that they can deal with their deep-seated feelings of being less powerful than others." This statement would most likely be made by:
a.	Alfred Adler.
b.	Karen Horney.
c.	Erik Erikson.
d.	John Bowlby.

6.	Rasheeda grew up in Hawaii, where there are no snakes. The first time she saw a snake, she reacted with fear. According to Jung, this reaction could be caused by:
a.	transference.
b.	repression.
c.	free association.
d.	an archetype.

7.	Paul, a 22-year-old, acts like a child when he experiences a stressful event. His behavior illustrates the defense mechanism of:
a.	regression.
b.	repression.
c.	denial.
d.	reaction formation.

8.	Deidre has just been diagnosed with terminal cancer. When her friend visits her, Deidre does not seem upset. She says that she hasn't thought about her health at all today. Freud would call Deidre's behavior:
a.	projection.
b.	repression.
c.	reaction formation.
d.	regression.

9.	According to Freud, male and female development differs in which of the following stages?
a.	oral
b.	phallic
c.	genital
d.	latency

10. It is difficult to understand the behavior of serial killers like Jeffrey Dahmer and Ted Bundy. In searching for explanations, object-relations theorists would be most interested in:
a. their early childhood attachments to their mothers.
b. their status in their school peer groups.
c. their deep-seated feelings of inferiority.
d. their basic anxiety.

11. Parents often tell their children that they should marry and have a family when they grow up. What would existential psychologists say about this advice?
a. They would reject it, since every person has to define his or her own meaning in life.
b. They would reject it, since the child's sexual orientation is unknown at an early age.
c. They would accept it, since the development of intimacy is considered a sign of maturity.
d. They would accept it, since marriage helps one to better understand the self.

12. Research psychologists sometimes criticize the psychodynamic approach on the basis of its:
a. poor educational value.
b. failure to address the depth of human behavior.
c. lack of scientific rigor.
d. failure to account for irrational behavior.

13. Three-year-old Donny constantly tries to imitate his father. According to Freud, he does so because:
a. he unconsciously fears his father.
b. he unconsciously hates his mother.
c. he is afraid of his own impulses.
d. he fears his feminine side.

14. Erikson's theory is similar to Freud's in its:
a. description of stages occurring throughout the lifespan.
b. emphasis on instinctual determinants of behavior.
c. assumption that people are inherently self-centered.
d. theory that a "crisis" must be resolved at each stage.

15. Horney's theory is similar to Adler's in its:
a. emphasis on identity crisis.
b. description of the child as helpless and vulnerable.
c. concept of "womb envy."
d. assumption that people strive for perfection.

16. Adler's theory is similar to Erikson's in its:
a. conception of personality development as a never-ending process.
b. emphasis on controlling the environment.
c. assumption that adult neurosis is the result of childhood fixation.
d. belief that all behavior is a compensation for unconscious negative feelings about the self.

17. According to some object-relations theorists, males may seem more independent than females because:
a. the collective unconscious contains archetypes of male hunters who spend large amounts of time alone.
b. boys must put rigid ego boundaries between themselves and their mothers at an early age.
c. society encourages males to deny their attachment to others.
d. males receive rewards for being independent more often than females do.

18. A major difference between existential psychology and most psychoanalytic theories is the existential emphasis on:
a. childhood events.
b. defensiveness.
c. self-determination.
d. instinct.

19. Horney believed that "womb envy":
a. causes women to feel superior.
b. encourages men to mistreat women in order to make up for their own sense of inadequacy.
c. makes men driven to father as many children as possible.
d. results in less anxiety than either penis envy or castration anxiety.

20. Children of abusive parents:
a. are no more likely than others to have psychological symptoms.
b. nearly always abuse their own children when they become adults.
c. usually are well adjusted by adulthood.
d. are likely to become better parents than nonabused children.

21. According to Freud, the biological part of the personality is the:
a. id.
b. ego.
c. superego.
d. conscious.

22. Based on available research, projective tests can be used to:
a. diagnose depression, but not anxiety disorders.
b. help make a decision in a child custody dispute.
c. develop rapport with a therapy client.
d. uncover repressed childhood abuse.

23. In the term "object-relations," the "object" usually refers to:
a. an early childhood toy.
b. an important person.
c. a life goal.
d. childhood protest against the parent.

24. According to existentialists, anxiety is the result of:
a. unfulfilled potential.
b. threats from the unconscious.
c. the harsh realities of life.
d. fear of mistreatment by others.

25. Of the perspectives discussed in the text, the best explanation for irrational behavior can be found in:
a. psychodynamic theory.
b. learning theory.
c. biological theory.
d. cognitive theory.

26. According to psychodynamic theory, what do accidents, jokes, and myths all have in common?
a. They are all learned during early interactions with parents.
b. They result from the breakdown of the ego.
c. They commonly occur during the anal stage of personality development.
d. They reveal unconscious impulses.

27. You are worried about your best friend because he won't admit that he has a serious drug problem. When you speak to your friend about his problem, you suggest that he is in denial about the effects that drugs have on his life. Which of the following psychological perspectives seems to have had the greatest influence on your understanding of your friend's problem?
a. the biological perspective
b. the cognitive perspective
c. the psychodynamic perspective
d. the sociocultural perspective

28. Alberta studied hard in her psychology course and she received an "A" at the end of the semester. What part of the personality, according to Freud, allowed Alberta to feel an enormous sense of pride in her accomplishment?
a. the id
b. the superego
c. the ego
d. the cognate

29. According to Freud, when is a child MOST likely to display hostility toward the same-sexed parent?
a. during the Oedipal stage
b. during the anal stage
c. during the stage of trust vs. mistrust
d. during the oral stage

30. Freud's concept of the "libido" is MOST similar to Karen Horney's concept of:
a. frustration.
b. basic anxiety.
c. suppression.
d. sexual spontaneity.

True-False Self-Test

T   F   1.   All psychodynamic theories involve speculations about intrapsychic events.

T   F   2.   Freud was a physician.

T   F   3.   The ego is driven by the pleasure principle.

T   F   4.   The ego controls the personality in a healthy person.

T   F   5.   Freud's view was that using defense mechanisms is always unhealthy.

T   F   6.   Scapegoating is an example of repression.

T   F   7.   Reaction formation involves converting unacceptable impulses into acceptable ones.

T   F   8.   The most basic defense mechanism is denial.

T   F   9.   Freud viewed human beings as forever dealing with conflicts within themselves.

T   F   10.   The phallic stage begins at puberty.

T   F   11.   Projective tests are useful in psychiatric diagnosis.

T   F   12.   Freud conducted many carefully controlled experiments.

T   F   13.   The idea of the Oedipus conflict is widely accepted among psychologists.

T F 14. Feminists tend to view Freud as something of a hero.

T F 15. According to Horney, people are driven by basic anxiety.

T F 16. Horney coined the term "inferiority complex."

T F 17. Adler had basic disagreements with Freud's theory.

T F 18. The collective unconscious contains archetypes.

T F 19. Erikson's first four stages reflect the same time periods as Freud's oral, anal, phallic, and latency periods.

T F 20. According to Erikson, most adolescents experience an "identity crisis."

T F 21. Object-relations theory focuses on a child's attachment to his or her parents.

T F 22. Object-relations theorists view internal representations of parents as a reflection of unhealthy defense.

T F 23. Most children rendered homeless in World War II failed to adjust to their adoptive homes.

T F 24. Existentialism emphasizes free will more than most psychodynamic theories.

T F 25. The psychodynamic perspective is often criticized for its overreliance on case studies.

T F 26. Psychodynamic hypotheses are difficult to test.

T F 27. Psychodynamic theories explain lost childhood memories as motivated by anxiety.

T F 28. Childhood sexual abuse was apparently quite rare in Freud's day.

T F 29. Freud pressured his patients to accept his theories.

T F 30. Sexual abuse in childhood inevitably causes adult emotional problems.

Key Terms

psychoanalysis A theory of personality and a method of psychotherapy developed by Sigmund Freud; it emphasizes unconscious motives and conflicts.

intrapsychic Within the mind (psyche) or self.

id In psychoanalysis, the part of the mind containing inherited psychic energy; particularly sexual and aggressive instincts.

libido (li-BEE-do) In psychoanalysis, the psychic energy that fuels the life or sexual instincts of the id.

ego In psychoanalysis, the part of the mind that represents reason, good sense, and rational self control; it mediates between id and superego.

superego In psychoanalysis, the part of the mind that represents conscience, morality, and social standards.

defense mechanisms Methods used by the ego to prevent unconscious anxiety or threatening thoughts from entering consciousness.

Oedipus complex In psychoanalysis, a conflict in which a child desires the parent of the other sex and views the same-sex parent as a rival; the key issue in the phallic stage of development.

castration anxiety In psychoanalysis, the boy's unconscious fear of castration by the powerful father; this anxiety motivates the resolution of the Oedipus complex.

inferiority complex To Alfred Adler, an inability to accept one's natural limitations; it occurs when the need for self-improvement is blocked or inhibited.

basic anxiety To Karen Horney, the feeling of being isolated and helpless in a hostile world; it is the motivating emotion in social relations.

collective unconscious To Carl Jung, the universal memories and experiences of humankind, represented in the symbols, stories, and images (archetypes) that occur across all cultures.

archetypes (AR-ki-tipes) Universal, symbolic images that appear in myths, art, stories, and dreams; to Carl Jung, they reflect the collective unconscious.

object-relations theory A psychodynamic approach that emphasizes the importance of the infant's first two years and the baby's formative relationships, especially with the mother.

splitting In object-relations theory, the division of qualities into their opposites, as in the Good Mother versus the Bad Mother; it reflects an inability to understand that people are made up of good and bad qualities.

humanist psychology A psychological approach that emphasizes personal growth and the achievement of human potential rather than the scientific understanding and assessment of behavior.

unconditional positive regard To Carl Rogers, love or support given to another person, with no conditions attached.

existential psychology An approach to psychology that emphasizes free will and responsibility for one's actions, and the importance of struggling with the harsh realities of existence, such as the need to find meaning in life and to accept suffering and death.

projective tests Psychological tests used to infer a person's motives, conflicts, and unconscious dynamics on the basis of the person's interpretations of ambiguous stimuli.

Rorschach Inkblot Test A projective personality test that asks respondents to interpret abstract, symmetrical inkblots.

Suggested Research Projects

1. Construct your own personality test. For example, you might be interested in measuring people's basic anxiety, as suggested by Horney's theory. Create some scenarios and allow people to choose a course of action from among several choices. Remember, you must first obtain their consent to be in an experiment.

2. Describe a character in a television show, movie, or novel in terms of psychoanalytic themes. Summarize the character's behavior, then try to explain why the person acted as he or she did, using a theory that interests you.

3. Take some psychological trait (like shyness, aggressiveness, alcoholism, or aloofness) and speculate on how Freud, Horney, Jung, or another psychodynamic theorist would talk about the development of that trait.

Suggested Readings

Freud, S., Gay, P. (ed.). (1995, reissue ed.). *The Freud reader*. New York: Norton. A large collection of Freud's most important writings.

Horney, K. (1967). *Feminine psychology*. New York: Norton. A collection of essays by one of the most influential women psychoanalysts.

Jung, C. G. (1964). *Man and his symbols*. New York: Doubleday. An illustrated description of the importance of art and religion to psychology.

May, R. (Ed.). (1961). *Existential psychology*. New York: Random House. A description of the application of existential philosophy to psychological functioning.

CHAPTER 12

Mental Disorders and Their Treatment

Learning Objectives

After reading and studying this chapter, you should be able to:

1. Define mental disorder.

2. Summarize the symptoms of the anxiety disorders, mood disorders, personality disorders, and schizophrenia.

3. Compare and contrast theories of various disorders from the viewpoints of the different psychological perspectives.

4. Discuss the sociocultural contexts of diagnoses and treatments of mental disorders.

5. Describe the procedures, uses, and misuses of psychosurgery and electroconvulsive therapy.

6. Describe the uses, sites of action, risks, and misuses of drugs that are prescribed for various mental disorders.

7. Compare and contrast behavioral, cognitive, biological, systems, humanist, existential, and psychodynamic therapies and their applications.

8. Discuss the controversy over dissociative identity disorder.

9. Describe biological, learning, cognitive, and sociocultural findings about music.

10. Summarize, compare, and contrast research about sex from the viewpoints of each of the major psychological perspectives.

Chapter Outline

I. Diagnosing Mental Disorder

    A. A **mental disorder** is any behavior or emotional state that causes an individual great suffering or worry, is self-defeating or self-destructive, or is maladaptive and disrupts the person's relationships or the larger community.

        1. The standard reference for diagnosis is the *Diagnostic and Statistical Manual of Mental Disorders* (DSM), which provides:

        a.   clear diagnostic categories for study and treatment.

        b.   symptoms for each disorder.

        c.   prevalence of the disorder.

   2.   Cultural consensus plays a role in defining mental disorder.

   3.   Some diagnoses appear to be universal across cultures.

II.   Some Major Disorders

   A.   Anxiety Disorders. Anxiety is a general state of apprehension or psychological tension.

   B.   Anxiety states.

      1.   **generalized anxiety disorder** is a continuous state of anxiety marked by feelings of worry and dread, apprehension, difficulties in concentration, and signs of motor tension.

        a.   According to researchers from the biological perspective, there is a physiological predisposition for some people.

        b.   Researchers from the learning perspective emphasize a history of uncontrollable and unpredictable environments and *precipitating factors* in the person's life.

      2.   **Posttraumatic stress disorder** is an anxiety disorder in which a person who has experienced a traumatic or life-threatening event has symptoms such as psychic numbing, reliving of the trauma, and increased physiological arousal.

      3.   **Panic disorder** is an anxiety disorder in which a person experiences recurring *panic attacks*, periods of intense fear and feelings of impending doom or death, accompanied by physiological symptoms such as rapid breathing and pulse, and dizziness.

        a.   Panic disorders are related to stress and other factors.

        b.   Cognitive research has revealed that panic sufferers interpret their bodily reactions as a sign of impending death or disaster.

        c.   Sociocultural researchers have shown that panic symptoms differ across cultures.

   C.   Fears and Phobias.

      1.   A **phobia** is an exaggerated, unrealistic fear of a specific situation, activity, or object.

      2.   The most disabling phobia is **agoraphobia**, a set of phobias, often set off by a panic attack, involving the basic fear of being away from a safe place or person.

   D.   Obsessions and Compulsions.

      1.   **obsessive-compulsive disorder (OCD)** is an anxiety disorder in which a person feels trapped in repetitive, persistent thoughts (obsessions) and repetitive, ritualized behaviors (compulsions) designed to reduce anxiety.

        a.   The most common compulsions are hand washing, counting, touching, and checking.

b.   PET scans reveal that several parts of the brain are overactive in OCD patients.

E.   Mood Disorders. The most widespread serious mood disorder is **major depression**, a mood disorder involving disturbances in emotion (excessive sadness), behavior (loss of interest in one's usual activities), cognition (thoughts of hopelessness), and body function (fatigue and loss of appetite).

    1.   **bipolar disorder** is a mood disorder in which episodes of both depression and mania (excessive euphoria) occur. It occurs about as frequently in men as in women.

    2.   Major depression occurs two to three times as often among women as among men. This may be an actual difference in rates of depression, or:

        a.   women are more likely to express negative emotions.

        b.   women are more likely to seek treatment.

        c.   depression in males may be overlooked or misdiagnosed, masked by denial, drug abuse, or violence.

F.   Theories of Depression.

    1.   Biological explanations emphasize genetics and brain chemistry.

        a.   Twin studies indicate the existence of a genetic component, although specific genes have not been identified.

        b.   Genes may create biochemical imbalances.

        c.   Depression may be caused by deficiencies in serotonin and norepinephrine, bipolar disorder by excesses in these two neurotransmitters.

        d.   Brain scans of depressed people show less active left frontal lobe activity, which could be a cause or an effect of the disorder.

    2.   Learning explanations emphasize how repeated experiences with failure and pain can "extinguish" the energy to cope and overcome setbacks.

        a.   The *learned helplessness* theory held that people become depressed when their efforts to avoid pain or control their environments consistently fail.

        b.   However, not all depressed people's backgrounds are like this.

    3.   Cognitive explanations emphasize particular habits of thinking and ways of interpreting events. Depressed people's thinking tends toward:

        a.   *Internality*, the belief that one's misery is entrenched in one's personality.

        b.   *Stability*, the belief that their situation is permanent.

        c.   Belief in a *lack of control* over their emotions or situations.

        d.   Brooding, or ruminating about their unhappiness. As women are more likely than men to develop this style, it may contribute to the sex difference in depression.

4. Social explanations emphasize the stressful circumstances of people's lives.
    a. From this perspective, women suffer from depression more often because they have less satisfying lives, lower status in society, and higher rates of poverty and sexual victimization.
        i. mothers are especially vulnerability to depression if they have many children and are unemployed.
        ii. men are more likely to be both married and working, a combination associated with low rates of depression.
    b. Violence is a risk factor, although most victims of violence do not become depressed.
5. Attachment and object-relations explanations emphasize problems with close relationships.
    a. Depression can be both a cause and an effect of relationship disruption.
    b. A longitudinal study indicated that marital problems tended to make wives depressed, but that for husbands, being depressed caused the marital problems.
6. Researchers are increasingly integrating all of these explanations into a *"vulnerability-stress"* approach.

G. Personality Disorders.
1. **personality disorders** are rigid, maladaptive personality patterns that cause personal distress or an inability to get along with others.
    a. **paranoid personality disorder** is a disorder characterized by habitually unreasonable and excessive suspiciousness or jealousy.
    b. **Narcissistic personality disorder** is a disorder characterized by an exaggerated sense of self-importance and self-absorption.
    c. **Antisocial personality disorder (APD)** is a disorder characterized by antisocial behavior such as lying, stealing, manipulating others, and sometimes violence; a lack of guilt, shame, and empathy. (Sometimes called *psychopathy* or *sociopathy*).
        i. People with APD are slow to develop physiological anxiety and fear responses and often fail to learn that their actions will have unpleasant consequences.
        ii. APD may involve an inability to control responses to frustration and provocation.
        iii. Children of parents with APD, substance-abuse problems, or impulsivity disorders are at a higher risk for developing these disorders, even if they are raised by others.
        iv. Many children who become violent have suffered brain injuries and neurological impairment.

          v.   According to the *vulnerability-stress model*, biological vulnerability combines with other environmental stresses to put people at high risk for APD.

H.   Schizophrenia. **Schizophrenia** is a psychotic disorder or group of disorders marked by positive symptoms (e.g., delusions, hallucinations, disorganized or incoherent speech, and inappropriate behavior) and negative symptoms (e.g., emotional flatness and loss of motivation).

     1.   It is a form of **psychosis**, an extreme mental disturbance involving distorted perceptions and irrational behavior; it may have psychological or organic causes. (Plural: *psychoses*.)

     2.   Positive symptoms of schizophrenia include:

          a.   bizarre delusions (false beliefs).

          b.   hallucinations and heightened sensory awareness.

          c.   disorganized, incoherent speech.

          d.   grossly disorganized and inappropriate behavior.

     3.   Negative symptoms include loss of motivation, poverty of speech, and emotional flatness. Some schizophrenics withdraw completely into a *catatonic stupor*.

     4.   Theories of Schizophrenia. Biological theories include:

          a.   Genetic predispositions. Data show that, the closer the genetic relationship to a person with schizophrenia, the greater the risk for developing the disorder. However, no specific gene has been identified.

          b.   Structural brain abnormalities. Some show signs of cerebral damage, enlargement of *ventricles*, or other abnormalities.

          c.   Neurotransmitter abnormalities. These include abnormalities in seratonin, glutamate, and especially dopamine.

          d.   Prenatal abnormalities. Fetal brain damage increases risk.

     5.   Researchers in the *vulnerability-stress model* have identified a combination of risk factors:

          a.   schizophrenia in the family.

          b.   physical trauma during childbirth.

          c.   exposure to prenatal trauma during the second trimester of pregnancy.

          d.   unstable, stressful environments.

III.   The Biological Perspective.

A.   **Psychosurgery** is any surgical procedure that destroys selected areas of the brain believed to be involved in emotional disorders or violent, impulsive behavior.

     1.   Prefrontal lobotomies were performed on tens of thousands of people, often with severe negative results.

B.   **Electroconvulsive therapy (ECT)** is a procedure used in cases of prolonged and severe major depression, in which a brief brain seizure is induced.

1. People have been treated successfully with ECT, but critics argue that ECT is often used improperly and can damage the brain.

C. Medicating the Mind. Drugs are widely prescribed for many mental disorders.

1. **Antipsychotic drugs**, also called *neuroleptics*, are used primarily in the treatment of schizophrenia and other psychotic disorders.
   a. Many reduce the sensitivity of dopamine receptors; some also increase levels of seratonin.
   b. These drugs can reduce agitation, delusions, and hallucinations, but give little relief from other symptoms.
   c. It is estimated that drugs help 60% of schizophrenics.
   d. There are unpleasant side effects. Many develop *tardive dyskinesia* – involuntary muscle movements.

2. **Antidepressant drugs** are used primarily in the treatment of mood disorders, especially depression and anxiety.
   a. Monoamine Oxidase (MAO) inhibitors elevate norepinephrine and seratonin levels by blocking an enzyme that deactivates these neurotransmitters.
   b. Tricyclic antidepressants boost these neurotransmitters by blocking reuptake.
   c. Selective seratonin reuptake inhibitors (SSRIs) specifically target seratonin.
   d. Antidepressants can produce unpleasant physical reactions.

3. **Tranquilizers** are drugs commonly but often inappropriately prescribed for patients who complain of unhappiness, anxiety, or worry.
   a. These drugs are not effective for depression or panic disorder and people who take them can also develop problems with withdrawal and tolerance.

4. **Lithium carbonate** is a drug frequently given to people suffering from bipolar disorder.
   a. It moderates levels of norepinephrine and protects the brain from being overstimulated by glutamate.
   b. Bloodstream Lithium levels must be carefully monitored -- too little is ineffective; too much is toxic.

D. Evaluating Medical Treatments. Drugs' potential risks and limitations include:

1. the **placebo effect**, the apparent success of a medication or treatment that is due to the patient's expectations or hopes rather than to the drug or treatment itself.
   a. A large amount of evidence questions the effectiveness of antidepressants.

2. high relapse and dropout rates. Half to two-thirds of people stop taking antidepressant or antipsychotic drugs.

3. dosage problems. It is a challenge to find the *therapeutic window*, the proper dosage. People of different ages, sexes, and ethnicities differ in the dosages they need and can tolerate.

4. long-term risks.
5. Many people have been helped by these drugs, but there are a number of problems:
   a. the overprescribing of drugs under pressure from managed-care organizations and drug companies.
   b. prescribing drugs for other-than-intended purposes.

IV. The Learning and Cognitive Perspectives

A. Behavior Therapy. Commonly used methods include:
   1. **Systematic desensitization**, a step-by-step process of desensitizing a client to a feared object or experience; based on the classical-conditioning procedure of *counterconditioning*.
   2. **aversive conditioning** In behavior therapy, a method in which punishment is substituted for the reinforcement that is perpetuating a bad habit.
   3. **exposure treatment** In behavior therapy, a method in which a person suffering from an anxiety disorder, such as a phobia or panic attacks, is taken directly into the feared situation until the anxiety subsides.
   4. Behavioral records and contracts help clients identify reinforcers that maintain unwanted habits. Then a treatment program can be designed to change the reinforcers and set behavioral goals.
   5. *Skills training* provides practice in behaviors that are necessary for achieving a person's goals.
B. Cognitive therapy. Cognitive therapy helps clients to identify and change beliefs and expectations that might be associated with problems.
   1. In *rational emotive behavior therapy*, the therapist uses rational arguments to challenge a clients unrealistic beliefs.
C. Evaluating Behavior and Cognitive Therapies. These therapies are particularly effective with:
   1. Depression. Cognitive therapy is often more effective and longer lasting than drug therapy.
   2. Anxiety disorders.
      a. Exposure techniques are more effective than other treatments for PTSD and phobia.
      b. Systematic desensitization is effective as a treatment for simple phobia.
      c. Cognitive-behavior therapy is more effective than drugs for panic, generalized anxiety, and obsessive-compulsive disorders.
   3. Anger and impulsive violence.
   4. Health problems.
   5. Childhood and adolescent behavior problems. Cognitive training also helps prevent depression in at-risk children.

V.   The Sociocultural Perspective

    A.   Therapy in Social Context. The sociocultural perspective emphasizes the
            effect of others on the client's behavior and the relationship with the
            therapist.
            1.   *Family therapy* helps couples and families to break out of negative
                    patterns of interaction. From a *family-systems* perspective, the
                    entire system can change if one member's behavior changes.
            2.   In *group therapy*, the influence of other people is used to effect
                    therapeutic change.
            3.   The success of therapy depends on the **therapeutic alliance**, the
                    bond of confidence and mutual understanding established between
                    therapist and client, which allows them to work together to solve
                    the client's problems.
    B.   Therapy in Cultural Context.
            1.   Therapists must be careful not to transform a cultural norm into a
                    pathological problem.
            2.   Sensitivity to cultural issues is not the same as stereotyping.
            3.   Therapists should take a client's cultural background into
                    consideration in diagnosis and treatment.
            4.   The goals of therapy reflect the values of the larger culture.
    C.   Evaluating the Sociocultural Contribution.
            1.   One of the greatest contributions of this perspective is the concept
                    of therapy as a social exchange in which a therapist uses
                    influence.
            2.   Some therapists have misused their influence, are ignorant about
                    cultural issues, or are biased toward those of different ethnicities or
                    sexual orientations than their own.
            3.   A therapist's influence can produce a disorder that the patient did
                    not have. This process may account for the increase in
                    dissociative identity disorder, a controversial disorder marked by
                    the appearance within one person of two or more distinct
                    personalities, each with its own name and traits; commonly known
                    as *multiple personality disorder (MPD)*.

VI.   The Psychodynamic Perspective

    A.   Therapies for the "Inner Life".
            1.   In *psychoanalysis*, the guiding assumption is that analysis of the
                    patient's past and unconscious motives will help to gain insight into
                    symptoms, which disappear with insight and emotional release.
                    a.   To bring unconscious conflicts into awareness, therapists
                            look at dreams, fantasies, and memories, and encourage
                            the patient to *free associate*, saying whatever comes to
                            mind.

        b.   A key element is **transference**, a critical step in which the client transfers unconscious emotions or reactions, such a emotional feelings about his or her parents, onto the therapist. The analysis of transference helps clients to resolve their emotional conflicts.

        c.   In orthodox psychoanalysis, the client and therapist meet several times a week for a period of years. More modern approaches are more goal-directed and time-limited.

2.   *Humanist therapies* start with the assumption that people seek self-actualization.

        a.   Humanist therapists want to know how clients perceive situations and help them feel better about themselves.

        b.   In client-centered therapy, the therapist's role is to listen with *unconditional positive regard*, a nonjudgmental, accepting attitude.

3.   *Existential therapy* helps clients explore the meaning of existence and confront questions such as death, freedom, and meaninglessness.

B.   The Scientist-Practitioner Gap. This gap is the major divide between psychodynamic assumptions and the methods of research-based perspectives.

1.   Many psychodynamic therapists see psychotherapy as an art, not a science, and see empirical research in this area as not useful.

2.   Scientists are concerned that therapists who do not follow the empirical research may be harming their clients. Clinical insight and experience are unreliable for predicting behavior.

3.   People with specific emotional problems should be treated with empirically validated approaches.

VII.   Therapy in Perspective

A.   Many therapists draw on multiple methods from cognitive, behavioral, family, and psychodynamic approaches.

1.   Some team up with psychiatrists so that their patients can also take medication. Some patients respond best to a combination of medication and psychotherapy.

2.   A promising treatment for sex offenders combines several approaches.

3.   Consumers should think critically about psychotherapy and be cautious about therapies that are not grounded in psychology's major perspectives.

VIII. Essay Six: The Whole Elephant. The Joy of Music.

A.   Music consists of pitch (melody), rhythm (sounds grouped according to a system), and timbre (tone qualities).

B.   According to Gardner, musical genius is in part heritable.

C. An appreciation of music may be biologically based.
    1.   Music is localized in a different part of the brain than language.
    2.   A few people are completely tone deaf (have *amusia*).
    3.   Different sets of neurons in the right hemisphere are activated when people are listening and playing music.
    3.   Brain development is affected by early musical training.
    4.   Perfect pitch appears to innate.
D. There are cultural differences in the relative emphases of pitch, rhythm, and timbre, as well as in attitudes and expectations about musical abilities.
E. Children develop cognitive schemas about music, and each generation partly defines itself around favorite music.
F. Cognitive psychologists are studying how rhythm and pitch are perceived and remembered. Learning affects all aspects of musical intelligence.

IX. The Joy of Sex

A. The Biological Perspective. Researchers study the physiology of sexual desire, arousal, and behavior.
    1.   A minimal level of testosterone seems to promote sexual desire in both sexes. Sexual activity also produces higher levels of testosterone.
    2.   Contrary to what Freud believed, there are not different kinds of female orgasms.
    3.   Male and female arousal and orgasms are physiologically similar; male and female genitals develop from the same tissue.
B. The Learning Perspective.
    1.   Sexuality is affected by:
        a.   parental lessons.
        b.   knowledge and attitudes.
    2.   People learn to follow *sexual scripts* that are influenced by:
        a.   gender roles.
        b.   cultural standards.
C. The Cognitive Perspective. This perspective holds that:
    1.   Sexual attitudes, beliefs, values, and expectations affect behavior.
    2.   Distracting thoughts interfere with sexual pleasure and arousal.
    3.   How a person interprets his or her physical states affects sexuality.
D. The Sociocultural Perspective. Researchers from this perspective have found that:
    1.   Cultural norms and group pressure affect people's sexual behavior.
    2.   External pressures affect the sexual behavior of both men and women.
    3.   Cultures vary in:
        a.   the clothing and body parts that are considered erotic.
        b.   sexual acts that are considered erotic or repulsive.
        c.   standards of beauty.
E. The Psychodynamic Perspective. Psychodynamic theorists suggest that:

1.   Sexual relationships involve unconscious dynamics.
2.   Sexuality is susceptible to defense mechanisms.
3.   Men and women have different unconscious sexual fears and vulnerabilities.

X.   Reflections on psychology

     A.   No single perspective can explain all psychological phenomena. Behavior is affected by:
         1.   biological influences such as physiology, heredity, and hormonal activity.
         2.   learning influences: environmental factors that encourage certain kinds of learning.
         3.   cognitive influences: the style and content of explanations for events.
         4.   sociocultural influences: the expectations and demands of others.
         5.   psychodynamic influences: unconscious intrapsychic forces.

Chapter Summary

A 1._____ is any behavior or emotional state that causes suffering, is self-defeating, maladaptive, or disruptive of relationships. 2._____ is a continuous state of feelings such as worry and dread. There is a biological predisposition for this problem, but researchers from the 3._____ perspective emphasize a history of unpredictable environments and precipitating factors in the person's life. Other anxiety disorders include 4._____ disorder, which is characterized by negative psychological reactions to a difficult or life-threatening event, 5._____, which involves attacks of intense fear and physiological symptoms, and 6._____, an exaggerated, unrealistic fear of a specific object or situation. The most disabling of the latter disorder is 7._____in which a person fears being away from a safe place or person. The symptoms of 8._____ are repetitive, persistent thoughts and repetitive, ritualized behaviors designed to reduce anxiety.

Major depression is the most serious type of 9._____ disorder. It involves disturbances in emotion, behavior, cognition, and physical functioning. When a person with these symptoms also has periods of excessive euphoria, the diagnosis is 10._____ disorder. There is a sex difference in depression, with 11._____ having the disorder more often than the other sex.

Biological explanations of depression emphasize genetics and brain chemistry, while 12._____ explanations emphasize repeated experiences with failure and lack of control over the environment, specifically referred to as the 13._____ theory. 14._____ explanations make reference to faulty ways of interpreting events. Depressed people tend to see negative events as stemming from sources that are 15._____ (within the personality) and 16._____ (not changing). Women are more likely than men to 17._____, or brood about their problems, which may prolong their unhappiness. The 18._____ perspective emphasizes the influence of stressful circumstances in people's lives. Attachment and 19._____ psychologists emphasize relationship disruption as both cause and effect of depression. No single explanation is adequate by itself, and researchers are increasingly integrating all of these explanations in a 20._____ approach.

21._____ disorders are marked by rigid and maladaptive patterns of behavior. These include 22._____ disorder, which is characterized by extreme suspiciousness, and 23._____ disorder, in which the person has an exaggerated sense of self-importance. 24._____ disorder, or APD, is of great concern to psychologists because of the propensity in these people for violence and other violations of people's rights. Research on APD indicates that biological abnormalities combine with environmental stresses to produce this disorder.

Symptoms such as hallucinations and delusions characterize the serious mental disorder called 25._____, which is classified as a 26._____ disorder because it involves distorted perceptions and thought processes. Biological explanations of this disorder include 27._____ predispositions, brain abnormalities, and abnormalities in 28._____ such as seratonin and dopamine. Researchers in the 29._____ model have identified a combination of risk factors that include a family history of the disorder, natal and prenatal trauma, and environmental factors.

30._____ is any medical procedure in which selected parts of the brain are intentionally destroyed. Historically, the most common of these operations was the 31._____, in which portions of the frontal part of the brain were destroyed. These procedures usually resulted in lifelong mental disturbances. In some cases of severe depression, a brain seizure is induced, a controversial treatment known as 32._____ therapy.

Drugs are widely prescribed to treat mental disorders. 33._____ drugs, also known as neuroleptics, are used in the treatment of schizophrenia and other like disorders. Although these drugs can reduce symptoms of the disorder, there are often unpleasant side effects, including a long-term loss of control over muscle movements called 34._____. MAO inhibitors, Tricyclics, and selective seratonin reuptake inhibitors (SSRIs) all belong to the class of drugs known as 35._____. Perhaps the most frequently mis-prescribed class of drugs are 36._____, which are sometimes inappropriately prescribed for people who complain about anxiety or worry. 37._____ is a drug used to treat bipolar disorder.

Drugs' potential risks include the 38._____ effect, which is a product of patients' expectations. It is also difficult to find the 39._____, or correct dosage of a drug, and there is pressure on physicians to prescribe drugs by companies that profit from the decision to do so.

The 40._____ perspective has led to a group of techniques known as behavior therapy, which include 41._____, a step-by-step process of treating phobia based on counterconditioning 42._____ conditioning, in which punishment is substituted for the reinforcement that sustains a bad habit, and 43._____ treatment, in which the phobia sufferer faces the feared situation until anxiety subsides. 44._____ is another technique that employs practicing desired behaviors. 45._____ therapies such as rational-emotive behavior therapy are used to challenge clients' unrealistic beliefs. Behavioral and cognitive therapies have demonstrated effective results for many disorders.

The sociocultural perspective emphasizes the social context of mental disorders. Two popular approaches from this perspective are family therapy and group therapy. Sociocultural psychologists also note that the success of therapy depends critically on the quality of the 46._____, a working bond between client and therapist. This perspective also emphasizes the need for therapists to be culturally sensitive to their clients and to understand how the goals of therapy reflect the values of the dominant culture. The therapeutic process is a process of influence, and therapists must take care not to misuse their power, which may be considerable enough to even produce a disorder that the patient does not have, as may be the case with 47._____ disorder, which has dramatically increased in diagnosis in recent years. This disorder is also commonly known as 48._____ disorder, or MPD.

The guiding assumption of the therapy known as 49._____ is that disorders are created by unconscious motives and past internal conflicts. The cure is to gain 50._____ into symptoms and facilitate emotional release. To bring these conflicts into awareness, therapists look at dreams, fantasies, and memories. They encourage clients to 51._____, saying whatever comes to mind in the moment. A key element of this therapeutic process is 52._____ in which the client's emotional feelings toward others become directed toward the therapist. Traditionally, therapist and client met several times a week for years, but more modern approaches apply traditional concepts of therapy in more goal-directed and time-limited fashion.

53._____ therapies start with the assumption that people seek self-actualization. In Carl Rogers approach, known as 54._____ therapy, the therapists role is to listen with an accepting, nonjudgmental attitude called 55._____. 56._____ therapy helps clients to struggle with large questions in life such as death, the meaning of existence, and freedom of choice.

The 57._____ gap is the major divide between psychologists who subscribe to psychodynamic assumptions and the methods of research-based perspectives. Many psychodynamic therapists see their work as art, and scientists are concerned about the potential for harm with therapists who do not keep up with the research on therapeutic outcome. Many therapists draw on multiple methods based on several approaches. Consumers should think critically about the claims made by therapists.

Music consists of 58._____ (melody), 59._____ (a system of sound grouping), and 60._____ (tone qualities). Music is universal and may well be biologically-based. It is localized in a different part of the brain than language. Some people are completely tone deaf, a condition called 61._____. Perfect pitch also appears to be innate. There are 62._____ differences in the relative emphases given to melody, tonal qualities, and sound groupings. Children develop cognitive 63._____ about music and each generation partly defines itself by its favorite music. 64._____ psychologists study how music is perceived and remembered. Learning affects all aspects of musical intelligence.

Researchers from the 65._____ perspective study the physiology of sexual desire, arousal, and behavior. A minimum level of the hormone 66._____ seems to promote sexual desire in both sexes. Contrary to what Freud believed, women do not experience different kinds of 67._____. Male and female arousal follows similar physiological patterns. Male and female 68._____ develop from the same tissue.

The 69._____ perspective sees sexuality as constructed from observation, parental lessons, knowledge, attitudes, and experiences. From this perspective, people learn and follow sexual 70._____ that are cultural and gendered. The cognitive perspective emphasizes the role of expectations, attitudes, and beliefs in sexual arousal and response. It is important, for instance, how a person interprets his or her physiological state. We also know that intrusive thoughts can interfere with sexual pleasure and response, and that people differ in their judgment of sexual signals.

The sociocultural perspective uses explanations that appeal to external influences on sexual behavior, such as peer pressure, relationship factors, and cultural practices. Cultures differ with regard to views of the sexualities of men and women, labeling of erotic dress and body parts, and acceptability of specific sexual practices. The psychodynamic perspective emphasizes the 71._____ dynamics of sexual relationships. For instance, sexuality seems particularly susceptible to the use of 72._____ mechanisms. From this perspective, men and women have different sexual fears and vulnerabilities.

No one psychological perspective can account for all behavior. Together, the five perspectives allow us to view people as being affected by physiology, environmental forces, thinking about and interpretation of events, culture, and forces that are beyond awareness.

Multiple Choice Self-Test

1. A behavior that causes marked psychological distress, is self-defeating, or disrupts relationships is called:
a. psychopathology.
b. insanity.
c. mental disorder.
d. psychosis.

2. Andrew is constantly "keyed-up" and worries most of the day that his parents will be injured in a car accident. He has trouble sitting still and has difficulty keeping his mind on his work. Andrew suffers from:

a. panic disorder.
b. trauma anticipation disorder.
c. obsessive-compulsive disorder.
d. generalized anxiety disorder.

3. Gerald was beaten severely and robbed last year by a group of 6 men. Now he has nightmares about the event and always seems on-guard in his daily life. Gerald suffers from:

a. posttraumatic stress disorder.
b. panic disorder.
c. generalized anxiety disorder.
d. chronic apprehensive disorder.

4. Marnie suffers from attacks in which her heart races, she has difficulty catching her breath, she becomes dizzy, and she thinks she is about to die. Marnie's symptoms indicate a diagnosis of:

a. generalized anxiety disorder.
b. panic disorder.
c. neurotic personality disorder.
d. psychotic disorder.

5. Zeke is afraid that someone will break into his house, so he checks his upstairs windows to make sure they are locked, goes downstairs to make sure that the doors and windows are locked there. Then, he can't be sure that he checked every window upstairs, so he checks them all again, returning downstairs so he can re-check there. Zeke's symptoms are consistent with:

a. agoraphobia.
b. generalized anxiety disorder.
c. obsessive-compulsive disorder.
d. amnesia.

6. Danny has had several panic attacks, and now he fears going to the grocery store, because he worries that he might have another attack and not receive help from anybody. Danny is suffering from:

a. agoraphobia.
b. nictophobia.
c. generalized anxiety disorder.
d. obsessive-compulsive disorder.

7. The distinction between major depression and bipolar disorder is in the presence or absence of:
a. self-defeating behavior.
b. biochemical imbalance.
c. mania.
d. excessive worry.

8. Genetic studies indicate that major depression:
a. is probably caused by a single gene.
b. is linked in identical twins.
c. has no genetic link.
d. is affected by a chemical enzyme.

9. "People become depressed when their efforts to control their worlds repeatedly fail, and so they have no faith in the future." This statement reflects the theory of:
a. cognitive dialectics.
b. learned biodeficiency.
c. compensatory conditioning.
d. learned helplessness.

10. According to cognitive theory, depression is the result of all of the following styles of thinking EXCEPT:
a. "Bad things happen because I'm stupid."
b. "It's not my fault that I'm often in bad situations."
c. "This terrible circumstance will never change."
d. "It doesn't matter what I do. I can't control my emotions."

11. A psychologist is giving a lecture on the causes of depression. She states that depression is the result of a biological predisposition to low seratonin levels combined with difficult life circumstances and a tendency to negatively interpret those circumstances. Her position is closest to the:
a. biological perspective.
b. cognitive perspective.
c. vulnerability-stress model.
d. sociocultural model.

12. Frankie is always on his guard, fearing that people will take advantage of him. He constantly confronts his wife, Annette, because he thinks she is having an extramarital affair, despite the fact that she is not, nor has she given any indication that she might be. A therapist evaluating Frankie might begin to suspect that Frankie suffers from:
a. narcissistic personality disorder.
b. antisocial personality disorder.
c. paranoid personality disorder.
d. partner-delusional behavior disorder.

13. Beginning early in childhood, Jeffrey has set fires, manipulated other people, and sometime engaged in violent behavior. He has never felt sorry about hurting others. Jeffrey's diagnosis is:
a. antisocial personality disorder.
b. asocial personality disorder.
c. narcissistic personality disorder.
d. psychoneurological personality disorder.

14. Schizophrenia is correctly classified as:
a. a mood disorder.
b. a neurosis.
c. a psychosis.
d. an anxiety disorder.

15. The positive symptoms of schizophrenia include all of the following EXCEPT:
a. hallucinations.
b. emotional flatness.
c. delusions.
d. incoherent speech.

16. Tardive dyskinesia is a side effect of:
a. tranquilizers.
b. psychodynamic therapy.
c. antidepressant drugs.
d. antipsychotic drugs.

17. A male and a female are likely to have different:
a. physical sensations at orgasm.
b. subjective descriptions of orgasm.
c. levels of sexual desire.
d. sexual scripts.

18. Depression can be effectively treated with all of the following EXCEPT:
a. SSRIs.
b. tranquilizers.
c. MAO inhibitors.
d. cognitive therapy.

19. Most antidepressant drugs affect the neurotransmitter:
a. glutamate.
b. seratonin.
c. dopamine.
d. acetylcholine.

20. Brad is sometimes depressed, but he also experiences periods of extreme elation. He gets so excited that he engages in behaviors that are self-defeating and even dangerous. The most likely treatment for Brad is:
a. neuroleptics.
b. lithium carbonate.
c. psychodynamic therapy.
d. behavior therapy.

21. John is afraid of flying, and his job as a national sportscaster requires him to travel long distances, so he seeks the help of a behavioral therapist. The therapist trains John in a relaxation technique while directing him to imagine progressively threatening situations, beginning with checking in at the airport and continuing to getting on the plane and taking off. This therapist is using a technique called:
a. exposure therapy.
b. aversive conditioning.
c. systematic desensitization.
d. rational-emotive therapy.

22. Alexandra seeks help from a behavioral therapist for her lack of assertiveness. The therapist has her participate in a group where people role play situations and rehearse assertive responses. Alexandra is undergoing:
a. exposure treatment.
b. systematic desensitization.
c. skills training.
d. aversive conditioning.

23. Zoie is a 22-year old who wants to develop perfect pitch. Based on the available research, what should she do?
a. Forget it; perfect pitch is biologically based.
b. Forget it; perfect pitch must be developed in early childhood.
c. Undergo extensive training at learning pitches in many different timbres.
d. Undergo intensive training on a single musical instrument.

24. Daniel is seeing a psychiatrist for help with his mental disorder. The psychiatrist prescribes a drug, but it doesn't help. Daniel reports this to his doctor, who increases the dosage of the drug, but then the side effects are too powerful for Daniel to tolerate. He returns again, and the dose is lowered. The drug is then effective because the dose is within the:
a. therapeutic window.
b. optimum dosage frame.
c. physiological parameters.
d. therapeutic boundaries.

25.   Steve procrastinates habitually, and he always does something pleasant instead
        of the work he wants to do. He enlists the help of a friend. Steve gives the
        friend $100, and the friend "fines" Steve $5 every time he procrastinates. This
        procedure is much like:
a.   systematic desensitization.
b.   exposure therapy.
c.   skills training.
d.   aversive conditioning.

26.   Behavior and cognitive therapies have been shown to be effective for all of the
        following disorders EXCEPT:
a.   depression.
b.   anxiety.
c.   phobia.
d.   psychosis.

27.   A dramatic increase in the incidence of diagnosis suggests that therapists may
        be producing in their clients the disorder called:
a.   schizophrenia.
b.   dissociative identity disorder.
c.   obsessive-compulsive disorder.
d.   antisocial personality disorder.

28.   Which of the following is considered by today's psychologists to be a major
        contribution of the biological perspective to our understanding of human
        sexuality?
a.   The biological perspective has validated the traditional concept of "right" versus
        "wrong" forms of orgasm.
b.   The biological perspective has identified the specific brain locations that
        interpret potentially sexual stimuli.
c.   The biological perspective has dispelled the pervasive myth that there is a "right"
        kind of orgasm.
d.   The biological perspective provided support for the Freudian interpretation of
        male and female anatomical differences.

29.   After experiencing difficulty becoming sexually aroused on several occasions,
        Felix decided to consult a cognitive psychologist. What will Felix's therapist
        attempt to do to help Felix?
a.   Perform physiological tests to determine the organic cause of his problem.
b.   Analyze his relationships with family members to determine the childhood roots
        of his problem.
c.   Identify and change the distracting thoughts that inhibit Felix from relaxing
        during sexual activities.
d.   Determine what factors Felix considers arousing or inhibiting, and train him to
        consciously relax.

30. Which of the following psychologists is MOST likely to emphasize that young men sometimes engage in unwanted sexual intercourse because of peer pressure, a desire for popularity, and a fear of not seeming masculine?
a.   a sociocultural psychologist
b.   a psychodynamic psychologist
c.   a cognitive psychologist
d.   a learning psychologist

True-False Self-Test

T   F   1.   Schizophrenia is a kind of psychosis.

T   F   2.   The family-systems perspective is consistent with the sociocultural perspective.

T   F   3.   Transference is a key element of psychodynamic therapy.

T   F   4.   Neuroleptics are used to treat anxiety disorders.

T   F   5.   The most disabling phobia is acrophobia.

T   F   6.   PET scans indicate no differences between the brains of people with and without obsessive-compulsive disorder.

T   F   7.   Major depression can be traced to a single gene.

T   F   8.   Learned helplessness is a cognitive theory of anxiety.

T   F   9.   Depressed people tend to believe that they have little or no control over their lives.

T   F   10. Rumination is related to duration of a depressive episode.

T   F   11. Antisocial personality disorder may be related to brain injury.

T   F   12. Hallucinations are a negative symptom of schizophrenia.

T   F   13. Testosterone appears to play an important role in the sexual response of females.

T   F   14. Male and female genitals develop from the same embryonic tissue.

T   F   15. In every culture, men are considered to be the more sexually responsive sex.

T F 16. Vaginal and clitoral orgasms are distinctly different.

T F 17. Delusions are false beliefs.

T F 18. Males and females in the United States learn distinctly different sexual scripts.

T F 19. Some cultures do not consider breasts to be sexy.

T F 20. The vulnerability-stress model combines several psychological perspectives.

T F 21. Psychosurgery repairs damaged brain tissue.

T F 22. Electroconvulsive therapy is a treatment for schizophrenia.

T F 23. Tranquilizers are frequently prescribed inappropriately.

T F 24. The best explanations of behavior are probably those that are based on information from several different psychological perspectives.

T F 25. Panic disorder involves striking physiological symptoms.

T F 26. Compulsions are repetitive, ritualized behaviors.

T F 27. Women are more prone to rumination than men.

T F 28. Poverty of speech is a negative symptom of schizophrenia.

T F 29. The placebo effect is an unusual reaction to a drug.

T F 30. Systematic desensitization is a treatment for phobia.

Key Terms

mental disorder Any behavior or emotional state that causes an individual great suffering or worry, is self-defeating or self-destructive, or is maladaptive and disrupts the person's relationships or the larger community.

generalized anxiety disorder A continuous state of anxiety marked by feelings of worry and dread, apprehension, difficulties in concentration, and signs of motor tension.

posttraumatic stress disorder An anxiety disorder in which a person who has experienced a traumatic or life-threatening event has symptoms such as psychic numbing, reliving of the trauma, and increased physiological arousal.

panic disorder An anxiety disorder in which a person experiences recurring *panic attacks*, periods of intense fear and feelings of impending doom or death, accompanied by physiological symptoms such as rapid breathing and pulse, and dizziness.

phobia An exaggerated, unrealistic fear of a specific situation, activity, or object.

agoraphobia A set of phobias, often set off by a panic attack, involving the basic fear of being away from a safe place or person.

obsessive-compulsive disorder (OCD) An anxiety disorder in which a person feels trapped in repetitive, persistent thoughts (obsessions) and repetitive, ritualized behaviors (compulsions) designed to reduce anxiety.

major depression A mood disorder involving disturbances in emotion (excessive sadness), behavior (loss of interest in one's usual activities), cognition (thoughts of hopelessness), and body function (fatigue and loss of appetite).

bipolar disorder A mood disorder in which episodes of both depression and mania (excessive euphoria) occur.

personality disorder Rigid, maladaptive personality patterns that cause personal distress or an inability to get along with others.

paranoid personality disorder A disorder characterized by habitually unreasonable and excessive suspiciousness or jealousy.

narcissistic personality disorder A disorder characterized by an exaggerated sense of self-importance and self-absorption.

antisocial personality disorder A disorder characterized by antisocial behavior such as lying, stealing, manipulating others, and sometimes violence; a lack of guilt, shame, and empathy. (Sometimes called *psychopathy* or *sociopathy*).

schizophrenia A psychotic disorder or group of disorders marked by positive symptoms (e.g., delusions, hallucinations, disorganized or incoherent speech, and inappropriate behavior) and negative symptoms (e.g., emotional flatness and loss of motivation).

psychosis An extreme mental disturbance involving distorted perceptions and irrational behavior; it may have psychological or organic causes. (Plural: *psychoses.*)

psychosurgery Any surgical procedure that destroys selected areas of the brain believed to be involved in emotional disorders or violent, impulsive behavior.

electroconvulsive therapy (ECT) A procedure used in cases of prolonged and severe major depression, in which a brief brain seizure is induced.

antipsychotic drugs Drugs used primarily in the treatment of schizophrenia and other psychotic disorders.

antidepressant drugs Drugs used primarily in the treatment of mood disorders, especially depression and anxiety.

tranquilizers Drugs commonly but often inappropriately prescribed for patients who complain of unhappiness, anxiety, or worry.

lithium carbonate A drug frequently given to people suffering from bipolar disorder.

placebo effect The apparent success of a medication or treatment that is due to the patient's expectations or hopes rather than to the drug or treatment itself.

systematic desensitization In behavior therapy, a step-by-step process of desensitizing a client to a feared object or experience; based on the classical-conditioning procedure of counterconditioning.

aversive conditioning In behavior therapy, a method in which punishment is substituted for the reinforcement that is perpetuating a bad habit.

exposure treatment In behavior therapy, a method in which a person suffering from an anxiety disorder, such as a phobia or panic attacks, is taken directly into the feared situation until the anxiety subsides.

therapeutic alliance The bond of confidence and mutual understanding established between therapist and client, which allows them to work together to solve the client's problems.

dissociative identity disorder A controversial disorder marked by the appearance within one person of two or more distinct personalities, each with its own name and traits; commonly known as *multiple personality disorder (MPD)*.

transference In psychodynamic therapies, a critical step in which the client transfers unconscious emotions or reactions, such a emotional feelings about his or her parents, onto the therapist.

Suggested Research Projects

1. Select a psychological phenomenon of interest to you, such as dreaming, aggression, or creativity. Look in your textbook and other sources, and attempt

to construct explanations and theories based on the five perspectives, just as your authors have done for sexual behavior.

2.   Do some library research on treatments for sexual dysfunctions. Identify the theoretical perspective or perspectives underlying the approach to treatment. For example, does the treatment involve changing biology, teaching new skills, educating about cultural beliefs, etc.?

Suggested Readings

Boston Women's Health Book Collective (1998). *Our bodies, ourselves for the new century: A book by and for women (revised and updated edition).* New York: Touchstone. A comprehensive sexual health guide for women.

Davis, M., Eshelman, E. R., & McKay, M. (2001). The relaxation and stress reduction workbook (5th ed.). Oakland, CA: New Harbinger. A popular guide to handling a range of anxiety symptoms.

Lynch, J., & Kilmartin, C. T. (1999). *The pain behind the mask: Overcoming masculine depression.* A view of depression as underdiagnosed in men and a guide to its treatment.

Mueser, K. T. (1995). *Coping with schizophrenia: A guide for families.* Help with managing symptoms and relationships with someone who has this mental disorder.

ANSWER KEYS

Chapter 1

Chapter Summary

1. behavior
2. mental processes
3. empirical
4. psychobabble
5. challenges
6. critical thinking
7. open-minded
8. concrete
9. evidence
10. assumptions
11. emotion
12. uncertainty
13. predict
14. nineteenth
15. empirical evidence
16. Wundt
17. trained introspection
18. objective
19. functionalism
20. adaptation
21. Darwin
22. James
23. psychotherapy
24. Freud
25. psychoanalysis
26. basic
27. applied
28. teaching
29. research
30. mental health
31. research
32. Clinical
33. psychotherapists
34. psychoanalysts
35. psychiatrists
36. community psychology
37. biological
38. psychoneuroimmunology
39. learning
40. Watson
41. Pavlov
42. Skinner
43. social-cognitive learning theory
44. cognitive
45. sociocultural
46. social
47. psychodynamic
48. humanistic
49. feminist
50. reductionism

Multiple Choice Self-Test

1. b	2. b	3. d	4. a	5. c
6. b	7. b	8. a	9. b	10. a
11. a	12. d	13. a	14. b	15. b
16. c	17. a	18. c	19. d	20. c
21. a	22. a	23. d	24. a	25. d
26. b	27. a	28. b	29. c	30. d

True-False Self-Test

1. F	2. T	3. F	4. T	5. T
6. F	7. F	8. T	9. T	10. T
11. T	12. T	13. F	14. T	15. F
16. F	17. F	18. F	19. T	20. T
21. T	22. T	23. T	24. F	25. F
26. T	27. T	28. T	29. F	30. F

Chapter 2

Chapter Summary

1. obtained	2. theory
3. hypothesis	4. operational
5. predictions	6. empirical
7. falsifiability	8. replicate
9. descriptive	10. case studies
11. inaccurate	12. tests
13. observational	14. naturalistic
15. laboratory	16. psychological tests
17. standardized	18. norms
19. reliable	20. valid
21. test-retest	22. alternate forms
23. Content	24. criterion
25. surveys	26. sample
27. representative	28. correlation
29. positive	30. negative
31. uncorrelated	32. correlation coefficient
33. +1.00	34. -1.00
35. 0.00	36. individual
37. cause	38. experimental
39. control	40. independent
41. dependent	42. experimental
43. control	44. random assignment
45. placebo	46. single-blind
47. experimenter	48. double-blind
49. field	50. descriptive
51. arithmetic mean	52. standard deviation
53. inferential	54. chance
55. significant	56. five
57. interpret	58. longitudinal
59. cross-sectional	60. Meta-analysis
61. informed consent	62. debrief
63. postmodernism	64. social constructionism

Multiple Choice Self-Test

1. b	2. a	3. c	4. a	5. d
6. a	7. b	8. c	9. a	10. b
11. d	12. d	13. d	14. a	15. c
16. b	17. c	18. d	19. a	20. c
21. c	22. c	23. b	24. d	25. b
26. a	27. c	28. b	29. c	30. d

True-False Self-Test

1. T	2. T	3. T	4. F	5. T
6. T	7. F	8. F	9. T	10. F
11. F	12. T	13. T	14. T	15. F
16. T	17. T	18. F	19. F	20. F
21. F	22. F	23. T	24. T	25. F
26. T	27. T	28. F	29. F	30. T

Chapter 3

Chapter Summary

1. nativists
2. empiricists
3. interact
4. overeating
5. evolutionary psychology
6. behavior genetics
7. Genes
8. chromosomes
9. DNA
10. mutate
11. linkage
12. Evolution
13. natural selection
14. Sensation
15. perception
16. critical periods
17. cliff
18. faces
19. synchrony
20. attachment
21. contact comfort
22. language
23. surface
24. deep
25. language acquisition
26. syntax
27. imitation
28. critical period
29. sociobiology
30. stereotypes
31. heritability
32. vary
33. individuals
34. environment
35. genes
36. monozygotic
37. dizygotic
38. apart
39. quotient
40. chronological
41. .50
42. Identical (monozygotic)
43. fraternal (dizygotic)
44. birth
45. adoptive
46. within
47. between
48. temperaments
49. traits
50. Big Five
51. underestimate
52. experience

Multiple Choice Self-Test

1. b	2. a	3. d	4. c	5. a
6. a	7. d	8. d	9. b	10. c
11. a	12. b	13. b	14. d	15. a
16. c	17. a	18. d	19. b	20. b
21. b	22. c	23. b	24. a	25. c
26. a	27. b	28. a	29. c	30. a

True-False Self-Test

1. F	2. T	3. T	4. T	5. F
6. T	7. T	8. F	9. T	10. F
11. T	12. T	13. T	14. F	15. T
16. F	17. F	18. F	19. T	20. T
21. F	22. F	23. F	24. F	25. F
26. T	27. T	28. T	29. T	30. F

Chapter 4

Chapter Summary

1. nervous	2. central
3. brain	4. spinal cord
5. peripheral	6. Sensory
7. spinal cord	8. Motor
9. hormones	10. somatic
11. autonomic	12. biofeedback
13. sympathetic	14. parasympathetic
15. neurons	16. glial
17. dendrites	18. cell body
19. axon	20. axon terminals
21. myelin	22. nerves
23. cranial	24. brain
25. synaptic cleft	26. axon terminal
27. synapse	28. action potential
29. vesicles	30. neurotransmitter
31. receptor	32. excitatory
33. inhibitory	34. seratonin
35. dopamine	36. acetylcholine
37. norepinephrine	38. glutamate
39. GABA	40. Alzheimer's disease
41. Parkinson's disease	42. endorphins
43. neuromodulators	44. Hormones
45. endocrine	46. Adrenal
47. melatonin	48. sex
49. lesion	50. electrodes
51. waves	52. electroencephalogram
53. PET scan	54. MRI
55. lower	56. higher
57. stem	58. medulla
59. pons	60. reticular activating
61. cerebellum	62. thalamus
63. smell	64. olfactory
65. hypothalamus	66. pituitary
67. limbic	68. amygdala
69. hippocampus	70. cerebrum
71. hemispheres	72. corpus callosum
73. lateralized	74. cerebral cortex
75. lobes	76. occipital lobes
77. parietal	78. left
79. temporal	80. frontal
81. association	82. split-brain surgery
83. corpus callosum	84. left
85. dominant	86. spatial

87. long-term
88. synaptic
89. procedural
90. declarative
91. epinephrine
92. REM
93. alpha
94. spindles
95. Delta
96. dreaming
97. activation-synthesis
98. reductionism

Multiple Choice Self-Test

1. a	2. b	3. d	4. b	5. c
6. c	7. d	8. a	9. b	10. b
11. d	12. b	13. c	14. c	15. a
16. a	17. d	18. d	19. d	20. b
21. d	22. a	23. b	24. b	25. c
26. c	27. c	28. d	29. a	30. b

True-False Self-Test

1. F	2. T	3. T	4. T	5. F
6. T	7. F	8. T	9. F	10. T
11. F	12. T	13. F	14. F	15. T
16. F	17. F	18. T	19. F	20. T
21. F	22. T	23. T	24. T	25. T
26. F	27. T	28. F	29. F	30. T

Chapter 5

Chapter Summary

1. Learning
2. conditioning
3. classical
4. unconditioned
5. unconditioned
6. conditioned
7. conditioned
8. precede
9. extinction
10. spontaneous recovery
11. higher order
12. generalization
13. discrimination
14. loud noise
15. white rat
16. counterconditioning
17. incompatible
18. operant
19. consequences
20. reinforcement
21. increases
22. punishment
23. decreases
24. positive
25. negative reinforcement
26. negative punishment
27. presented
28. removed
29. increases
30. decreases
31. primary
32. Secondary
33. extinction
34. spurt
35. generalization
36. discrimination
37. discriminative
38. stimulus control
39. continuous
40. extinction
41. schedules
42. Ratio
43. Interval
44. fixed
45. variable
46. curves
47. shaping
48. successive approximations
49. behavior modification
50. immediate
51. consistency
52. emotional
53. attention
54. extrinsic
55. intrinsic
56. extrinsic
57. intrinsic
58. reinforcement
59. intermittently
60. confirming
61. insight

Multiple Choice Self-Test

1. a	2. b	3. a	4. d	5. c
6. b	7. a	8. d	9. b	10. a
11. b	12. d	13. d	14. a	15. a
16. b	17. c	18. c	19. a	20. d
21. c	22. b	23. d	24. b	25. d
26. a	27. c	28. a	29. d	30. a
31. d	32. a	33. c	34. c	35. a

True-False Self-Test

1.	F	2.	T	3.	T	4.	T	5.	T
6.	T	7.	F	8.	F	9.	F	10.	F
11.	F	12.	T	13.	T	14.	T	15.	T
16.	F	17.	F	18.	F	19.	F	20.	T
21.	F	22.	T	23.	T	24.	T	25.	T
26.	F	27.	F	28.	F	29.	T	30.	T

Chapter 6

Chapter Summary

1. interaction	2. behaviorists
3. latent	4. observational
5. model	6. vicariously
7. interpretations	8. motivation
9. expectations	10. locus of control
11. external	12. self-fulfilling prophecy
13. explanatory	14. pessimistic
15. internal	16. stable
17. global	18. optimistic
19. external	20. unstable
21. limited in impact	22. achievement
23. Self-efficacy	24. mastering
25. role models	26. physiological
27. positively	28. mastery
29. performance	30. gender
31. psychological	32. gender identity
33. gender socialization	34. schemas
35. maintenance	36. morality
37. preconventional	38. Conventional
39. postconventional	40. verbal
41. behavior	42. situations
43. distress	44. Power
45. induction	46. explanations
47. reductionism	48. instinctive drift

Multiple Choice Self-Test

1. c	2. b	3. a	4. c	5. b
6. d	7. d	8. a	9. c	10. b
11. c	12. b	13. a	14. c	15. d
16. b	17. b	18. d	19. a	20. d
21. b	22. d	23. c	24. a	25. d
26. c	27. c	28. a	29. c	30. c

True-False Self-Test

1. F	2. T	3. F	4. F	5. F
6. T	7. T	8. F	9. T	10. T
11. F	12. T	13. F	14. F	15. T
16. F	17. F	18. F	19. T	20. T
21. T	22. F	23. T	24. T	25. T
26. F	27. T	28. F	29. F	30. F

Chapter 7

Chapter Summary

1. Concepts
2. basic concepts
3. prototype
4. cognitive schemas
5. Subconscious
6. unconscious
7. Reasoning
8. algorithm
9. deductive
10. syllogism
11. inductive
12. heuristic
13. Dialectical
14. convergent
15. divergent
16. adaptation
17. assimilation
18. accommodation
19. sensory-motor
20. object permanence
21. mental imagery
22. preoperational
23. egocentric
24. concrete operations
25. conservation
26. formal operations
27. abstract
28. theory of mind
29. reflective reasoning
30. prereflective
31. quasi-reflective
32. twenties
33. hindsight
34. availability
35. loss
36. confirmation
37. dissonance
38. justification of effort
39. Cognitive ethology
40. language
41. meaningful
42. displacement
43. productivity
44. anthropomorphism
45. anthropocentrism

Multiple Choice Self-Test

1. b	2. a	3. a	4. c	5. c
6. c	7. b	8. a	9. a	10. a
11. b	12. b	13. a	14. d	15. c
16. d	17. d	18. b	19. d	20. b
21. a	22. d	23. b	24. d	25. c
26. a	27. a	28. d	29. c	30. c

True-False Self-Test

1. T	2. T	3. F	4. T	5. F
6. T	7. T	8. F	9. F	10. F
11. F	12. T	13. T	14. T	15. F
16. T	17. F	18. F	19. T	20. T
21. T	22. F	23. F	24. T	25. T
26. T	27. T	28. F	29. F	30. T

Chapter 8

Chapter Summary

1.	reconstructive	2.	Source
3.	flashbulb	4.	confabulation
5.	ethnicity	6.	hypnosis
7.	explicit	8.	recognition
9.	implicit	10.	relearning
11.	priming	12.	information-processing
13.	encoding	14.	storage
15.	retrieval	16.	sensory
17.	short-term	18.	working
19.	long-term	20.	parallel distributed
21.	chunks	22.	procedural
23.	declarative	24.	semantic
25.	episodic	26.	serial position
27.	primacy	28.	recency
29.	maintenance rehearsal	30.	elaborative rehearsal
31.	Mnemonics	32.	massed
33.	overlearning	34.	decay
35.	Interference	36.	retroactive
37.	Proactive	38.	cue-dependent
39.	state-dependent	40.	psychogenic
41.	childhood amnesia	42.	reminiscence bump
43.	metaphors	44.	reductionism
45.	relativism		

Multiple Choice Self-Test

1. a	2. a	3. b	4. c	5. c
6. a	7. b	8. b	9. a	10. c
11. d	12. d	13. b	14. c	15. a
16. d	17. a	18. c	19. b	20. d
21. b	22. a	23. b	24. a	25. c
26. b	27. d	28. c	29. a	30. a

True-False Self-Test

1. F	2. F	3. F	4. T	5. T
6. T	7. F	8. T	9. T	10. F
11. T	12. F	13. T	14. T	15. T
16. F	17. F	18. F	19. T	20. T
21. T	22. T	23. F	24. F	25. T
26. T	27. T	28. T	29. T	30. T

Chapter 9

Chapter Summary

1. individual
2. norms
3. roles
4. victim
5. decreased
6. unethical
7. artificial
8. entrapped
9. conformity
10. groupthink
11. ethnicities
12. generational
13. diffusion of responsibility
14. bystander apathy
15. social loafing
16. deindividuation
17. social cognition
18. attribution theory
19. situational
20. dispositional
21. fundamental attribution error
22. self-serving bias
23. just-world hypothesis
24. situational
25. dispositional
26. validity
27. coercive
28. need for achievement
29. Thematic Apperception
30. incentive pay
31. cooperation

Multiple Choice Self-Test

1. d	2. a	3. b	4. d	5. c
6. b	7. a	8. b	9. c	10. d
11. c	12. c	13. b	14. a	15. b
16. d	17. d	18. a	19. b	20. b
21. b	22. a	23. c	24. d	25. c
26. a	27. b	28. b	29. b	30. c

True-False Self-Test

1. T	2. F	3. F	4. T	5. F
6. T	7. T	8. T	9. F	10. T
11. T	12. T	13. T	14. T	15. T
16. F	17. F	18. F	19. T	20. F
21. F	22. T	23. T	24. F	25. T
26. F	27. T	28. F	29. F	30. T

Chapter 10

Chapter Summary

1. culture
2. cross-cultural
3. cultural anthropology
4. equivalence
5. stereotype
6. body language
7. conversational distance
8. monochronic
9. polychronic
10. individualism
11. collectivist
12. social
13. ethnic
14. acculturation
15. bicultural
16. assimilation
17. ethnic separatists
18. marginal
19. deductively
20. permanent
21. innate
22. stereotype threat
23. industrialized
24. ethnocentrism
25. stereotyping
26. selective perception
27. prejudiced
28. economic
29. reductionism
30. stereotyping
31. relativism
32. ethnocentrism
33. assimilated
34. deficit
35. family

Multiple Choice Self-Test

1. b	2. c	3. d	4. b	5. a
6. c	7. a	8. c	9. d	10. c
11. b	12. a	13. b	14. d	15. a
16. c	17. d	18. a	19. c	20. a
21. b	22. a	23. a	24. d	25. c
26. a	27. b	28. a	29. c	30. b

True-False Self-Test

1. F	2. T	3. T	4. F	5. F
6. T	7. F	8. F	9. T	10. T
11. T	12. T	13. F	14. F	15. T
16. T	17. F	18. T	19. F	20. T
21. F	22. T	23. F	24. T	25. T
26. F	27. T	28. F	29. F	30. F

Chapter 11

Chapter Summary

1. childhood	2. Freud
3. instincts	4. id
5. ego	6. superego
7. defense mechanisms	8. neurotic
9. fixation	10. neurosis
11. oral	12. anal
13. phallic	14. genital
15. latency	16. Oedipus
17. phallic	18. Dora
19. Adler	20. inferiority
21. Karen Horney	22. penis envy
23. womb envy	24. basic anxiety
25. Carl Jung	26. collective unconscious
27. archetypes	28. Erik Erikson
29. psychosocial	30. adolescence
31. object-relations	32. two
33. representation	34. splitting
35. attachment	36. ego boundaries
37. existential	38. Abraham Maslow
39. peak	40. self-actualized
41. Carl Rogers	42. congruence
43. unconditional positive regard	44. Rollo May
45. existential	46. subjective
47. testable	48. research
49. unconscious	50. case
51. overgeneralized	52. retrospective
53. longitudinal	54. projective
55. Rorschach Inkblot Test	

Multiple Choice Self-Test

1. a	2. b	3. d	4. a	5. a
6. d	7. a	8. b	9. b	10. a
11. a	12. c	13. a	14. d	15. b
16. a	17. b	18. c	19. b	20. c
21. a	22. c	23. b	24. c	25. a
26. d	27. c	28. b	29. a	30. b

True-False Self-Test

1. T	2. T	3. F	4. T	5. F
6. F	7. T	8. T	9. T	10. F
11. F	12. F	13. F	14. F	15. T
16. F	17. F	18. T	19. T	20. T
21. T	22. F	23. F	24. T	25. T
26. T	27. T	28. F	29. T	30. F

Chapter 12

Chapter Summary

1. mental disorder	2. generalized anxiety disorder
3. learning	4. posttraumatic stress
5. panic disorder	6. phobia
7. agoraphobia	8. obsessive-compulsive disorder
9. mood	10. bipolar
11. women	12. learning
13. learned helplessness	14. cognitive
15. internal	16. stable
17. ruminate	18. social
19. object-relations	20. vulnerability-stress
21. personality	22. paranoid personality
23. narcissistic personality	24. antisocial personality
25. schizophrenia	26. psychotic
27. genetic	28. neurotransmitters
29. vulnerability-stress	30. psychosurgery
31. prefrontal lobotomy	32. electroconvulsive
33. antipsychotic	34. tardive dyskinesia
35. antidepressants	36. tranquilizers
37. lithium carbonate	38. placebo
39. therapeutic window	40. learning
41. systematic desensitization	42. aversive
43. exposure	44. skills training
45. cognitive	46. therapeutic alliance
47. dissociative identity	48. multiple personality
49. psychoanalysis	50. insight
51. free associate	52. transference
53. humanist	54. client-centered
55. unconditional positive regard	56. existential
57. scientist-practitioner	58. melody
59. rhythm	60. timbre
61. amusia	62. cultural
63. schemas	64. cognitive
65. biological	66. testosterone
67. orgasms	68. genitals
69. learning	70. scripts
71. unconscious	72. defense

Multiple Choice Self-Test

1. c	2. d	3. a	4. b	5. c
6. a	7. c	8. b	9. d	10. b
11. c	12. c	13. a	14. c	15. b
16. d	17. d	18. b	19. b	20. b
21. c	22. c	23. a	24. a	25. d
26. d	27. b	28. c	29. c	30. a

True-False Self-Test

1. T	2. T	3. T	4. F	5. F
6. F	7. F	8. F	9. T	10. T
11. T	12. F	13. F	14. T	15. F
16. F	17. F	18. T	19. F	20. T
21. F	22. F	23. T	24. T	25. T
26. T	27. T	28. T	29. F	30. T